JOSEPH QUINN

Perfection
and
Progress

The MIT Press
Cambridge,
Massachusetts,
and London,
England

Perfection and Progress:

Two Modes of Utopian Thought

Elisabeth Hansot

This book was set in VIP Optima
by DEKR Corporation,
printed on Fernwood Opaque,
and bound in Columbia Millbank Vellum MBV-4259
by The Colonial Press, Inc.
in the United States of America.

Library of Congress Cataloging in Publication Data

Hansot, Elisabeth.
    Perfection and progress: two modes of utopian thought.

    Bibliography: p.
    1. Utopias—History. I. Title.
HX806.H3   335'.02'09   74-7106
ISBN 0-262-08077-X

To My Parents
and
to the
Memory
of
Otto Kirchheimer

Contents

Preface

"Actually, perfectibility is something almost as undetermined as mutability in general; it is without aim and purpose and without a standard of change." It is not surprising that Hegel, equally concerned with progress and perfectibility, should have so precisely pinpointed the paradox of utopian thought. Perfectibility *is* unimaginable; notwithstanding, men have continued to imagine it and frame societies according to its specifications.

My experience of utopias has an uncertain quality to it, for while I have found it a pleasant pastime to attempt their construction, the prospect of living in a completed utopia has never been attractive to me. The impetus for this book came from a desire to explain this disinclination and to discover why perfectibility appeared without aim and purpose. As I read among utopias, I developed some sense of why they leave the reader unsatisfied, and I discovered other human needs that these societies do fulfill. The result of my reflections and the purpose of this book are not only to indicate the difficulties that burden the authors of utopias when they begin to conceive of their future societies as viable but also, by questioning such claims, to reaffirm the importance of utopias as a distinctive mode of thought in which values are examined and displayed.

I am indebted to those friends and colleagues whose support and interest helped make this study possible. It gives me great pleasure to thank Herbert A. Deane, Julian H. Franklin, and Otto Kirchheimer for their generous help and encouragement. I am grateful to Robert D. Cumming, Maurice M. Goldsmith, and J. G. A. Pocock, from whose suggestions and comments I have benefited. I am also indebted to Carole Parsons, Oreste Ranum, Eugene F. Rice, and Robert J. McShea for help at various stages. My thanks are also due to Ene Sirvet and Barry J. Naughton for their assistance with the manuscript.

Perfection
and
Progress

Introduction

1

The Utopian Tradition

The utopian tradition is recognized as having had a long career within Western political thought. According to the interests of the commentator, the tradition may be said to have begun as early as Isaiah's prophecies or Homer's description of the Phaeacians and to have persisted to the present either in the work of those engaged in projecting alternate futures or in science fiction fantasies.

This study is neither a survey of utopian thought nor an analysis of all the salient features of this form of writing. Its purpose is rather to describe certain changes in the enterprise of constructing ideal commonwealths that come into focus in the seventeenth and eighteenth centuries and that mark the difference between classical and modern utopian thought.

Definition of Utopia

The most prominent difference between classical and modern utopian thought is to be found in the different purposes they seek to accomplish. This difference is exemplified in the attempt of modern utopians to incorporate change into the ideal society and thereby to establish at least a congruence between utopia and reality with a view to changing the latter. This new purpose has, in turn, changed the impact, sense, and significance of utopia. The derogatory sense of "utopian" as impractical, irresponsible thinking in a void, though perhaps already implicit in More's ambiguous coinage of the word, is now normal usage.[1] Such usage reflects the fact that the static character of utopia had become a problem for the modern utopian author, intent upon bringing his vision of the future into existence. For the classical utopian author, the static nature of utopia presented no such difficulties. Rather, it complemented his purpose: to provide a fixed standard of judgment and to articulate an ideal in thought.

Any attempt to confine the variety and complexity of utopias within one definition is an invitation to failure. Certainly any work dealing with social phenomena which purports to do more than narrate, describe, or explain present conditions has elements in common with utopias. To take only one example, Erasmus' *The Praise of Folly* resembles More's *Utopia* in that both are satiric comments on their times; critical of contemporary

[1] *Eu-topos,* "place where all is well," or *ou-topos,* "nowhere." Surtz and Hexter note that it is not certain that More intended the prefix to bear a double meaning; in earlier correspondence More used only the negative sense. Thomas More, *The Complete Works of St. Thomas More,* Vol. IV: *Utopia,* ed. Edward Surtz and J. H. Hexter (New Haven: Yale University Press, 1965), p. 385.

ideals to which only lip service is paid, they both have a vision of a better world to juxtapose to the existing one.

There is also a close connection between saturnalia, satire, Cockaigne, and utopia.[2] Bacon's saturnalia, *Gesta Grayorum,* which was written for the twelve days of Christmas license at Gray's Inn, is a first draft of Salomon's House. There are, moreover, similarities between utopian and Robinsonade literature (the latter involve an enforced exile) and between utopian and apocalyptic literature, but such discussions go beyond the competence of this study.[3]

Utopias are somewhat more easily distinguished from fantasy because they presuppose no miracles of nature or improbable physiological developments. Utopias that are primitive in character, however, shift very easily into fantasy and the tradition of the land of Cockaigne. In Iambulus' work (ca. third century B.C.), utopia and fantasy merge: there is neither day nor night, and men live to the age of 150 in an environment of spontaneous abundance without themselves growing soft.[4]

To distinguish utopias from the previously mentioned genres, the term will be used to designate totally fictive constructions or reconstructions of society. A proposal for changing only one or several institutions would not constitute a utopia for the purposes of this study. To be a utopia, such a proposal would have to describe all the major social arrangements an author thinks are necessary and desirable for the good life.

Utopias in Relation to Other Forms of Political Thought
Utopias have in common with other modes of social or political thought the attempt to construct or depict a functioning society. That is to say, most

[2]Robert C. Elliott, "Saturnalia, Satire, and Utopia," *The Yale Review,* LV (Summer 1966), 521–536. The section in the *Statesman* (272^{c-e}) in which Plato suggests that in the age of Cronus men might have led a debauched life instead of using their reason wisely is reminiscent of the tradition of utopia as saturnalia. The passage suggests that Plato was aware that in a state of ease and plenty where all problems have been eliminated, what is distinctively human in men may not come into existence.
[3]For differences between utopia and Robinsonade literature, see Fritz Brüggemann, *Utopie und Robinsonade* (Weimar: A. Duncker, 1914). For differences between utopia and apocalyptic literature, see H. H. Rowley, *The Relevance of Apocalyptic: A Study of Jewish and Christian Apocalypses from Daniel to the Revelation* (2nd ed. rev.; New York: Association Press, 1963), pp. 38 ff.
[4]Iambulus, *Heliopolis,* cited from Ernest Barker, *From Alexander to Constantine* (Oxford: At the Clarendon Press, 1956), pp. 61–64. For a discussion of primitive utopias in the Middle Ages, see George Boas, *Essays on Primitivism and Related Ideas in the Middle Ages* (Baltimore: The Johns Hopkins Press, 1948), pp. 138–167.

such theories attempt, if only in a cursory fashion, to deal with what they conceive to be the main prerequisites of a viable social system.

Utopian thinking, conceived in its paradigmatic classical form, would be placed at one end of a spectrum of political thought because its criticism of society is indirect. Although classical utopias (most notably More's) frequently contain topical criticism, they aim primarily at a change in the individual. While the critical utopian endeavor may prepare the way for social change by changing individuals, both Plato and Andreae, as well as More, are pessimistic about their ability to influence men who have political power.

At the other end of the spectrum would be political thought at its most pragmatic: limited projects for specific changes in given areas of society. This mode of thinking considers criticism of social reality useful mainly in order to draw attention to areas in which change is imperative or impending. It is commonly faulted for its inability to do more than react to present or anticipated needs, for its tendency to acquiesce in the direction in which social change is occurring. In its concern to control the extent of social change and to remedy its less fortunate by-products, pragmatic thought is liable to criticism for neglecting standards or ideals by which the direction of social change can be judged. Thus it may be tentatively placed at the other end of this spectrum of political thought. To the extent that modern utopias offer only a critique of existing society, the change they propose is very closely tied to the problems of the present, and they tend in the direction of pragmatic thought.

In between these two extremes will be found the broad range of political theory as one normally conceives of it: thinking that combines criticism of existing social arrangements with provisions for change and derives both of these from an ideal of (or assumption about) man's nature and activity in society.

While utopias can be seen as part of a spectrum of political thought, they may also be viewed as a particular kind of political theory if the latter is not considered entirely as a cognitive enterprise. At its best, political theory is also the proposal in vivid terms of priorities among possible forms of social life, and utopias are one form these proposals may take. If one conceives of political argument as beginning at a quite specific level of disagreement concerning the desirability or adequacy of empirical social phenomena and working back to disagreements based on different value schemata, there comes a point at which direct argument is no longer effective. This is not in the least because all values are seen as relative but because any of various values or value schemata, once chosen, can provide a more or less satisfactory basis for explaining the present and mapping its relation to the past and future.

When such an opposition of principle arises, one way to break through the impasse is by describing how one's ideals would *actually* work if given free rein; one tries to persuade by means of a picture or a concrete description. I have called the utopian attempt to employ this mode of political persuasion a thought experiment, but in the forms of metaphor, analogy, or fictive reconstructions of the past or present, this type of argument is found widely in political writing. Classical utopias, to the extent that they are successful, are a method of reaching agreement about ideals, thereby establishing a nonprivate standard of judgment. Modern utopian authors also describe how their ideals would work if reality could be made to conform to them. But to the extent that the modern author views man's nature as characterized by a *diversity* of legitimate values and ends to be sought, he cannot expect that the values he pictures in utopia will necessarily evoke recognition and eventual assent. When an opposition of principle or of value arises, the new universe of discourse that the modern utopia establishes cannot solve the problems leading to the breakdown of political argument at a more theoretical level. If it is, at present, almost a truism to believe that man's future environment will influence the nature and delineate the scope of the values available to its citizens, the modern utopia's dilemma points all the more vividly to the need to obtain prior assent to the values men use as guides in shaping their common environment.

Selection of Utopias

Six utopian commonwealths are examined in this study. Plato's *Republic*, More's *Utopia*, and Andreae's *Christianopolis* are studied as modes of classical utopian thought; Bellamy's *Looking Backward*, Wells's *A Modern Utopia*, and Howells's *A Traveller from Altruria* and *Through the Eye of the Needle* are used as examples of modern utopian thought. The decision to study Plato and More needs no justification; they are the giants of utopian thought, and no work that omitted them for lesser men could claim to have sufficiently dealt with classical utopias. Although less well known, Andreae's utopia warrants study because it is unambiguously built on the premises of Christianity. Although More's work has been interpreted as a Christian utopia, this study does not accept that view; his utopians, guided only by natural reason, may arrive at Christian truths, but without benefit of the sacraments they cannot properly be Christians. Andreae's *Christianopolis* is the utopia of a committed Christian, written for the edification of fellow believers. And although he is writing in the same century as the better-known Bacon and Campanella, Andreae's utopia remains, as theirs do not, ahistorical.

Among modern authors the choice was more difficult. In the seventeenth and eighteenth centuries utopias were transitional in nature, retaining some of the assumptions of the classical form while, at the same time, moving in the direction of the moderns by offering themselves as models for future change. By the nineteenth century the modern utopian form has clearly emerged. *Looking Backward* was selected because it offers one of the best models of a utopia organized along economic lines, the existence of which was thought to be the inevitable result of historical development. Wells's inclusion was dictated by his valiant attempt to demonstrate that a utopia can be dynamic. Aware that the static quality of the prior utopian tradition was a defect if utopia was ever to be realized, Wells made every effort to include mechanisms and incentives for change within the organization of utopian society. The choice of Howells was somewhat idiosyncratic, for he is among the least confident of modern utopian authors. Howells's attitude toward utopia is ambiguous: he has misgivings about the quality of life that his utopia offers without, for all of that, wishing to abandon the enterprise. His interest for this study derives from his awareness—caught possibly by the novelist's fine sense for revealing nuance and detail—that what is specifically human may not be able to survive in utopia.

Among the works that have been omitted, the most famous of modern visionaries, Marx, never wrote a fully developed utopia. By and large, Marx wrote social criticism and histories in which economic and technological events were determining forces. The weight of Marx's attention and the explanatory power of his theory are focused on the past, with the complex and (some would say) conflicting purposes of establishing the primacy of economic causality and calling men to action in terms of it.

Marx's descriptions in the *German Ideology* and the *Communist Manifesto* of what a nonexploitative society would be like are suggestive and evocative statements but not fully developed utopias. Their function is to give weight and substance to Marx's technical economic critique of the present rather than to spell out an alternative working society for the future. Marx's critique of utopian socialism makes the same point: to describe the solution to social problems that arise under bad economic conditions leads men "to discover a new and more perfect system of social order and to impose this from without by propaganda," but "the more completely they were worked out in detail, the more [these social systems] could not avoid drifting off into phantasy."[5]

The Marxist concept of the state centers on those functions of government that thwart the interests of the working class and that "wither away" once the proletariat is in control. This vision of the future links Marx with anarchist rather than utopian strains of thought. His criticism of Feuerbach, like his criticism of the utopian socialists, stresses one theme: to the present "philosophers have only interpreted the world in various ways; the point, however, is to change it."[6]

Marx was so conscious of the complex process of social change and so skilled in persuading others of its inevitability that it is tempting to conclude that he deliberately avoided a detailed exposition of a final state that would put an end to history as men knew it. Certainly utopia's ability to serve as a thought experiment would have been of little interest to Marx, for the values that other men explore through utopia he discovered in the very process of change itself.

The exclusion of other noted utopian authors such as Saint-Simon, Comte, Cabet, Morris, Hertzka, Skinner, and Huxley can only be partially justified. To have multiplied the study of modern utopias to reflect the variety that the last two centuries have produced would have stretched this work to unmanageable lengths. The purpose of this study is not to analyze utopias comprehensively, but rather to describe two distinct utopian traditions, depending upon whether or not utopia is thought of as a historical phenomenon, and to point out the striking differences these two traditions make in our understanding of utopian thought. The study of several utopias in each genre is sufficient to make clear the lines of the argument; I shall be satisfied if it persuades the reader that this analysis is a useful tool for understanding the countless other utopias not mentioned or only alluded to in this study.

A word about the amount of detail included in the exposition is in order. It was assumed that the reader would be familiar with Plato's and More's work, but not necessarily with either Andreae's utopia or any of the

[5]Friedrich Engels, *Socialism: Utopian and Scientific*, in Karl Marx and Friedrich Engels, *Selected Works*, 2 vols. (Moscow: Foreign Language Publishing House, 1962), II, 79.
[6]Karl Marx, *Theses on Feuerbach* (Moscow: Progress Publishers, 1972), p. 94.

modern ones. An attempt was therefore made to include along with the analysis of the less familiar works a certain amount of description so that the reader could obtain a sense of the quality and tone of these works. A more economical form of organization would have been to discuss the utopias, not as single works, but divided into the categories used to analyze them. This format was tempting because it would have reduced the risk of repetition that can result from analyzing each utopia separately. It was rejected because it required chopping up the utopias in a manner that would prevent the reader from acquiring any sense of each society's distinctive character and coherence.

    This study draws attention to certain characteristics of utopias which, to the present, have not been sufficiently remarked upon. Too frequently in the past, utopias have been judged by the sole criterion of realization, even when utopia's realization is not of paramount concern to the author. In an attempt to redress this imbalance, I have treated utopias as a complex mode of thought, raising questions about the nature of human values, the process of change, and the basis for value judgments. Briefly, this study contends that utopias provide a standard by which existing societies may be judged to the extent that they do not, at the same time, offer proposals for future change. They also fill another, little-noticed function: they provide alternate means of carrying on a dialogue that has become stalemated because the interlocutors hold divergent or incompatible values.[7] The following sections of this chapter sketch out these contentions in more detail. The reader without a large appetite for abstraction may

---

[7]Judith Shklar's analysis of classical utopias is, in some respects, similar to mine:

For them, utopia was a model, an ideal pattern that invited contemplation and judgment but did not entail any other activity. It is a perfection that the mind's eye recognizes as true and which is described as such, and so serves as a standard of moral judgment.

Judith Shklar, "The Political Theory of Utopia: From Melancholy to Nostalgia," *Utopias and Utopian Thought*, ed. Frank E. Manuel (Boston: Houghton Mifflin Company, 1966), p. 105. Shklar considers Rousseau to be the last of the true utopians; his ideal societies serve to condemn change, which is seen as a source of imperfection, because it prevents men from living in the present and from prolonging the present by inactivity. Judith Shklar, "Rousseau's Two Models: Sparta and the Age of Gold," *Political Science Quarterly*, LXXXI (March 1966), 25–51. My study differs from Shklar's in several key respects. It argues that the critical shift in utopian thought occurs much earlier than Rousseau. Moreover, Shklar does not consider modern action-minded utopias like Bellamy's to be utopias at all. My study does, and because modern and classical utopias have in common the attempt to function as thought experiments, I am more optimistic than is Shklar about the viability of utopian thinking in the present.

prefer to move directly to the chapters following it in which specific utopias are examined in the light of these hypotheses.

Differences between Classical and Modern Utopias

The different controlling assumptions within the utopian tradition which this study investigates are not derived from differences in the variety of utopian institutional arrangements; they follow from changing assessments of what is valuable in man's nature and how he is to realize or conserve those values. Prior to the seventeenth century, utopias were not written primarily as models for societal change. Classical utopian criticism addressed itself first and foremost to changing individual men and concerned itself only secondarily with the societal arrangements in which men live.

By the nineteenth century, however, the terms of the equation were reversed: modern utopias address themselves primarily to changing the arrangements of society and are only indirectly concerned with changing man. In ideal societies such as Bellamy's, in which the change predicted in utopia is thought to be inevitable, men become better when their environment improves. While in Wells's utopia change is not thought to be inevitable, it is argued that men will become better as they deliberately attempt to change their society in the direction indicated by utopia. In both cases, attention is focused primarily on the process of change leading to utopia and only indirectly upon changes in the character of the men destined to live in utopia.

The basic assumption used to distinguish modern from classical utopian thought is man's recognition of his ability to initiate social change and use it for ends of his own devising. Before the seventeenth century, according to E. A. Burtt, space and time were accidental and not essential categories of scientific thought: "Instead of spatial connexions of things, men were seeking their logical connexions; instead of the onward march of time, men thought of the eternal passage of potentiality into actuality."[8] The essential categories were predetermined; they adhered in the nature of things and were not subject to man's volition. Extending this distinction to utopias, I suggest that modern utopias were written with the hope or expectation that they would come into existence in the near future; modern utopias are essentially time oriented. Classical utopias, less obsessed with

[8]E. A. Burtt, *The Metaphysical Foundations of Modern Physical Science* (New York: Doubleday & Company, Inc., Anchor paperback, 1932), p. 27.

actualization in time, were self-contained entities, in which an ideal or value was treated *as if* it were fully actualized.

A related measure of the difference between classical and modern utopias is the latter's attempt to make change an integral part of utopian reality. H. G. Wells calls his ideal state "A Modern Utopia" in a deliberate attempt to distinguish its dynamic, progressive character from the static perfection of previous utopias. If utopia is to be an attractive goal for future societal development, Wells thinks its values must not be static; utopia must be able to incorporate change within it. It follows that a major concern of the modern utopian author is how to portray significant change in a society that has already solved all its important problems. For classical utopias the static, nondevelopmental character of perfection poses no problem. The fully real, like the Platonic forms, need not be thought of as part of the phenomenal world, which is subject to change. (Were a utopia such as Plato's actually to come into existence, it would belong to the world of appearance and be subject to flux and decay.) Because the nature of the ideal portrayed in classical utopias is a changeless one, the immobility of utopian reality does not become the problem it is for modern utopias.

The static character of utopias has been widely recognized. George Kateb, for instance, has noted that the changelessness of classical utopias was concomitant with the view that human nature was immutable and that change was decay or decline.[9] But such immobility is not merely, as Kateb suggests, an acceptable price to pay for securing other values. It is implicit in any attempt to describe the "best"—that which by definition does not allow of change to a better state. Frank and Fritzie Manuel have observed that trouble comes to the nineteenth-century utopia "when differences and distinctions multiply and unregulated innovations disrupt the rational social forms . . . ," but they do not discuss the nature of the trouble.[10] This study suggests that these difficulties start to occur within the utopian tradition when it shifts from being an appeal to individuals to make actual the potential values they carry within them to being a theory of action in which the static utopian format is a liability to be overcome rather than an asset.

[9] George Kateb, *Utopia and Its Enemies* (New York: The Free Press of Glencoe, 1963), pp. 78–80. See also George Kateb, "Utopia and the Good Life," *Utopias and Utopian Thought*, ed. Frank E. Manuel (Boston: Houghton Mifflin Company, 1966), pp. 239–259.
[10] Frank E. Manuel and Fritzie P. Manuel, eds., *French Utopias: An Anthology of Ideal Societies* (New York: The Free Press, 1966), p. 9.

Classical and Modern Utopian Ideals

Despite the risk of an overly theoretical exposition, it may be useful for the reader, as a point of orientation, to have a map of the arguments to be developed later in detail. Among the characteristics that distinguish classical from modern utopian ideals, a most important feature of the classical utopian ideal is that its existence does not *directly* depend on a particular form of social organization but hinges rather upon the existence of a suprasensible reality. In other words, the activity of the inhabitants of utopia, which is how the primary utopian ideal is portrayed, cannot be adequately understood simply in terms of utopian social organization.

The social organization itself contains "secondary" or supporting ideals that emphasize a facet or make concrete some of the implications of the primary transcendent ideal. They are "secondary" ideals because their existence as virtues in the utopian universe depends upon a primary set of ideals that reflect the ends men should pursue. Typically, the classical utopia's emphasis is on the primary ideal, which transcends the utopia proper and under which the secondary ideal can be subsumed.

The modern utopia, by contrast, has only one ideal, which is directly dependent on the utopian social organization. The ideal is "social" because both the necessary and sufficient conditions for understanding the activities of a modern utopian citizen can be found in the arrangements of utopian society which determine the ways in which men will interact. Indeed, it is difficult to distinguish the ideal activity of a modern utopia from the social organization within which it takes place. The ideal of Bellamy's utopia, economic equality, can be described equally well in terms of the structure of utopian society or in terms of the activity of utopian citizens within that society.

What has been called the secondary ideal of classical utopias resembles the modern ideal in that they are both portrayed through utopia's social arrangements. But the differences are more important than the similarity. The secondary ideal of the classical utopia is not autonomous, and social arrangements are correspondingly unimportant; they serve to delineate an appropriate space in which something else takes place. The secondary classical ideal either prepares for the primary ideal (as in the case of More's utopians, in whom an absence of pride prepares the way for true pleasure) or exemplifies one of the facets of the ideal (as in Andreae's utopia, where knowledge is an alternate way of recognizing a deity whose existence is attested to primarily by a virtuous life). In both cases, the secondary ideal derives its significance from the primary ideal, which is addressed not to changing society but rather to measuring its worth by a fixed standard of value.

The modern utopian ideal is not transcendent and appears indistinguishable from the social organization through which it is described. Its value gains persuasiveness from the past: the prior undesirable social organization that utopia has superseded. And when this ideal is severed from its roots in the past, it appears to be an arbitrary creation, ungrounded in man's nature or his history. W. D. Howells's ideal of creative work fits this pattern, for it derives its persuasiveness from knowledge of a past in which work was too often mechanical and shoddy. When this knowledge is no longer alive, the social ideal loses its intelligibility for the men who live by it. The persuasiveness of the social ideal likewise resides in its call for change; the criticism of existing society which it offers is significant to the extent that it prepares the way for such change. But again, once the change has occurred and the author brings his utopia into existence, the persuasiveness that adheres to a call to action evaporates.

To illustrate further the difference between the classical and modern ideal or activity within utopia, one can contrast Aristotle's description of contemplation with Adam Smith's portrayal of economic activity. Aristotle's philosopher is distinguished from the just or virtuous man who functions entirely within the city-state. The philosopher needs the city-state in order to enjoy both the necessities and the goods of life, but he is not directly dependent on it for his contemplative activity. While practical wisdom is necessary for Aristotle's virtuous man, it is not sufficient to make him a philosopher capable of speculative wisdom.[11]

A good example of the social ideal or activity of modern utopias is found in Adam Smith's *The Wealth of Nations*. Smith describes a society in which men act in relation to each other because their objective, the production of certain goods, can be more efficiently achieved in this manner. The division of labor is attributed to a propensity in human nature to barter and exchange goods; but that propensity is not further explained, at least in *The Wealth of Nations*. The economic order is treated explicitly; the moral order that Smith considered coextensive with it is barely mentioned. The reason (in Glenn Morrow's interpretation) is that after Smith had described the

[11]Aristotle *Ethics* x. 6. 1177ª–1178ª and vi. 12. 1144ᵇ–1145ª. See *The Basic Works of Aristotle*, ed. Richard McKeon (New York: Random House, 1941).

moral order in *A Theory of Moral Sentiments,* he was unable to relate it by a study of jurisprudence to his description of the economic organization of society.[12] As a result, the motive of the actors does not appear in *The Wealth of Nations;* their activity is described only in terms of the social organization in which it takes place.

Classical utopian activity, then, depends for its existence directly on a suprasensible, transcendent reality, while modern utopian activity depends on a certain set of social arrangements. Although both types of activity point to an underlying order of a different nature (transcendent or historical), modern utopias encounter difficulty to the extent that they claim an enduring validity for the activity that takes place within utopia.

The distinction between classical and modern ideals is intended for purposes of analysis. Historically, the distinction could be seen to be between ideals that have an ontological standing considered to be objective and determinate, corresponding to requirements of man's nature but not created by him (classical), and ideals that have an ontological standing considered to be subjective and indeterminate, not required by man's nature, but created by him and able in turn to change his nature (modern). Polanyi describes secularism, man's attempt to conceive the meaning of life in immanent terms in this world, in comparable terms to those I have used to define modern utopian ideals.[13]

The Relation of Classical and Modern Utopias to Society
The relation of classical and modern utopias to their authors' societies is every bit as different as the ideals they embody. While classical utopias are critical of existing society, they aim primarily at changing the individual rather than society. Plato's utopia, for example, depends on a monarch being converted to philosophy *before* society can be altered by bringing the Republic into existence. Socrates begins by inquiring what justice is in the individual and, almost incidentally, to aid him in that inquiry, constructs a state in which justice is writ large. As noted previously, modern utopias attempt to change man by remaking the society in which he will live. Con-

[12]Glenn Morrow, *The Ethical and Economic Theories of Adam Smith: A Study in the Social Philosophy of the Eighteenth Century* (Cornell Studies in Philosophy, No. 13; New York: Longmans, Green, and Co., 1923), pp. 59 ff. and 45 ff.
[13]Michael Polanyi, *History and Hope: Progress in Freedom,* ed, K. A. Jelenski (London: Routledge and Kegan Paul, 1962), pp. 18–24. As this treatment is not primarily historical, and as the authors' nonutopian works are not considered, the distinction is used analytically rather than historically.

sequently, they are much more dependent on the society they criticize, for in it they must locate the critical impetus for change which is to bring utopia into being and maintain it over time. Bellamy typifies the modern position: for all his distaste of cutthroat economic conditions, it is these very conditions that create individuals capable of desiring the saner society of his utopia.

To underscore the contrasting relationship of classical and modern utopias to their own society, I have described the role of one as a standard of judgment and the role of the other as a vehicle for social criticism. The classical utopia's standard of judgment provides an unchanging criterion by which to measure man and his society. It condemns the direction of change in the present but does not *directly* offer utopia as an alternative. While it may prepare the way for change, a standard of judgment is not the same as a proposal for change, for it does not specify either the form or the degree of change which is to be brought about. The modern utopia's social criticism is much nearer a critique than a judgment; its description of the ills of the body politic is relentless but never despairing. Its criticism of existing society is inevitably an ambiguous one, for without present injustices the future utopia would not be possible.

The differences between a standard and a critique are very closely linked to the differences between the classical and modern utopian ideals. In classical utopias, both primary and secondary activity is linked to or grounded in a reality that transcends them. As a result of this linkage, the social activity or organization depicted in classical utopias is based on and justified by a transcendent ideal, conceived to be different in kind and not just in degree from the way existing society is organized. Classical utopias are standards of judgment not merely because they offer a static society to contrast to the flux and change of the present but also because they offer a picture of social arrangements that are radically different in character from the ones to be found in existing society.

The modern utopian critique, by contrast, is based on the single ideal these societies exemplify. The cluster of activities describing this ideal is social in nature and serves as the basis for all other apparently unrelated activities within the utopia. The modern utopian ideal is "pervasive" as well as social—that is to say, all other activities in utopia (activities that are not necessarily social in nature) take on the character and imprint of the social ideal. *Looking Backward* contains a striking example. Bellamy describes his ideal state as undergoing a second renaissance, in which literature and the arts flourish as never before. Yet his description of artistic activity, closely examined, is little more than a description of his social ideal, economic equality, under another name. Bellamy describes the way artists earn their living in utopia. As he does not describe any other, independent criterion by which to evaluate the results of the artists' activities, the merit of artistic work is measured (almost by default) by the artists' abilities to support themselves.

In contrast to the transcendent nature of the classical ideal, the modern utopian ideal is different only in degree, not in kind, from the rationale that the author believes determines his own society. Modern utopias depict more rational and more humane social arrangements than those the author criticizes. Typically, poverty and prejudice are eliminated, and men are no longer penalized for what is not their fault. It is not at all surprising that the modern utopia, which is intended to come into existence as soon as conditions permit, should find its source of change in dissatisfaction with preutopian conditions. The consequence is, however, that the utopian ideal is understood and justified in terms of the preutopian reality that it has superseded. It is rather as if a motion picture began with its characters in a very unpleasant predicament that resolved itself as the picture progressed. Once the problems are solved, the picture stops, leaving the last image on the screen. The modern utopia is rather like this final film frame; it really makes sense only in terms of the preceding and now resolved predicament. In an effort to provide men with a continued full development in the utopian future, modern authors claim to incorporate change in their societies. But when the incentives for change within utopia are examined, they appear to be of the same nature as those that were responsible for the injustice of preutopian society. The difference is that within utopia such incentives no longer result in inequitable social arrangements. If, to continue the analogy, the film director were to behave like a utopian author, he would claim that the film is still going on. Because his characters have shown themselves capable of decisive action in the past, they are, he would claim, still capable of significant action in the present.

In sum, the modern utopia is a critique rather than a standard of judgment because its social ideal is of similar nature to the principle that organizes preutopian reality and because its significance depends on the preutopian reality it is designed to replace.

It should be apparent that in claiming that classical utopias portray a society different in kind, and not merely in degree, from existing social reality, much more is meant than that classical utopian thought is self-contained, formal, and abstract, while social reality is subject to different and less orderly criteria: change, novelty, custom, and irrational belief. Modern utopian thought is also very abstract and formal in comparison to existing reality; it likewise presents a simplified world in which social arrangements are worked out logically, unimpeded by such complicating factors at work in the present as habit or irrational belief. Classical and modern utopias are both abstract verbal constructions, but because of the different nature and grounding of their ideals classical utopias differ in kind, and modern utopias only in degree, from existing reality.

A standard of judgment may thus be said to transcend existing society, whereas the modern critique does not. The social activity displayed in the modern utopia is the basis for its critique of contemporary society; the ideal on which this activity is grounded may be called immanent in contemporary society because it is, of course, the source of the impetus responsible for bringing utopia into existence. The modern utopian ideal can differ only in degree from current reality; were the hiatus more absolute, there would be no possibility of going from one to the other. Both utopia and reality are, from the modern perspective, capable of change. But within the modern utopia the social ideal appears pervasive; it organizes the entire utopian reality and is not limited by another ideal of a different nature because that other possible ideal—change in the direction of utopia—has already been achieved.

A standard of judgment, therefore, is based on ideals that transcend both existing social reality and utopian reality. A critique is based on ideals immanent in existing social reality and fully expressed in utopian reality. In the course of examining these differences in particular utopias, the question arises whether or not the modern utopia is as effective as an instrument for changing the present as the classical utopia was for judging it. Timeliness is not intrinsic to the nature of the modern utopian idea; change is appropriate to it and could serve as a model for effecting change in the real world if the author were able to express such change within the constraints of utopian thought.

Characteristics Common to Classical and Modern Utopian Thought
Despite the different presuppositions on which classical and modern utopias are built, there are important continuities within utopian thought.

The critique of existing society made by a modern utopia serves a function similar to that of the standard of judgment afforded by the classical utopia. In the *process* of constructing a modern utopia, the author is led to ponder some of the implications of his ideal and to understand it better by embodying it in a hypothetical society. The author expands and specifies his social ideal until it is fully exemplified in "facts," in this case the institutions and organization of his utopia. These "facts" all refer to, and are justified by, the ideal. The result is to make the institutions and social arrangements of utopia a counterpart of the ideal, a replica of the ideal at a level of greater specificity.

This process is a form of thought experiment, *similar* but not *identical* to the manner in which classical utopias articulate their ideals in thought. The experiment is similar insofar as it involves the process of drawing out and making concrete the implications of an ideal. The difference lies in the different nature of the ideals articulated.

The classical ideal corresponds to that which is thought to be most permanent and valuable in men's natures. The ideal is public, or can become public, in the sense that it is capable of offering permanent satisfaction, and some men are capable of recognizing this when it is pointed out to them. The classical utopia attempts to make the reader recognize this ideal by showing him what it would be like to live in a reality determined by it and in which no complicating or contradictory factors are present.

Like its classical counterpart, the modern utopia tries to elicit the reader's assent by drawing a verbal picture. But there is a difficulty. The social ideal of the modern utopia addresses itself, not to men's common nature, but to their common environment. Thus, when change in the direction of utopia is thought to be inevitable, the effect is to constrain rather than to persuade the reader to accept the utopian ideal, for to refuse the inevitable is to risk being judged not merely mistaken but, more important, immoral by the standards of future utopians. It is arguable that to postulate a common future history is no more or less arbitrary than to postulate a common human nature. The issue is not the validity but the different grounds on which these claims are based. Plato holds that men have a common human nature that is as necessary to their well-being as lungs or vocal cords. Bellamy argues (from the vantage point of utopia) that change in the direction of the ideal society is inevitable; his is really an argument that the future will vindicate his ideals. These ideals are not "necessary" either in the sense that events could develop only in this manner or in the sense that human nature is truly satisfied only when adhering to one set of common values.

If the reader, then, should choose to reject either the inevitability of change or the correctness of the modern utopian author's description of it, he is free to imagine another utopia, to perform his own thought experiment. Compared with the classical utopian ideal, the modern social ideal appears to be private. If the reader happens to hold the same beliefs as the author, he may find the latter's argument convincing. If not, he can construct a counterutopia in which he feels more at ease and which, at the same time, vindicates his own view of the future.

The phenomenon of counterutopias does not appear before the seventeenth century. While More's utopia aroused considerable comment in humanist circles, it provoked no further efforts at utopian creation. But Bacon's unfinished utopia, *New Atlantis,* was the stimulus for a number of similarly named utopias, elaborating upon or criticizing his proposals for a scientific college.[14] Bacon's utopia and the reactions it elicited are part of a transitional period in utopian thought. It was only Bacon's idea of scientific development, rather than any vision he offered of complete and coordinated social arrangements, that aroused comment. However, by the time Bellamy wrote *Looking Backward,* he provoked his contemporaries into a barrage of counterutopias criticizing the entire scope and tenor of his social arrangements.[15]

Thought experiments are a persistent feature of utopias, recognizable in the *finished* utopia by the abstract, somewhat schematic quality of its thought. This quality seems to be present in all utopias irrespective of their content and helps utopias to maintain their distance from the real world. Insofar as the thought experiment is similar in classical and modern utopian thought, it is distinct from any attempt to provide a model for future change. It is much nearer to the philosophic effort, as seen, for example, in Spinoza, to articulate certain principles coherently and according to logical norms into a system.

---

[14] See H. R. Trevor-Roper, *The Crisis of the Seventeenth Century: Religion, the Reformation and Social Change* (New York: Harper & Row, Publishers, 1968), pp. 237 ff.; A. L. Morton, *The English Utopia* (London: Lawrence and Wishart, Ltd., 1952), pp. 79 ff.
[15] Some of the titles themselves indicate the tenor of the criticism: *Looking Further Backward* (A. D. Vinton, 1890); *Looking Further Forward* (R. Michaelis, ca. 1890); and *Looking Within* (J. W. Roberts, 1893).

While I do not intend to suggest that a thought experiment is related to a particular position about the nature of truth, in an essay on truth as coherence Harold Joachim gives a good account of what is involved in the process of investigating an ideal in thought:

A "significant whole" is an organized individual experience, self-fulfilling and self-fulfilled. Its organization *is* the process of its self-fulfillment, and the concrete manifestation of its individuality. But the process is no mere surface-play between static parts within the whole. . . . The coherence—if we call it a "form"—is a form which through and through interpenetrates its materials; and they . . . are materials which retain no inner privacy for themselves in independence of the form. They hold their distinctive being in and through, and not in sheer defiance of, their identical form; and its identity is the concrete sameness of different materials.[16]

What Raymond Ruyer calls a mental exercise also comes very near to describing what is meant by a thought experiment. Ruyer, however, considers the "lateral possibilities" of an event or fact (alternative modes of procedure), rather than ideals, to be the subject matter of such a mental exercise:

It is not by their variety of purpose, nor is it by their imaginativeness that utopias should be defined. . . . The essence [or unifying principle] is the use of the utopian method or mode of thought. . . . there is a utopian mode of thought, which can be defined as a *mental exercise on lateral possibilities.*
The utopian mode of thought belongs by nature to the realm of theory and speculation. But unlike theory, which seeks knowledge of that which is, the utopian mode of thought is an exercise or a playing with the possibilities lateral to reality. In the utopian mode of thought intellect becomes "a power of concrete operation"; it amuses itself in trying out mentally the possibilities which it sees overflowing reality. The utopian mode of thought is related to "understanding"; it depends on an initial understanding of reality, and in its turn it helps toward a better comprehension. . . .[17]

The static quality of utopia is necessary to utopia if it is to remain a simplified, schematic construct through which the author can investigate the implications of his ideal and see the ideal reflected in a society molded to its specifications. This effort of abstraction or articulation, central to classical utopian thought, continues to be exhibited in modern utopias. But I shall

[16]Harold Joachim, "Truth as Coherence," *Contemporary Philosophic Problems: Selected Readings,* ed. Abraham Edel and Yervant Krikorian (New York: The Macmillan Company, 1959), pp. 218–219 (Joachim's italics).
[17]Raymond Ruyer, *L'utopie et les utopies* (Paris: Presses universitaires de France, 1950), p. 9 (Ruyer's italics; my translation).

argue that the modern effort to incorporate change into the static utopian structure, though successful in portraying only the weakest form of change, serves to distract attention from one of utopia's continuing assets: its ability to serve as a thought experiment.

My study will explore the differences that distinguish the classical from the modern utopian enterprise: the character of the utopian ideal and utopia's attitude toward change both within utopia and in relation to contemporary society. I shall try to show why modern utopias are not as successful in their multiple enterprise of attempting to criticize contemporary society, change it into utopia, and accommodate within utopia the valuable characteristics of preutopian reality as classical utopias are in their more modest endeavor to provide a standard that allows men to measure and judge the adequacy of their society.

Although the classical and the modern utopia, as finished products, are very different in nature, the type of thought experiment that occurs in the process of creating a utopia remains characteristic of the entire utopian tradition. The consequences of such exercises will, of course, vary, depending upon whether or not human nature is seen as requiring a plurality of values for its development or satisfaction. While neither classical nor modern utopian thought offers criteria by which to rank or judge different sets of values, in the process of investigating ideals in thought a special sort of knowledge is acquired: a concrete awareness of the possible implications of one set of values. This knowledge, the result of an exercise—a thought experiment of sorts—is a way of becoming alert to the implications of values, what they exclude as well as what they permit.

The *Republic*
of
Plato

2

The view that Plato did not expect the Republic to be brought into being is a common one. Werner Jaeger calls the Republic a paradigm of virtue, and John Burnet describes it as a standard by which existing and possible institutions may be judged.[1] Most commentators indicate uncertainty about Plato's intention in writing the *Republic*. Whether or not Plato's Republic is an unsuccessful blueprint for future change is not crucial; the Republic's importance for this study lies in the character of the utopian ideals and their relationship to the Greek polis.

Classical utopias have been said to exhibit two ideals: one primary, the other secondary. In the *Republic* these two ideals are contemplation of the Good and justice. Plato's ideal of contemplation both requires a just society to be understood at its full value and transcends the just society, pointing to a greater reality beyond it. The Republic is a static society in which, when change does occur, it takes the weakest possible form—that of specifying already established principles. Although the unchanging character of Plato's society makes it difficult to conceive of utopia being brought into existence, it is well adapted to a classical utopia's primary purposes: to function as a thought experiment and as a standard of justice.

The Two Ideals of the Republic
The most important feature of the classical utopia is that its existence is not directly dependent on a particular form of social organization but instead relies upon the existence of a transcendent ideal. In the Republic this ideal is the form of the Good. The secondary or supporting ideal, justice, is necessary to the full and continued contemplation of the Good, for without justice the philosopher lacks an environment that remains congruent with his contemplative activity by adopting one facet of the Good, justice, as its ruling principle.

The task that Socrates sets himself in the *Republic* is to show Glaucon and Adeimantus why justice is valuable in itself whether or not it is seen and acknowledged by gods or by men. The manner in which he pro-

---

[1]Werner Jaeger, *Paideia: The Ideals of Greek Culture,* trans. Gilbert Highet (New York: Oxford University Press, 1943–1945), II, 260; John Burnet, *Greek Philosophy: Plato to Thales* (London: Macmillan & Co., Ltd., paperback, 1961), p. 292. See also Francis M. Cornford, trans., *The Republic of Plato* (New York: Oxford University Press, 1945), p. 1; David Grene, *Greek Political Theory: The Image of Man in Thucydides and Plato* (Chicago: The University of Chicago Press, 1965), p. 191; Robert Cushman, *Therapeia: Plato's Concept of Philosophy* (Chapel Hill: University of North Carolina Press, 1958), pp. 32–34; *The Collected Dialogues of Plato,* ed. Edith Hamilton and Huntington Cairns (New York: Bollingen Foundation, 1963).

ceeds with his task is worth investigating, because while Socrates teaches his companions a great deal about the nature of justice, he does not really show that justice, isolated from the Good, is valuable in itself. What he does succeed in demonstrating is that both in the soul and in the state justice cannot be understood in isolation from the other virtues. In the soul justice expresses an internal harmony, the rule of reason over the passions. In the state justice stands for the harmonious relationship between the different classes and appears as a form of social organization in which the Good can be pursued for its own sake while at the same time benefiting the state. In both cases, justice is the precondition for the philosopher's contemplative activity, and its value derives from its relation to the Good.

As Socrates explains justice, it is not a substantive virtue with its own specific field of activity but the right organization of the other three virtues: wisdom, courage, and temperance. Wisdom is knowledge of the best conduct for the entire state; courage is knowledge of what really is to be feared; and temperance is unanimous agreement about who shall rule. In the state justice is the proper performance of one's function; it stands for the principle of the division of labor and is the condition for the existence of the other three virtues.

In the soul the distinctions between the virtues are less rigorously maintained. Justice is self-mastery: the maintenance of right order and internal harmony. In this respect, justice is very similar to temperance, for when the latter is described in the soul, it also serves as a principle of unification. Likewise, courage and wisdom appear to merge in the soul when courage is defined as obedience to reason concerning what one should fear. As wisdom itself is described as knowledge of what is good for the three elements of the soul, separately and in common, the main distinction that appears to remain between the virtues is that temperance and, presumably, justice are fully present in the souls of all the citizens, whereas courage and wisdom are exemplified primarily in the Auxiliary and Guardian classes. (To avoid confusion, those whose function is to defend the state will be called Auxiliaries, and the philosopher-rulers will be referred to as Guardians.)

When Socrates describes the virtues in the individual, all four are present (although courage and wisdom in different degrees) in each soul. But when one looks at the structure of Plato's state and asks where knowledge resides, the distinction between the virtues is more sharply evident, separating the craftsmen from the rulers, and within the ruling class separating the right opinion *(ortha doxa)* of the Auxiliaries from the knowledge, *(epistēmē)* of the Guardians. Although the distinction is made more sharply, it is not as crucial in the *Republic,* where carefully designed institutions and a coherent educational system serve to stabilize right opinions, as in the badly ordered state where individuals are subjected to the flux and change that are characteristic of appearances. It is when the virtues express qualities within the soul that the interdependence of the three classes is most clearly seen. Both courage and wisdom work *directly* for the good of the entire state, while temperance and justice characterize the unity and harmony of the entire state, which depend on a separation of functions. Justice, the right performance of an activity resulting from a rightly ordered soul, may be said to characterize all classes in the *Republic,* as all classes have the same order (but not degree of development) of faculties within the soul.

In other words, when Plato describes justice in the state and temperance in the soul, he seems to be emphasizing the common purposes of a rightly ordered state, to which all classes contribute, rather than the different functions of each class, by which they make their contribution. The perfectly just man is the one who is aware of the difference of function and the unity of purpose within the state and acts on that awareness, while the perfectly unjust man is the despot who, ruled by the worst of his appetites, has purged the state of all classes that are better than he is and has remade the state in his own image.

At times Plato treats justice as if it could be equally well described as a state of knowledge or as an activity.

In all these fields when he speaks of just and honourable conduct, he will mean the behaviour that helps to produce and to preserve this habit of mind; and by wisdom he will mean the knowledge which presides over such conduct. Any action which tends to break down this habit will be for him unjust; and the notions governing it he will call ignorance and folly.[2]

There is no gap, requiring a special effort of the will to be bridged, between knowing one's craft and practicing it for Plato. All four virtues, like the *technai,* can be described as skills involving both knowledge of the true end of the activity and knowledge of how to attain the end.[3] Like the distinction

[2]Cornford, *The Republic of Plato,* p. 142; *Republic* iv. 443ᵉ. All direct quotations are from Cornford's translation of the *Republic* and will be cited both from the Cornford edition and by Stephanos' pagination.
[3]See Cornford, *The Republic of Plato,* p. 8, for the comparison between justice and the *technai.*

between virtue in the soul and virtue in the state, the distinction between
virtuous conduct issuing from within or imposed from without is not an
important one. "It is better," Socrates says, "for everyone, . . . to be subject
to a godlike wisdom residing within him, or failing that, imposed from
without, in order that all of us, being under one guidance, may be so far as
possible equal and united."[4]

This lack of sharp separation between being and doing is the reason
why cobblers and warriors cannot exchange tasks in Plato's *Republic* while
cobblers and carpenters may, for to change the nature of the activity performed by any class would disrupt the right order within the soul. It is the
same dislike of disorientation within the soul, the result of playing different
roles, which leads to Plato's strictures on the desirability of drama in the
Republic. So when Plato describes the three classes within the state as
interdependent and as working for the common well-being, their activities
can equally well be understood in terms of their special knowledge. Thus
Plato calls the philosopher just when he recognizes the requirements of the
common good and reluctantly accepts the rulership of the state for which
his knowledge has qualified him.

Justice is a secondary virtue, supporting well-tempered souls and
maintaining the harmonious social structure necessary to the philosopher's
activity. While it is true that for the Guardians a rightly ordered soul is not
entirely dependent on the wise organization of the state (philosophers are
found in corrupt states), it is only in the just state that their existence is
assured and their activity unhampered. The philosopher owes his training in
philosophy to the state, and it is only within the state that he can attain his
full stature, although once his training has led him to see the Good, he is no
longer dependent on instruction to continue his contemplative activity. The
philosopher must be just (and know the form of justice) before he can
understand the nature of the Good, but once he has understood the Good,
justice and all other forms are derived from and confirmed by his vision of
the Good.

The Good, insofar as Socrates is able to convey knowledge of it, is of
a different nature from justice. It is apprehended through dialectic that
starts from assumptions and ascends to that which requires no assumptions.
It is dialectic alone that has the peculiar power of disclosing the truth, but
the truth, once revealed, needs no explanation or justification outside itself.

[4]Ibid., p. 318; *Republic* ix. 590[d].

In other words, reason, strictly trained, is the means by which to arrive at contemplation, but contemplation is a state altogether different from reason itself.

This, then, which gives to the objects of knowledge their truth, and to him who knows them his power of knowing, is the Form or essential nature of Goodness. . . . while you may think of it as an object of knowledge, you will do well to regard it as something *beyond* truth and knowledge and, precious as these are, of still higher worth.[5]

In comparing the Good to the sun, however, Plato indicates that "beyond" does not signify cut off but means greater in dignity and power. The Good transcends the other forms and is their ground and being. Likewise, although dialectic is the method used to ascend to a vision of the Good, the Good itself is known by contemplation *(theoria)*. The Good is intrinsically intelligible and self-evident because human reason *(nous)* is axiological in its structure and inclination and therefore essentially conformed to the Good. Intelligence and Good are mutually self-defining, and to be dissatisfied with the Good is either to deny the essential nature of intelligence or to require a standpoint outside existence by which to interpret existence.[6]

Plato marks the difference between the philosopher and the other classes in his Republic by suggesting that there is an essential affinity between the philosopher's soul and the reality he attempts to grasp. The philosopher contemplates, and reproduces as much as is possible in his own soul, a divinely harmonious and unchanging order where reason governs and nothing can do or suffer harm. Were the philosopher to attempt to direct any state but the perfectly just one, he would risk disrupting the harmony in his soul by attempting to rule in a society hostile to reason and its ordering function; the consequence of attempting to rule such a state would be to make his soul unfit to understand the Good. In short, the philosopher requires the just society not only for training in philosophy but also because it provides him with a field of activity in which reason and its ruling function are preserved and valued.

It is possible to treat the *Republic* as a dialogue that, like dialectic, attempts to give a rational account *(logos)* of justice. The vision of the Good, which can be described only in images, is an activity that is different in kind

[5]Cornford, *The Republic of Plato*, p. 220; *Republic* vi. 508^d–509^b (my italics).
[6]Cushman, *Therapeia*, pp. 43, 160, 179. My discussion is indebted to Robert Cushman's interpretation, which posits an essential congruity between the knowing faculty and the object known.

from the just activity of the rightly ordered society. It is because the vision of the Good transcends the social order and confers understanding of a quality and purity not to be found in the social order that the philosopher must be "persuaded" or "constrained" by the laws of the state to turn away from contemplation of the Good.[7] The end of the rightly ordered society is its own harmonious functioning and that of the citizens who comprise it, while the end of the philosopher is a form of understanding that includes and surpasses justice.[8] In other words, the Good has reality apart from the state that serves it and reflects one of its aspects, justice, in the rightly ordered society. Similarly, the contemplative activity of the philosopher (as distinct from the training in different stages of knowledge leading to contemplation) can be said to occur "outside" the state. Although it can be described as supremely active, contemplation does not issue in actions; it is essentially a solitary activity and does not even require the presence of other philosophers.

Socrates admits that, of itself, his description of justice is insufficient to show why it, and no other principle, offers the best form of organization for the state. It is only when justice is related to the nature of the Good that the full significance of a rightly ordered soul and the full validity of justice's claim to rule in the state can be understood. Viewed in isolation from the Good, justice would appear to be arbitrarily chosen as an organizing principle. While it might be recommended as more consistent or efficient than the contradictory practices by which existing states are managed, Adeimantus has, from the outset, stipulated that justice is to be defended in itself, independent of its consequences and its relation to injustice.

The description of the Good meets part of Adeimantus' demand. It grounds justice in a reality transcending the Republic Socrates has created and, by the same token, transcends the actual states he criticizes. Justice becomes increasingly self-validating when it conforms to, and is seen as a part of, an objective good that both supports and makes intelligible the

[7]*Republic* vii. 519[e]. The tension between justice and the Good, between the philosopher's responsibility to rule and his desire to continue his contemplation of the forms, is not fully resolved in the *Republic*. It is possible to reduce the tension between these two goods by describing the Guardians' rule as a means of perpetuating a state of affairs congenial to their own interests. To overemphasize this element, however, is to make justice into enlightened self-interest, which is Thrasymachus' position. For a discussion of this problem, see N. R. Murphy, *The Interpretation of Plato's Republic* (Oxford: At the Clarendon Press, 1960), pp. 16–22.

[8]When the special position of the philosopher is taken into account, it becomes understandable why the "bottom part" of Plato's state is treated so sketchily. It would be difficult to explain Plato's neglect of the education of the artisans were his state constructed only to exhibit justice.

virtues whose right organization constitutes justice. When it is viewed in the light of the Good, the relation of justice to the Good is more than the one of indirect dependence, suggested by Plato's description of the ascent from various subordinate forms to the vision of the Good, which includes them. As an aspect of the Good, justice transcends the ideal state, and to a far greater and almost incommensurable degree, it transcends existing states. Both justice and the utopia devised to exhibit its principles derive their justification from the unchanging nature of the transcendent Good.

The Static Character of the Republic

The changelessness of utopian society is part of its transcendence, signaling that the nature of its ideals is different in kind from those of contemporary societies. For Plato the permanent is the real, and the immobility of the ideal society is meant to be in sharp contrast to a world of flux and change—a world alien, even inimical, to the true nature of thought. In the *Republic*, more clearly than in any other utopia, change is a liability, for the satisfaction of reason in the permanency of the forms is the most real satisfaction for Plato and includes all other satisfactions within it.

The static character of the Republic follows, of itself, from Socrates' description of perfection:

. . . is his [a god's] nature simple and of all things the least likely to depart from its proper form? . . .

So this immunity to change from outside is characteristic of anything which, thanks to art or nature or both, is in a satisfactory state. . . .

Then a god cannot desire to change himself. Being as perfect as he can be, . . . [he] remains simply and forever in his own form.[9]

Perfection, quite naturally, cannot be improved upon. In other words, there is little room for change in a society in which, thanks to a judicious use of art and nature, all goods for men have been identified and incorporated in the most adequate institutions of which the author can conceive.

Were one to look for change in Plato's utopia, one might expect to find it in the latitude he gives to the military. But material gains provide no incentive for aggression in Plato's self-sufficient state. The Auxiliaries exist only to protect the state against the danger of change brought about by the threat of aggression from "outside." They are men initially selected for their qualities of endurance and steadfastness, who are then given a rigorous training in gentleness and humaneness as well as in the more martial qual-

[9]Cornford, *The Republic of Plato*, pp. 72–73; *Republic* ii. 380^e–381^c.

ities. The communism under which they live precludes the unsettling extremes of both wealth and poverty and prevents the Auxiliaries from falling prey to the idleness and luxurious mode of life typical of wealthier states. Such a regime creates, almost as a matter of course, stable character traits that prevent the Auxiliaries from being tempted to subvert their own or other cities. Plato notes, furthermore, that any state with which his Republic might be at war is, in fact, at least two states—the rich and the poor. Such states are easily subverted from within by promising to either class the entire wealth and power of the city. Without rancor between classes, the Republic itself would be immune to any such subversion. Shirking one's duty in such a state would seem barely conceivable if the Guardians had done their job of selection adequately, but Plato mentions that its occurrence would be punished by demotion to the artisan-farmer class.

Protected from change imposed from "outside," any change within the Republic would require a decision from the Guardians, who are, in Plato's words, primarily preservers and protectors. He does not conceive of their making numerous laws, which might then need to be amended. Guided by the principles already embodied in their institutions, the Guardians' primary duty is to interpret particular cases in the spirit of the institutions already created. Socrates compares a host of petty regulations to a doctor who caters to an invalid rather than curing him, and he notes that in a well-ordered state some laws "are such as anyone could devise, and the rest will follow of themselves from the practices we have already instituted."[10] In other words, once justice is embodied in a few key precepts, all that remains is to adapt the already established principles to existing cases, what would today be called administrative law. Without private possessions among the directing classes, lawsuits and prosecutions will be almost nonexistent; cases of assault or outrage, should they occur, will be dealt with by the victim, whose physical training makes him quite able to defend himself.

Plato preferred rule by men, rather than by laws, when wise men could be found.[11] One explanation lies in his view of the legislator as a

[10]*Republic* v. 464[c-e].
[11]Cornford, *The Republic of Plato*, p. 118; *Republic* iv. 427[a-b]. In the *Statesman*, the rigidity and generality of law are cited as its major defects, but when states lack men with sufficient political wisdom to rule without laws, they will "owe their very preservation to their following a code of laws . . . and to a strict adherence to a rule. . . ." *Statesman* 297[d-e]. In the *Republic*, where the Guardians have direct access to the Good, there is a much greater emphasis on character training, or shaping a fit receptacle for the reception of the Good, than in either the *Statesman* or the

craftsman who makes the law like any man-made material object and departs once the work is done.[12] Law, because of the lack of generality of the cases to which it applies, is not completely susceptible to rational formulation. It is thus unwise to require any craftsman to produce rigid, formalized rules if he is to obtain the best results. In the ideal state, the administrator will not need to innovate, but he will be expected to rule wisely, which means adapting the general to the specific with tact and understanding.

The process of establishing basic laws or principles occurs while the Republic is being constructed, and it is completed before the Republic is described as a functioning state. Socrates tells Glaucon that it is the latter's obligation, as lawgiver, to select men and women who will be faithful to the law in spirit and detail. Any innovations that are to be made should occur in the process of constructing utopia, for the finished society operates in such a way as to preserve itself intact.

The aim of politics, according to Plato, is to make citizens as good as possible. Within the completed commonwealth, politics becomes the province of education, for which, of course, the properly designed institutions already exist. Political activity, so defined, may be said to occur in the creation of the ideal state; but once utopia is created, existing institutions are designed to maintain utopian ends, and politics become superfluous. As the preservers of educational arrangements (most laws in the Republic are expressed through institutions), the Guardians are, once again, best seen as administrators, applying already established principles to specific cases.

Punishment, as a method of preserving the status quo, is given scant treatment in the *Republic*. Plato notes that with proper training there will be as little need for legal correction as for medicine. There does exist, in the soul of a man who has become identified with and committed to his own errors, a sort of willful ignorance. This may be what Plato has in mind when he mentions the incurably corrupt in mind, who will be put to death. Such drastic punishment is best seen in terms of the ideal conditions in which men are reared in Plato's society. Their upbringing offers little excuse for wrongdoing. It offers even less possibility of reeducating a person (changing a pattern of behavior for which there is insufficient motive) who has not

---

Laws. The *Republic* might be compared to the preludes to laws in the *Laws:* where the preludes are effective, laws themselves are unnecessary. *Laws* iv. 722^d–723^d.

[12]Hannah Arendt, *The Human Condition* (New York: Doubleday and Company, Anchor Paperback, 1959), pp. 173–175.

been exposed to temptations, and who has already received the best education of which his nature is capable. When punishment is capable of improving the citizen, it becomes part of the educational process for Plato. Such an
identification of punishment and education is quite in accord with Plato's
concept of evil. Evil is not a lack, in the sense of noncompletion, but a lack
of something that can be obtained.[13]

   After being told the myth of the three metals, Glaucon comments
that although the first generation of Socrates' ideal state will not believe
such a story, their sons and descendants will. Glaucon's statement can be
made more explicit by a passage from the *Laws*. The Athenian describes a
state in which the laws, by the blessing of heaven, have remained un-
changed for centuries. The result of such stability is that there exists in that
state no recollection or report of the laws ever having been different from
what they are now. In such a state, the Athenian continues, reverence and
fear prevent anyone from altering the laws. By contrast, states that permit
innovation in education will raise children who are different from their
parents, and who will seek a different mode of life with novel institutions
and laws.

   Although the Athenian's description is intended to point out the
dangers of change, it provides an excellent description of what will occur
after the first generation dies in Plato's utopia. The original citizens of the
Republic, having experienced a different reality and having been acquainted
with other beliefs and modes of thought, will be skeptical of Plato's myth.
The second generation (excluding the Guardians) have no experience of any
reality outside the Republic. Their beliefs and values derive from the Republic and therefore cannot serve either to establish a critical perspective on
that society or to judge particular institutions within it. The second generation will believe the myth of the three races of metal.

   . . . when a community has once made a good start, its growth proceeds in a
sort of cycle. If a sound system of nurture and education is maintained, it

---

[13]Plato's theory of punishment, as sketched in the *Protagoras* (323^c–324^d), is a restorative one.
Punishment is both justly deserved and justly proportioned; it is designed to eradicate the evil by
calling the doer's attention to the fact that what he has done *is* evil and not the presumed good he
thought it to be. The impersonality of Plato's theory of punishment derives from his view that
moral questions, like mathematical ones, are capable of definite answers. Punishment is not
aimed at the individual *qua* individual and specific author of his misdemeanors but is designed to
evoke the "right nature," which he should desire.

produces men of a good disposition; and these in their turn, taking advantage of such education, develop into better men than their forebears. . . .[14]

Were Plato's ideal society actually brought into being, the only decisive change the author would accept precedes its existence. Change would be part of the process of designing and bringing utopia into existence, such change being understood only by those acquainted with the reality that utopia superseded.

Plato's psychology is uniquely adapted to the innocence that would result from living in the perfect, changeless reality of his utopia. Such innocence is part of the nature of a good man and is both moral and intellectual in nature. Plato contrasts the physician, who may "experience" the disease he cures in someone else and remain unaffected, as it is his mind he uses to cure the body, with the judge who cannot be brought up with the experience of evil, because his is the jurisdiction of mind over mind. The judge's knowledge of evil will come late in life and only from observation and insight, for without right order in his own soul, the judge would be incapable of understanding the Good. The implication is dire: even a temporary experience of wrongdoing can impair the quality or adequacy of mind.[15]

In other words, the innocence found in the *Republic* is a desirable psychological state; while its purpose is to create rightly ordered souls, its effect is to secure the citizens of utopia from any and all avoidable forms of change. Such innocence reinforces and in turn is reinforced by the static character of reality inherent in the utopian format. The order embodied in utopia is profoundly ahistorical and a perfectly adequate receptacle for human nature conceived as having an end that is unchanging, objectively real, and identical for all men.

The static character of Plato's utopian reality can be seen to flow from its military preparedness, the nature of law and rulership, the educational system, the psychological desideratum, and, finally, the nature of the

[14]Cornford, *The Republic of Plato*, pp. 114–115. *Republic* iv. 424[a–b]. Nettleship interprets this passage to suggest that progress is a natural tendency. Richard L. Nettleship, *Lectures on the Republic of Plato* (London: Macmillan and Co., Ltd., 1963), p. 115. But it accords better with Plato's view of change to interpret it as describing a decisive change for the better such that, once it is achieved, it will not be endangered by further innovation.

[15]In Book ix of the *Republic* (580[d]–583[b]) Plato appears to be saying the opposite. He claims that the philosopher is the best judge of the worth of different kinds of lives because he has had experience of the life of gain and of ambition and is unique in being acquainted with the life of reason. But in this discussion Plato is referring to the philosopher living in a corrupted state (583[b]) and not in the Republic. And even in the unjust state it is experience seconded by insight which makes the philosopher the best judge.

activity of the philosophers. The supremely rational and unchanging ideas afford the philosopher a frame of reference that transcends utopia, while the unchanging nature of his contemplative activity in no way disrupts the stability of the state, which allows him this activity in return for ruling it. The secondary ideal of justice expresses a facet of the Good: right order in the soul, along with separation and hierarchy of function in the state. Such an order, in society and in the soul, results in virtue's becoming a second nature, an effortless habit. Justice within the state and the happiness of the philosopher's contemplation "outside" the state are both attainable states of being; neither implies a constant effort of the will to reach the unattainable. Seen as an inner freedom, or a nondependence upon accident and external circumstance, both justice and contemplation require a changeless framework in which to be properly exhibited.

The Republic as a Standard of Judgment
Classical utopias have been described as offering a standard for judging the societies with which they are contemporaneous in contrast to the modern utopia's critique. A standard of judgment transcends existing society and is rooted in an ideal that is different in nature, not just in degree, from those that order ordinary human institutions. When the Republic is seen as a standard of judgment, it is the related notions of permanence, intelligibility, and completeness that are paramount. While a standard of judgment may prepare the way for change, its own functioning does not require such change to occur. Likewise, the Republic is sufficient as an intellectual inquiry, whether or not it is ever approximated in reality.

Indeed, Socrates is quite ambivalent about the possibility of his imaginary commonwealth ever coming into existence. A king with an uncorrupted philosophic nature is not, he thinks, inconceivable if one postulates a long enough time span.

It would be no miracle if others should think as we do; and we have, I believe, sufficiently shown that our plan, if practicable, is the best. So, to conclude: our institutions would be the best, if they could be realized, and to realize them, though hard, is not impossible.[16]

But in other parts of the dialogue, Socrates claims he would be satisfied with only an approximation of his ideal, which would occur if there were men who exhibited a greater degree of justice than is commonly found in the world.

[16]Cornford, The Republic of Plato, pp. 210–211; Republic vi. 502^{b-c}.

. . . when we set out to discover the essential nature of justice and injustice and what a perfectly just and a perfectly unjust man would be like, supposing them to exist, our purpose was to use them as ideal patterns: we were to observe the degree of happiness or unhappiness that each exhibited, and to draw the necessary inference that our own destiny would be like that of the one we most resembled. We did not set out to show that these ideals could exist in fact.[17]

The problem of how to bring about utopia is one that Socrates deliberately sets aside. Although he jestingly calls this maneuver the weakness of a lazy mind, a passage in the *Laws* suggests a more basic reason. The model that a legislator prepares "should omit no detail of perfect beauty and truth. . . ."[18] The model must be, in all respects, consistent with itself if it is to have any value at all. Only after the full model is constructed can one debate what part of it to omit or leave unexecuted. To attempt at the same time to exhibit the ideal and to modify that ideal in the light of unstable and transitory phenomena is to undertake an enterprise with conflicting aims.

Plato is indicating by such strictures that the standard by which one measures contemporary reality is not identical with a program to replace that reality when it is found wanting. The basis for judgment is not the same as a proposal for change. Such a standard may, by providing the basis for a critical judgment, prepare the way for change, but it does not of itself specify either the form or the degree of change which should be brought about. While the ideal used to judge existing societies and the proposals for changing such societies may have much in common, the latter involve a compromise that can never be justified on its own terms but is defended only in terms of its approximation to the ideal.

Socrates claims, moreover, that the impossibility of proving that a state could be governed in accordance with his picture of the ideal does not invalidate the conception.

. . . we have been constructing in discourse the pattern of an ideal state. Is our theory any the worse, if we cannot prove it possible that a state so organized should be actually founded? . . .
Can theory ever be fully realized in practice? Is it not in the nature of things that action should come less close to truth than thought?[19]

Plato does not claim that it is the essence of his Republic that it comes into existence. He does claim, however, that it is the essence of the Good to

[17]Cornford, *The Republic of Plato*, p. 177; *Republic* v. 472^{c-d}.
[18]*Laws* v. 746^b.
[19]Cornford, *The Republic of Plato*, pp. 177–178; *Republic* v. 472^e–473^b.

serve as a pattern or model for the right ordering of the state and of the individual. The utopian model, because of its perfection, serves as a measure: "No measure that falls in the least degree short of the whole truth can be quite fair in so important a matter. What is imperfect can never serve as a measure. . . ."[20]

The value Plato attributes to reason depends upon the ability of thought to offer men a standard by which to measure the flux of sensible qualities. Like a yardstick, the measure must be different from what it measures. The difference is like that existing between forms and appearances. The forms serve as an unchanging standard from which one obtains the knowledge with which to judge a wide variety of appearances without the appearances ever being able to attain to the nature of the forms. In the *Protagoras* Socrates alludes to a supreme art of measurement which is the philosopher's knowledge of objective values. Thrasymachus, at the other extreme, cannot show that his view of justice is even advantageous, much less right, because he does not admit any limit or standard by which to measure unlimited self-assertion.

While the concept of measure points to the requirements of thought when it serves as a standard of judgment, the notion of model *(paradeigma)* indicates the character of the knowledge necessary to make such judgments. Blindness, or lack of knowledge, is described as a condition in which men

. . . have in their soul no clear pattern of perfect truth, which they might study in every detail and constantly refer to, as a painter looks at his model, before they proceed to embody notions of justice, honour, and goodness in earthly institutions or, in their character of Guardians, to preserve such institutions as already exist.[21]

The type of knowledge the model offers depends upon the belief that there exists something fully rational that is the end *(telos)* of knowledge. A thing is not fully known unless its end is known. Rationality, so understood, means having ideals that are never fully present in particulars. Man is so constructed that he must aim at something beyond phenomena if he is to understand them, and reason is the faculty that seeks such intelligibility and identifies it with permanence and stability. The ignorant, by contrast, are described as

[20]Cornford, *The Republic of Plato*, p. 214; *Republic* vi. 504^{c-d}. Cf. *Republic* iv. 426^{d-e}.
[21]Cornford, *The Republic of Plato*, p. 190; *Republic* vi. 484^{c-d}. Jaeger notes that the concept of education *(paideia)* is founded on the ideal of model and of imitation. Jaeger, *Paideia*, II, 259.

those without a single mark before their eyes at which to aim. Such ignorance is opinion *(doxa)* that cannot render an account *(logos)* of its knowledge because, lacking knowledge of the forms, it cannot see particulars in their light. Ignorance is characterized by lack of stability; what it calls knowledge is always changing, uncertain, and hence incommunicable. The coherence of the model or measure derives from its stability; it offers a fixed standard in contrast to the flux of appearances. When the Republic is considered as a model or paradigm, its value for thought lies in its immutability, its refusal to allow change, and the distance it thus obtains from the world of appearances.

The two ideals of justice and the Good are central to Plato's utopia when it is used as a standard of judgment. To harm human beings, Socrates says, is to make them worse men by the standard of human excellence, which is justice. The very possibility of a standard of justice, for Plato, depends upon the vision of a social organization radically different in kind from existing ones. The contrast is between justice and the frenzied lawlessness of the multitude, expressed in their unbounded ambition and limitless appetites. Justice, the principle of organization both within the state and within the soul, appears to Plato so radically different from the usage of actual states that he calls it madness to try to produce a different type of character in the average man. The Athenians, the example closest to Plato, are illustrative: they use fines, banishment, or the death penalty as such effective deterrents to dissent that Plato calls it a miracle for a man to remain uncorrupted in that state. His description of the philosopher scraping the canvas clean or, more mundanely, rusticating the population above the age of ten gives another indication of how ineffective Plato believes his standards will be for men whose souls have been turned for so long in the other direction.

It has been suggested that to consider Plato's utopia as a standard of judgment need not imply the corollary that utopia should be brought into existence. Whenever Socrates tries to envision the existence of utopia, he encounters the problem that change is imperfection. In answer to Glaucon's question, whether the state is perfect, Socrates says: "Yes, in all points but one: our state must always contain some authority which will hold to the same idea of its constitution that you had before you in framing its laws."[22] The point of imperfection occurs if the state is conceived to be brought into existence, for any existing state, even the best, is subject to decline. Soc-

[22]*Republic* vi. 497^{c-d}.

rates invokes the Muses to explain how this decline begins: "Hard as it may
be for a state so framed to be shaken, yet since all that comes into being
must decay, even a fabric like this will not endure for ever, but will suffer
dissolution."[23] This speech is attributed to the Muses; the implication is
that, like the Platonic myths, it describes something that cannot be adequately understood by reason alone. Socrates goes on to remind Glaucon
that they have already discussed the need for an authority within the state
with knowledge equal to that of its founders. The discussion referred to is
the education of the Guardians, designed to produce a reverence for law
which will enable them to restore any institutions that fall into decay. There
appears to be an irresolvable difference between the ideal state and actual
states, corrupt or reformed, for the latter are always subject to change in the
form of decline and decay. When Plato calls the ideal state divine and other
ways of life merely human, it would seem that a good part of what he meant
by the divine is the immutable and unchanging.[24]

For Socrates the least change necessary to reform the state depends
on the existence of a philosopher-king, and the philosopher-king is a
paradox. The substance of the paradox is that the power needed to reform
the state cannot be obtained in an unreformed state. There is a deep pessimism in this interlocking of opposites. A standard of judgment exists, but
it seems almost as if that standard makes sense only when used in a state
already prepared to accept its relevance. The philosopher who lives in an
actual state is fortunate if he can keep clear of iniquity and go his own way
quietly. He has no obligation to attempt the reform of existing states, for the
judge's jurisdiction is that of mind over mind, and the public that Plato is
talking about is mindless. It is described as a great beast, to whose humors
the Sophists pander with deadly sophistication, and who can give no other
account of good or bad than that which pleases or vexes it.

Plato's *Republic*, then, can be seen as presenting a coherent and
stable arrangement of ideals and norms, not primarily as a proposal for
changing existing states, but as a basis for judging them.

---

[23]Cornford, *The Republic of Plato*, pp. 268–269; *Republic* viii. 545^d–546^b".
[24]*Republic* vi. 497^{b-c}. Neither the age of Cronus nor the age of Zeus in the myth of the *Statesman*
(269^a–275^b) is divine in the sense of being immune to change. If either is interpreted as referring
to a society that, even hypothetically, did exist, the myth can be seen as indicating the impossibility of ever attaining utopia rather than as an expression of Plato's later disillusionment with his
ideal.

Such, then, is the type of constitution that I call good and right. . . . By this standard, the other forms in which a state or an individual character may be organized are depraved and wrong.[25]

The imperfections of the timocratic, oligarchic, democratic, and despotic states and their corresponding types of man can be understood by comparing them to the ideal state. Plato's paradox repeats itself, for it is only the philosopher, with his ability to reason as well as his insight into the nature of unjust lives, who is equipped to make such comparisons. But paradox requires extreme formulations and will not admit, as Plato at times does, of degrees of rightness. If the degeneration of the state has not reached its last term in the perfectly unjust despotic man, and if some degree of right opinion remains available to men living in the intermediate forms of the state, a standard of judgment might serve as a means to arrest or retard the inevitable direction of change. Political wisdom might then consist in the attempt to reduce the disparity between form and flux, between the ideal and the actual.

The Republic as a Thought Experiment

The process of building a utopia is as important as the finished product, for it permits the author both to explore the implications of his ideals and to attempt to convince the reader, in the process, that these ideals answer the real requirements of human nature. As a thought experiment, utopia is an effort to increase man's knowledge and to persuade; in the course of the dialogue, Socrates attempts, with varying success, to do both.

The age when the gods ruled Athens is described as one in which persuasion, not force, held sway.

Only they would not coerce body with body in the fashion of shepherds who drive their flocks to pasture with blows; they set the course of the living creature from that part about which it turns most readily, its prow, controlling its soul after their own mind by persuasion as by a rudder, and so moving and steering the whole mortal fabric.[26]

In the development of the *Republic,* Socrates tries several modes of persuasion, which are not altogether successful. The *Republic* begins with an exposition of traditional morality by Cephalus, for whom right conduct is telling the truth and restoring to their owners those things with which one

[25]Cornford, *The Republic of Plato,* pp. 145–146; *Republic* iv. 449[a–b].
[26]*Critias* 109[c].

has been entrusted. Cephalus has performed the duties required by the traditional view of justice without knowing why, and by not challenging his assumptions Socrates suggests that this type of man has nothing of value to say any longer. If one were to look for an indirect reply to Cephalus, it could be found in the description, in the Myth of Er, of the man who is virtuous only by habit, without pursuing wisdom, and who ends by choosing a superficially attractive life of despotism without examining it closely.

Polemarchus offers as another definition of justice the maxim, borrowed from the poet Simonides, of giving to each man his due. Socrates shows rather easily that Polemarchus does not understand the implications of his definition and that the definition itself is inadequate. Justice does not have a limited and specific field of action, as does horse trading or medicine; it cannot involve injustice in its consequences, such as injuring an enemy. In the process of persuading Polemarchus that his definition is a poor one, Socrates empties justice of everything that is of immediate practical value. At the same time the concept of justice is broadened to include not only the action and its effects but also the motive of the agent, and it becomes required of all these factors that they reflect the character of justice.

The form of Socrates' argument with Thrasymachus resembles the discussion with Polemarchus. In both cases Socrates uses an abstract or ideal concept to force his respondent into a self-contradictory position. For instance, Socrates maintains that "it can no more be the function of goodness to do harm than of heat to cool or of drought to produce moisture."[27] A thing cannot partake of itself and its opposite. Already Socrates has established an ideal, controlled situation in which the consequences of an action are congruent with the intent and the intent is fully expressed and intelligible in the act and its consequences. It is the disparity between Socrates' ideal of a craftsman and Thrasymachus' argument from how people really act that makes the argument appear unreal. Because Socrates' refutation remains a logical one, Thrasymachus can be made to contradict himself by a superior dialectician, but he cannot be made to change his belief.

Despite Socrates' apparent victory, the dialogue with Thrasymachus is not convincing, and Glaucon says as much when he tells Socrates that while he has made a show of proving justice to be better than injustice, in fact, he has shown only what justice is not. Socrates acknowledges the fairness of the complaint by agreeing to Glaucon's and Adeimantus' request to continue the discussion. The basis on which the discussion continues is,

[27]Cornford, *The Republic of Plato*, p. 14; *Republic* i. 335^{d-e}.

however, changed. The interlocutors agree to eliminate from their discussion the consequences of justice, to treat justice in itself, and to examine its effects on the possessor whether or not they are seen by gods or men. The consequences of justice are, in the short run, ambiguous; by eliminating them, Adeimantus and Socrates establish and agree upon a universe of discourse.

This new universe of discourse is the one from which Socrates has already been arguing by reducing consequences to actions, and actions to motives described normatively. As long as consequences are included in the argument, Socrates runs the risk that his interlocutor will believe, as Thrasymachus did, that justice can be discussed by referring to consequences outside morality. This method, at best, leads to an "honesty is the best policy" answer; it does not meet the real issue of why Thrasymachus should be moral. By agreeing to discuss justice in itself, Socrates eliminates both chance and indifferent things—the accidental connection of justice with wealth or with power over other men.

When Socrates constructs the ideal state, he is not only looking for justice writ large in the state. He is also designing a state in which the nature of justice can be seen isolated from all extraneous circumstances. He is attempting a thought experiment in which justice, the Good, and their interrelation are rendered intelligible by being isolated from nonideal factors. If the *Republic* is viewed primarily as a thought experiment, it cannot be faulted for excluding a variety of other conceivable goods for man and concentrating exclusively on justice and the Good. The exclusion is necessary if Socrates' purpose is to be accomplished: to understand the nature of his ideals more fully by isolating them and treating them as if they were fully realized.

To understand justice is to see its harmony and proportion as perfectly exhibited as its nature allows. In this sense to investigate an ideal in thought means to draw out what is implicit in a concept, showing the content of the concept to be both coherent and comprehensive. The hoped-for result is a fuller understanding—moral and aesthetic as well as intellectual. To be able to give a true account implies the ability to convey stable knowledge and occurs when an ideal is expanded and exhibited in a framework from which the contingent and the transitory have been eliminated, thus precluding a partial and incomplete understanding.[28]

[28]In a similar interpretation Walsh describes the successive departures from the ideal state as a logical, not a historical, sequence—a sequence that one would find if everything happened as it

Socrates, then, creates a picture of justice for Glaucon and Adeiman-tus. The method he uses to create his picture is one in which the principle and its consequences for the ideal state are developed side by side. When he begins this enterprise, Socrates shifts from the position of an ironic, detached questioner to that of a guide who knows in rough outline the terrain to be covered. Aware of this shift, in an interlude in his argument with Thrasymachus, Socrates calls the new method one that combines the functions of advocate and judge. At every step in the discussion, the agreement of Glaucon and Adeimantus must be obtained. The finished picture is one that will have taken account of their reservations and objections and consequently allows them to give it their complete assent. The questioners have retained their freedom to object to the picture while it is being constructed; as a result their acceptance of the finished product can be a complete one, not unlike a conversion.

This procedure can be contrasted to the set speech and rejoinder that Thrasymachus prefers. Thrasymachus counts upon the cumulative effect of his impassioned harangue to override any possible objections and compel assent, while for Socrates it is the process of reasoning together that guarantees the intelligibility of the result. Nor is Socrates the loser when he agrees to explore new routes and bypaths and show why they do, or do not, lead to the desired destination, for by the end of the journey Socrates also knows the terrain better for having had new features in it brought to this attention.

You need not hesitate, he [Glaucon] replied. This is not an unsympathetic audience; we are neither incredulous nor hostile.

Thank you, I said, I suppose that remark is meant to be encouraging. Certainly it is.

Well, I said, it has just the opposite effect. . . . If one knows the truth, there is no risk to be feared in speaking about the things one has most at heart among intelligent friends; but if one is still in the position of a doubting inquirer, as I am now, talking becomes a slippery venture. . . . I am afraid I may miss my footing just where a false step is most to be dreaded and drag my friends down with me in my fall.[29]

---

theoretically should. He compares Plato's theoretical treatment of political decline to an ideal experiment in mechanics where all extraneous factors are eliminated until one has a pure case of the change or motion in question. "The simplified account may serve to illustrate more complex cases, and can do so just because it is simplified." W. H. Walsh, "Plato and the Philosophy of History: History and Theory in the Republic," History and Theory: Studies in the Philosophy of History, II (1962), 12.

[29]Cornford, The Republic of Plato, p. 147; Republic v. 450^d–451^b.

An account, Plato says, must be of the same order as that which it sets forth. A construct of reason will be as abiding and stable as reason, while an account of appearances can attain to no more than the uncertainty and instability of belief. An art such as poetry is misleading because it presents appearances as having a reality they do not possess. Art performs its function most truly when the images of the good and the beautiful which it offers guide the mind beyond the images themselves to a recognition of the eternal and changeless forms on which they are based.

The picture of the ideal state which Socrates sketches is art of this sort, designed to draw the mind toward the reality it attempts to portray. Such art might be compared to the two higher stages of knowledge described by Plato's image of the divided line. Like the model or diagram of mathematical thought *(dianoia),* the ideal state is an abstraction from any of its visible counterparts. At this stage the mind assumes that abstract principles are self-evident, and attempts to draw conclusions from them. At the higher stage of reasoning called dialectic, the mind is forced to mount to the nonhypothetical first principle, which confirms the assumption left unexamined by mathematical reasoning. An assumption is made intelligible and shown to be true when it is connected with, or grounded in, its first principle.

The picture or diagram of justice which Socrates draws might be compared to mathematical reasoning. Justice is assumed to be desirable, and its nature is portrayed as it would appear in an ideal universe where nothing either does or suffers harm. But the picture of justice includes within it images of the first principle needed to confirm justice. The investigation of justice as an ideal points beyond justice to the Good, leaving the mind unsatisfied with the image and prepared for knowledge that cannot be conveyed by dialectic. But unlike the picture of justice which has visible but inadequate counterparts, the Good can be pointed to only by analogy.[30]

As a verbal picture, Plato's ideal of justice can be best seen as a frame that draws attention to something of a different nature within it. The investigation of an ideal takes place over a period of time, whereas the words used to refer to the eternal objects of knowledge (*eidos* and *idea* both have the root meaning of vision) imply a type of knowledge ap-

---

[30]*Timaeus* 29[b]. Analogy should be distinguished from example. Plato describes the latter in the *Statesman* 278[c–e]. An example occurs when two identical elements found in widely separated areas are brought together so that a true judgment can be made about both.

prehended immediately in its entirety.[31] The Good, then, is conveyed as an image of a different order from the picture of justice which is its frame. The Good can be spoken of only by analogy; there are no actual elements that can be identified as reoccurring in both the model of the Good and its exemplar, the sun.

In a discussion of Plato's dialectic, Cushman observes that truth does not avail in the absence of a moral temper suitable to the truth.[32] The dialectic is designed to induce, and yet at the same time presupposes, a condition of character suitable to the truth. The ignorance of Glaucon and Adeimantus is not an ignorance that clings to error but ignorance resulting from their inability to defend the supposition that justice is better than injustice. It is with just this sort of ignorance, which is not a clinging to error, that dialectic is effective:

. . . the soul of every man does possess the power of learning the truth and the organ to see it with; . . . there may well be an art whose aim would be . . . not to put the power of sight into the soul's eye, which already has it, but to ensure that, instead of looking in the wrong direction, it is turned the way it ought to be.[33]

Such wisdom cannot be produced in a person who, like Thrasymachus, is not willing to suspend belief in his previous judgments. Ill temper and malice, Socrates remarks rather heatedly, call forth those qualities in others. It is because Glaucon and Adeimantus are willing to suspend final judgment without suspending their critical faculties that they are able to enter into Socrates' universe of discourse.

Knowledge of the type Socrates tries to portray is possible because of a likeness between the knowing mind and the reality to be known. In the process of investigating ideals by articulating them in thought, the mind might be described as becoming more akin to the objects of its thought. Plato calls such a mind well proportioned, having a sort of mental symmetry that makes it adaptable to truth. It is this initial inclination to the truth that Socrates reinforces by embodying justice in the most perfect form he can conceive. By articulating justice in an ideal, empty space that in the process takes on the character and imprint of justice, Socrates points to a universal

[31]For a discussion of the meaning of *eidos* and *idea*, see Paul Friedländer, *Plato: An Introduction*, trans. Hans Meyerhoff (Bollingen Series LIX; New York: Bollingen Foundation, 1958), pp. 16 ff.
[32]Cushman, *Therapeia*, p. 150.
[33]Cornford, *The Republic of Plato*, p. 232; *Republic* vii. 518^{d-e}.

applied universally. Reason is a method of articulating ideals in thought while retaining intact, as much as possible, the universal character of the ideal. In Plato's portrayal, when this method of obtaining knowledge reaches its end, it finds that the end has qualities akin to the tool used to reach it.

Utopias are myths as well as thought experiments, and myths, Plato believes, are needed for the enchantment of souls. Although the authenticity of the just and the Good does not depend on obtaining agreement to the picture drawn of them, the picture does serve to clarify and support the ideals it portrays.[34]

The ideals Socrates articulates exist apart from the activity of articulating them. They exist in reality as requirements without which man's truest nature cannot be satisfied. Plato suggests that Glaucon's and Adeimantus' assent to the picture Socrates draws will remain when that universe of discourse no longer exists. If justice in the state remains a standard of judgment to measure a society it cannot hope to order, justice in the soul need not.

. . . this commonwealth we have been founding in the realm of discourse . . . nowhere exists on earth.

No, . . . but perhaps there is a pattern set up in the heavens for one who desires to see it and, seeing it, to found one in himself.[35]

[34]In Greek "hypostatization" means that which stands under and serves as a support. Friedländer describes myths in terms that might equally well serve to characterize the picture of an ideal state that Socrates has made for Glaucon and Adeimantus. Myths are both a preparation for dialectic and a view beyond the limits to which dialectic leads. Both revealing and concealing, myth is akin to transcendence and occurs when transcendence penetrates into the world of appearances. Friedländer, *Plato: An Introduction,* pp. 184–209.
[35]Cornford, *The Republic of Plato,* p. 319; *Republic* ix. 592[a–c].

From Plato to the Renaissance: A Historical Overview

3

Between the time that Plato wrote his utopia and More and Andreae developed theirs, crucial assumptions about the nature of man and the conditions under which he must live had changed. Some of these changed assumptions are reflected in the utopias of More and Andreae. Although the categories used to analyze classical utopias remain applicable, the content of some of the categories—transcendence, for instance—changes according to the age and its assumptions.

This overview is intended to provide a transition from Plato to his successors by sketching in some of the changed assumptions and altered premises of thought. There is no attempt to present a comprehensive survey of these changes or to treat in depth the issues raised. While Andreae and More are properly considered as belonging to the Renaissance, they are treated here in the context of late medieval Christian thought because their utopias (as this study interprets them) are influenced primarily by this tradition. A study concerned—as this one is not—with the entirety of these men's works would be obliged to consider, in much more detail, the influence of both humanism and the Reformation on More's and Andreae's development.

Much has been written about the impact of Judeo-Christian ideas upon Greek and Hellenistic thought. This chapter is limited to an overview of a few changes that are the key to an understanding of More's and Andreae's utopias. The Christian understanding of the significance of time and space, of stability and change, is powerfully influenced by the belief in an omnipotent creator. The tradition of discourse within which (and to a certain extent against which) these authors wrote is itself important. And finally, the Greek understanding of human nature as primarily a cognitive enterprise in which knowing and doing cannot be clearly separated was radically changed by the Christian concept of original sin with its corollary of men's fundamental inadequacy and interdependence.

Concepts of Space
One of the most striking differences between Plato's utopia and More's and Andreae's works is the fact that the latter are much more specifically located in time and in space. More was well acquainted with accounts of Amerigo Vespucci's voyages, and Hythlodaeus is said to have traveled with Amerigo Vespucci on three of his four trips to the New World. No doubt, interest in the New World provided More with a plausible framework for his utopia, to which the reports of Epicureanism and communism among the American

aborigines gave an additional touch of the exotic. The more sober Andreae eschews this type of contemporary reference for allegorical coordinates, but Christianopolis is also a definite city situated, like More's utopia, on an island. Andreae's voyager is a Christian pilgrim who arrives in the city after the traditional utopian shipwreck and observes in detail the intelligence and harmony of the inhabitants' lives. Plato's utopia has no such concrete location. Such was the Greek pride in the polis and such was their disdain for barbarian culture that a city—even an imaginary one—situated concretely outside the "civilized world" would not be a model worthy of their attention.

In both More's and Andreae's work utopia is concretely situated and already a going concern. Plato's Republic, by comparison, is spatially unsituated. It exists in a universe of discourse; it is a hypothesis rather than a pretended reality. These differing concepts of space have important consequences. For More and Andreae the visitor to the city is, for narrative purposes, a different person from its founder. For Plato, the building of the city *is* the method of examining it, and if one recalls the Greek saying that beginnings are divine, to be present at the construction of the Republic is to be witness to its perfect moment. Andreae, by contrast, tells us that he was not admitted to the inside of Christianopolis' government and that, debarred from its secrets of statesmanship, he had to be content with reporting the external elegance of that city. To summarize, one might say that, for a Christian, beginnings are not only divine but also mysterious and impenetrable, reflecting the first act of creation ex nihilo, whereas, for the Greeks, accustomed to the idea of the mother city's deliberately founding colonies according to a predetermined plan, what was critical was the adequacy of the model for the new settlement.

Another equally important reason why Plato chose to build his utopia in the process of describing it is that he valued dialectical more highly than discursive thought. Plato's Republic is an elaborate thought experiment, involving an ascent from the initial rudimentary state to the ideally just state and then to the Good that validates the idea of justice. In Plato's philosophy, discursive thought (*epistēmē*) is so remote from dialectical thought that merely to describe an ideal state—from the outside, so to speak, and without prior preparation of the reader—would fail drastically to convey any comprehension of the ideal. At the risk of superficiality, one might say that Plato's unreconstituted man is turned toward the Good in the process of learning to understand it, whereas More's and Andreae's citizens are invited to re-cognize a good the value of which they already accept, or to which they at least pay lip service.

Concepts of Time

Not only are More's and Andreae's utopias much more concretely situated in space than is Plato's, but they are also differently related to time. In Greek thought there is little connection between history and philosophy, between time and eternity: perfection is outside the realm of time.[1] But Christianity, heir to Hebrew millennial expectations, did believe in the restoration of the divine kingdom on earth, if not *in* time, then at the *end* of time. And if Christianity judged it impious for reason to inquire into the beginnings of events or into first causes, the origins of which rest in God's inscrutable will, it was thought both proper and desirable to inquire into history, one of the instruments whereby God reveals his will to man. Instead of the eternal repetition of events assumed by the classical view, God's decrees are future oriented, known in history by means of the phenomenon of typology in which, as the Old Testament prefigures the New, later events are thought to perfect and accomplish earlier ones.[2]

W. Den Boer has observed that the historian within the Christian tradition writes as a witness of God's acts. The difference between the contemporaneity of "witnessing" and "giving an account," the Greek search for fixed laws and immutable essences behind the phenomena, is central to utopian thought. Hythlodaeus and Andreae are both witnesses and vivid raconteurs; the harmonious and happy cities they observe contain a message intimately connected with man's future salvation in the world. Christianopolis' existence is thus repeatedly explained as an awesome and unmerited act of God's grace, and Utopia's inhabitants find their lives to be perfectly in accord with Scripture when it later becomes known to them.

The Renaissance utopias, then, are oriented more distinctly toward a

[1] Arnaldo Momigliano, "Time in Ancient Historiography," *History and Theory: Studies in the Philosophy of History*, Beiheft 6, Vol. 5 (1966), pp. 20–22. Momigliano notes that another difference between the classical and the Renaissance sense of the past is that the Greeks appreciated what lasted a long time but did not admire what was ancient, or antiquity independent of its durability.

[2] W. Den Boer, "Graeco-Roman Historiography in Its Relation to Biblical and Modern Thinking," *History and Theory: Studies in the Philosophy of History*, VII (1968), 73–74. See also John G. Gunnell, *Political Philosophy and Time* (Middletown, Conn.: Wesleyan University Press, 1968), for a detailed working out of the difference between the Hellenic sense of time as the realm of human finitude and disorder and the Hebrew view of time as the working out of God's acts in the world.

future dimension of time than is their Greek counterpart. This future orientation parallels each man's individual concern with salvation; it does not, by
any means, entail the necessary realization of utopia itself in time. The
source of error for More and Andreae is man's flawed moral nature rather
than the institutional arrangements that later utopian writers were to
emphasize.[3] Society is created, and like other parts of God's creation, it too
must be redeemed.[4] Here the difference between Plato and his successors is
felt most clearly. There is a sense of tension within the Christian utopias.
While Plato's philosophers appear to attain an almost Godlike perfection,
for More's Utopians and Andreae's Christians virtue can never become an
established habit; it must remain a continual effort of the will, supported by
a faith itself constantly under trial, in God's redemptive message.[5]

The Christian's understanding of utopia is colored by the millennial
and apocalyptic traditions of his faith. Utopia is clearly related to men's
salvation, and if from this perspective Christianopolis is much closer than
More's utopia to the Bensalem of Bacon's New Atlantis (both are based on
fictitious acts of grace), what continues to separate More and Andreae by a
wide gulf from later "transitional" utopias is that their works are not ani-
mated by any expectation that their societies will be brought about in historical time.[6] Just as men could prepare for the millennium but could not bring
it about, the time in which these utopias are located is sacred, not secular,
time.

Concepts of Change and Stability

Both Andreae and More emphasize the need for stability in society, for it is
only within stable situations that intentions can be adequately expressed in
actions and actions freed of unintended and undesirable consequences.
Utopia and Christianopolis are authoritarian societies, and Peter Laslett has
shown the importance of such societies for men's sense of social stability:

[3]Arthur B. Ferguson, Review of The Complete Works of St. Thomas More, Vol. IV: Utopia, in
Journal of the History of Ideas, XXIX (April–June 1968), 307 ff. For a discussion of Christian and
secular concepts of progress, see Ernest Lee Tuveson, Millennium and Utopia: A Study in the
Background of the Idea of Progress (New York: Harper & Row, Publishers, paperback, 1964),
pp. 6 ff.
[4]A. J. Close, "Commonplace Theories of Art and Nature in Classical Antiquity and in the
Renaissance," Journal of the History of Ideas, XXX (October–December 1969), 480 ff.
[5]See Chapter 4 for a discussion of utopian beliefs not arrived at through the use of reason.
[6]See Chapter 6. H. R. Trevor-Roper gives an excellent description of the influence of Andreae
and of Bacon upon Hartlib and his circle, for whom the possibility that at least the beginnings of
a utopian plan might be set in motion is increasingly plausible. H. R. Trevor-Roper, The Crisis of
the Seventeenth Century (New York: Harper & Row, Publishers, 1968), pp. 250 ff., 269 ff.

The ancient order of society was felt to be eternal and unchangeable. . . .
There was no expectation of reform. How could there be when economic
organization and relationships were rigidly regulated by the social system,
by the content of Christianity itself? . . . Social revolution, meaning an
irreversible changing of the pattern of social relationships, never happened
in traditional, patriarchical, pre-industrial human society. It was almost impossible to contemplate.[7]

In addition to reaffirming an important tradition within Christianity, the
patriarchal authoritarianism of More and Andreae reflects a deliberate
desire to arrest the perceived process of social change, to reaffirm the
congruence of intentions with actions, and of actions with their consequences.

Plato most certainly had no such experience of an ancient order of
society felt to be eternal and unchangeable. His awareness of the instability,
revolution, and incipient chaos to which the polis tended is better compared to the later use of *fortuna*—that favored figure of speech by which
Renaissance men described their own fear of uncontrollable change. While
Plato viewed change no less skeptically than did More and Andreae, he
portrays it differently. In the *Republic* change is a series of successively
greater departures from the controlling idea of the Good exemplified in the
ideal state, and in the *Critias* Atlantis, although its past was virtuous and
glorious, declined from an excess of wealth and power even before the city
was overwhelmed by a flood.

The stability that Plato sought in his concept of justice was not the
stability of custom or ancestral habit. It was akin to the unity and concord he
found in the natural universe. The order of nature *(physis)* and the order of
true being for which the Ideas stood were identical: both signaled "an order
of occurrences . . . independent of human contrivance, something primal,
unchanging, and universal."[8]

Traditions of Discourse
The tradition of discourse within and against which Plato writes would be
quite alien to More and Andreae. Homer and the Sophists had set a tradition

[7]Peter Laslett, *The World We Have Lost* (London: Methuen & Co., Ltd., University paperback,
1965), p. 4. Cf. Thomas More, *The Complete Works of St. Thomas More,* Vol. IV: *Utopia,* ed.
Edward Surtz and J. H. Hexter (New Haven: Yale University Press, 1965), pp. xli–xlv (Hexter
introduction).
[8]Glenn R. Morrow, "Plato and the Law of Nature," *Essays in Political Theory,* ed. M. R. Konvitz
and A. E. Murphy (Ithaca, N.Y.: Cornell University Press, 1948), p. 19; cf. pp. 28–33.

of discourse profoundly at variance with Plato's desire to show what justice is in itself, independent of its consequences. Both Homer and the Sophists, despite their differences, would have agreed that the merit of an action should be judged by its consequences—by its success in this world.[9] Socrates' paradoxical formulation "it is better to do than to suffer wrong" would seem much more shocking to a Greek raised within the Homeric tradition than to the heirs of Christianity. And it might be argued that Plato never entirely succeeded in freeing himself from this earlier view, that he was able to answer the claim that the worth of an action be judged by its success only (as in the Myth of Er) by stretching out the period of time in which the consequences of action made themselves felt beyond this life and into the next.

Because the Christian has no doubt that the virtues enjoined upon him have weighty consequences—salvation or damnation—he has much less difficulty conceiving that values exist "in themselves" and independently of their long- or short-range benefits. Every act of goodness—and its opposite—is within the purview of an omniscient deity. Christian values are expressed in the form of commandments, imperatives whose very formulation invokes a higher authority. The terms in which Plato struggled with the problem—to validate justice whether or not it is seen by gods or by men—created far less difficulty within the Christian universe.

The concept of *aretē*, which meant both skill and excellence, was another focus in the quarrel over terms of discourse between Plato and the proponents of traditional culture. As the Sophists used the word, it referred to excellence of performance, whether this was the performance of an athlete, a doctor, or a skilled rhetorician.[10] Socrates' new use of *aretē* referred to an excellence derived from a right order within the soul. But this new understanding of what constituted well-being relied so heavily upon a state of internal equilibrium that its consequences for the action-oriented polis remained negligible. Its practitioners were, by Plato's own admission, ridiculed for being unmanly, and this reaction led him to warn philosophers to stay aloof from the corrupting affairs of the polis.

Part of Plato's difficulty lay in trying to convince a society only recently tribal in nature that what was important could not be measured by standards of success in this world. In its paramount need to provide effec-

---

[9]Arthur W. H. Adkins, *Merit and Responsibility: A Study in Greek Values* (Oxford: At the Clarendon Press, 1960), pp. 46 ff., 68 ff.
[10]Ibid., pp. 210 ff., 225 ff.

tive protection against outsiders, tribal society resembled feudal society. In both societies defensive and juridical functions were decentralized and the visible responsibility of those charged with leadership. Weakness was dangerous and therefore culpable; it endangered the community by putting it at the mercy of any stronger power. Such a community could no more expect clemency than the hapless Melians when they found themselves at the mercy of the Athenians.

More and Andreae faced problems of a different order in attempting to persuade their readers that virtue is valuable whether rewarded in this world or not. Both men wrote within a Christian tradition and, unlike Plato, could assume that their ideals were familiar to their audiences. Both were critical of the worldliness of their societies and interpreted societal injustices not as the result of social forces beyond men's control but as a sign that Christianity was observed more in the breach than in the performance. A good example of the dilemma faced by More and Andreae is to be found in the argument between *persona* More and Hythlodaeus in Book I of *Utopia*. The argument is a debate, not about how a private man should live, but rather about how much he should publicly champion Christian ideals to a nonsympathetic world. Andreae, likewise, does not doubt that good Christians are to be found in this world; his concern is that their voices will not be heard above the din of wordly affairs.

What both men confront may be described as a breakdown of the medieval assumption that political knowledge enables men to establish stable situations within which ethical behavior becomes possible. Medieval thought operated on the assumption that the result of ethical conduct would be the creation of a more desirable state of affairs, that to act honestly would produce situations characterized by honesty. Wolin suggests that when Machiavelli came to reject the literal translation of ethical acts into ethical situations, he substituted for it a notion of the irony of the political condition.[11]

Irony abounds in More and attests to his consciousness of an increasingly overt discrepancy between fact and value, between what is and what should be done. Hythlodaeus expresses just such an awareness when, at the beginning of Book I, he rejects *persona* More's assumption that "from the monarch, as from a never-failing spring, flows a stream of all that is good

[11]Sheldon Wolin, *Politics and Vision* (Boston: Little, Brown and Company, 1960), pp. 224–228.

or evil over the whole nation."[12] And it is in a similar vein that Erasmus has Folly observe that "all human affairs, like the Sileni of Alcibiades, have two aspects, each quite different from the other; . . . what at first sight is beautiful may really be ugly; . . . the noble, base; . . . and what is wholesome, poisonous."[13]

Like the church, the Christian monarch traditionally had been assigned the capacity and function of Christianizing the customary practices of society. In Hexter's words, this attempt to Christianize society "affects with a presumption of rightness, or at least of nonwrongness, the things that at any time men are currently doing and customarily have done."[14] More's thinking reflects these traditional views when he advises Hythlodaeus that an indirect, accommodating approach is appropriate in the councils of kings. Such an approach can be compared to the Mirror of Princes genre. Both are strategies that attempt through praise to paint the picture of the perfect prince in the hope that he will be led to desire some of the virtues attributed to him. Hythlodaeus vehemently condemns such an approach as oversubtle and ineffective. But, curiously enough, utopia embodies in a different form the very assumptions upon which the Mirrors of Princes were based, for in it ethical acts *do* create ethical situations. The difference lies in the fact that the picture of virtue is directed no longer to a prince but to the learned circle of More's acquaintance.

Concepts of Human Nature and Society

Nature, the general cosmic order seen as both good and intelligible to man, is for Plato a standard by which the polis was measured. It was also the substance of Plato's natural religion which resembles that of the Utopians in requiring a belief in the immortality of the human soul and in the providential direction of the world. But in their assumption that the knowledge of the divine is accessible to all men, More's and Andreae's utopias are more egalitarian than Plato's. Plato's reliance on trained intellect entails an elitism that is quite foreign to the Christian tradition.

The Christian tradition accounts for some of the most important differences between Plato's concept of human development and that of his

---

[12]More, *Works*, IV, 57.
[13]Desiderius Erasmus, *The Praise of Folly*, ed. Hoyt H. Hudson (Princeton: Princeton University Press, 1941), p. 36.
[14]More, *Works*, IV, cxv.(Hexter introduction).

utopian successors. Murphy has commented on Plato's "deliberate unwillingness to admit any serious form of personal development, any ideal of improvement, other than through philosophical proficiency."[15] The highest development of human nature is portrayed as apprehension of a nonhuman supratemporal reality. And for the nonphilosopher a definite but subordinate good, justice or self-control, is the greatest degree of development that is possible.

In both Utopia and Christianopolis there is a much closer relation than in the Republic between the primary and the secondary ideal. Neither More's absence of pride nor Andreae's pursuit of knowledge should be seen as merely a preparation for pleasure and the worship of God. The absence of pride *enables* men to seek pleasure; the pursuit of knowledge *is* a form of worshiping God. Plato's just man, if he is not a philosopher, has reached his maximum development, and although his nature exhibits a harmony analogous to that of the philosopher's, it is only the latter who is capable of understanding the full significance of justice in the light of the Good.

In addition, neither the virtue of Plato's just man nor the wisdom of his philosopher depends upon a relation with other human beings; justice and wisdom are and remain self-contained and self-sufficient states. More and Andreae—the latter albeit in a more stylized fashion—both depict human beings in utopia as requiring other human beings in order to achieve their own good. The pleasure that is the Utopians' prime concern is really a form of charity, which establishes right relationships among men as well as between men and the deity. For Andreae, likewise, it is the cultivation of Christian virtue which determines and gives value to men's relations with each other.

Plato has been frequently criticized because his philosophers are said to rule over automatons, capable of performing only one function and with knowledge of only the one virtue that characterizes their task. This criticism depends upon a distinction between having knowledge and being conscious of having knowledge, and it differentiates between justice and wisdom on these grounds. Only in the latter case is the agent conscious of having knowledge of the form to which he is subject.[16]

[15]N. R. Murphy, *The Interpretation of Plato's Republic* (Oxford: At the Clarendon Press, 1960), p. 44.
[16]M. B. Foster, *The Political Philosophies of Plato and Hegel* (Oxford: At the Clarendon Press, 1935), pp. 28–29.

This interpretation, while intriguing, is basically misleading because it does not consider whether the value of being able to give an account of the forms does not consist in showing the stability and permanence of knowledge rather than in demonstrating degrees of self-consciousness. The Kantian distinction between actions determined in accordance with a law and actions according to the conception of a law, to which justice and wisdom are compared, implies that virtue is more virtuous by being self-conscious.[17] But, as Jagu has noted, Plato did not think analyzing the content of consciousness with its accompanying self-awareness results in self-knowledge.[18] For Plato, self-knowledge results from questioning the role of consciousness and the significance of the problems with which consciousness deals.

The type of self-awareness that is lacking in Plato is properly found in Christian thought, for it is in part the result of conceiving human nature to be divided against itself. When man's will is thought to be defective, analyzing the content of consciousness serves a critically important purpose. It becomes a method of sorting out different impulses, assigning them different values, and attempting, in the light of Christian dogma, to encourage some at the expense of others. More's citizens typically arrive at a "true" notion of pleasure after having subordinated, modified, or discarded its more obvious and less satisfying physical forms.

In addition to marking a defective will, the doctrine of original sin causes the split, found, for instance, in St. Paul, between understanding and doing.[19] This distinction is foreign to Plato and incompatible with the claim that no man does wrong voluntarily. That claim is predicated on the assumptions that (1) all men will what they believe to be good and (2) no man who knows what is good will do wrong (knowledge being taken in the highest sense and therefore used to denote a cognition that controls the will).[20] Knowledge for Plato involves a practical capacity; to do wrong is not so much a failure of the will as either a failure of one's ability to discern truly what is good for oneself or a failure of training (paideia).[21] To do wrong

[17]Ibid., p. 16.
[18]A. Jagu, "La conception platonicienne de la liberté," Mélanges de Philosophie Grecque offerts à Mgr Dies (Paris: Librairie Philosophique J. Vrin, 1956), p. 133.
[19]Erich Frank, Philosophical Understanding and Religious Truth (New York: Oxford University Press, 1945), pp. 155–156, 174, n. 30.
[20]Paul Shorey, The Unity of Plato's Thought (Chicago: University of Chicago Press, 1903), pp. 9–10.
[21]John Gould, The Development of Plato's Ethics (Cambridge: At the University Press, 1955), pp. 54 ff.

indicates that one has not achieved moral certainty rather than that moral certainty has been overcome.

Free will is not a concept that Plato employs; it develops out of two later conceptions: the infinite foreknowledge of God and the absolute continuity of physical causation. The idea of a free moral will, as expressed in Genesis, implies that God created the world out of his unfathomable volition and is free to change the laws of the universe, which are likewise a product of his will.[22]

The Platonic *demiurgos* has no such power at his disposal. He is an artificer who creates the world according to a preexisting pattern. In the cosmos, called *ananke* (necessity) or *moira* (fate), everything happens with absolute necessity.[23] Such necessity is divine and is expressed in order and regularity; the typical is the essential, and not the single and unique act. Cochrane has observed, in discussing the Greek concept of human nature, that the individual is not intelligible to the Greeks. The typical alone is seen as permanent, essential, and intelligible.[24] The Christian notion of the free personality, by contrast, posits a cleavage of the soul into two antagonistic parts in which what becomes valuable is each individual's struggle, given infinite worth by Christ's redemptive mission.

The distinction that Andreae and More draw between moral or private and political or public virtue, like the concept of the individual, depends on a perception of society as alien or at best neutral to the true concerns of the individual. It was not a distinction congenial to Greek culture and would not have been understood by men for whom the polis was prior to the individual. Within the new Christian perspectives society was no longer thought capable of forming and perfecting man—at best it could present a neutral space in which such processes might take place by other means. Thus when More and Andreae downgrade the importance of society, their skepticism is similar to Plato's, but its causes are different.

The differences between Plato and his Renaissance successors are profound, but they should not obscure the existence of broad lines of similarity. Teleological explanation, common to both traditions, presupposed a purposive universe intelligible to man. Change—understood as a

[22]Frank, *Philosophical Understanding,* p. 156.
[23]Karl Löwith, "The Philosophical Concepts of Good and Evil," *Evil,* ed. The Curatorium of the C. G. Jung Institute (Evanston, Ill.: Northwestern University Press, 1967), p. 205.
[24]Charles N. Cochrane, *Christianity and Classical Culture: A Study of Thought and Action from Augustus to Augustine* (New York: Oxford University Press, 1957), p. 82.

force for novelty and creativity—was alien to both outlooks; like Plato's craftsman, the Christian artisan only imitates an order that he cannot create. The need to understand the state historically was also a later phenomenon, arising from the perception that the state had neither a rational essence nor a natural existence. When the state does become understood historically, it becomes susceptible to men's attempt to change it in history, and when these attitudes take root, one is already outside the frame of mind in which classical utopias, in all their variety, were possible.

The *Utopia* of Thomas More

4

In the *Rhetoric* Aristotle says that for purposes of praise and blame a speaker may identify a man's actual qualities with qualities bordering on them. In More's hands, Aristotle's device becomes a subtle method of conveying blame, for whether or not More meant the Utopians to be paragons of Christian virtue, it is more than likely that he intended them as a heuristic device capable of turning men to a reexamination of themselves and their society. The qualities that the Utopians possess in such abundance are, by implication, lacking in More's own countrymen, and *Utopia* is the device by which More points up the discrepancy.

More is aware that the comparisons he draws between his countrymen and the Utopians are oblique, even playful and fanciful, and he is quite able to justify this. He points out, in defense of *The Praise of Folly*, that biting wit, when it is mingled with truth, rankles in the memory and serves as an excellent device for combating stupidity.[1] His own comment on Utopia is very similar: it is "a fiction whereby the truth, as if smeared with honey, might a little more pleasantly slide into men's minds."[2] And as a good disciple of Lucian, More would not hesitate to apply to his writing of *Utopia* the lessons that he learned from his master:

Refraining from both the arrogant teachings of the philosophers and the more dissolute dallyings of the poets, he everywhere remarks and censures, with very honest and at the same time, very amusing wit, the shortcomings of mortals.[3]

In Book I of *Utopia* More uses satire directly to attack and ridicule the folly and vices of contemporary society. But it is only in the utopia proper, described by Hythlodaeus in Book II, that a positive standard of excellence is offered, one that serves, at the same time, as a critical commentary on the present.[4]

[1]*St. Thomas More: Selected Letters*, ed. Elizabeth F. Rogers (New Haven: Yale University Press, 1961), p. 55.

[2]Thomas More, *The Complete Works of St. Thomas More*, Vol. IV: *Utopia*, ed. Edward Surtz and J. H. Hexter (New Haven: Yale University Press, 1965), p. 251. For an excellent discussion of the comic element, see Surtz introduction in ibid., pp. cxlvii–cliii.

[3]C. R. Thompson, *The Translations of Lucian by Erasmus and St. Thomas More* (Ithaca, N.Y.: Vail-Ballou Press Inc., 1940), pp. 24–25.

[4]Elliott notes that it is characteristic of literary utopias to reverse the proportions of formal verse to satire and give greater weight to the positive part, which establishes a norm or standard of excellence, over the negative part, which attacks folly or vice. Robert C. Elliott, "Saturnalia, Satire, and Utopia," *Yale Review*, LV (Summer 1966), 534. For a different view, see A. R. Heiserman, "Satire in the *Utopia*," *Publications of the Modern Language Association of America*, LXXVIII (December 1963), 163–174.

More's use of satire makes largely irrelevant the controversy over whether *Utopia* is a revolutionary or a reactionary document. In the *Utopia* satire is used to achieve a critical distance from society by viewing it through both ends of a telescope, observing its vices writ large and its virtues writ small.[5] *Utopia* can equally well be called radical, because it offers an absolute standard by which to criticize the present, or conservative, because it offers no realistic proposals for changing the present it criticizes.[6]

This interpretation of *Utopia* differs from those who argue that the Utopians exemplify that degree of virtue which men can obtain by natural reason and without the help of revelation.[7] It follows much more closely the reasoning of Hexter and Surtz, who view the Utopians as essentially Christian in their spirit and mode of life and see More as contrasting their true Christianity to the nominal Christianity of Europeans.[8] The Christian interpretation does not postulate any serious discrepancy between Utopian beliefs and attitudes and those More could espouse. Impressive support for this view can be found in More's famous letter to Oxford University which, at the same time, is a revealing description of how Utopia itself functions in relation to existing society:

[5]Erasmus uses a similar distancing technique when he has Folly speak as if she were a wise man dropped from heaven. Desiderius Erasmus, *The Praise of Folly*, trans. Hoyt Hopewell Hudson (Princeton: Princeton University Press, 1941), p. 37.

[6]Hexter concurs that More offers no suggestions about how a corrupt Christian commonwealth could be transformed into a utopian one. The description of utopian society, which he thinks was completed before More wrote the Dialogue on Counsel, is, in Hexter's words, an "ideal standard," attributable to the humanist faith that "mere verbal utterance, effectively arranged, appropriately varied, and frequently repeated" performs work in the world. J. H. Hexter, *More's Utopia: The Biography of an Idea* (New York: Harper & Row, Publishers, Torchbook edition, 1965), p. 123. See also pp. 59 ff., 142 ff.

[7]Chambers is the best-known expositor of this view. See R. W. Chambers, *Thomas More* (New York: Harcourt, Brace and Co., 1935). For more recent commentators who take substantially the same position as Chambers, see H. W. Donner, *Introduction to Utopia* (Upsala: Sidgwick & Jackson, Ltd., 1945), and A. P. Duhamel, "Medievalism of More's *Utopia*," *Studies in Philology*, LII (April 1965), 99–126. It should be noted that Chambers's interpretation is also compatible with the argument of this study. If the Utopians are pagan and arrive at a knowledge of the deity solely by use of their reason, they resemble more closely Plato's philosophers. What is important for the purposes of this study is that they have knowledge of a supratemporal reality; the pagan interpretation would alter the character of the knowledge, but not the fact of its transcendence.

[8]St. Thomas More, *Utopia*, ed. Edward Surtz (New Haven: Yale University Press, Yale paperback, 1964), pp. xxvii ff.; More, *Works*, IV (Hexter introduction), lxxv–lxxvi. The Utopians may be considered Christian in spirit but not in a strict or literal sense, for among the essentials of Christianity they lack sacraments, a doctrine of the Trinity, and a belief in the Incarnation.

Moreover, there are some who through knowledge of things natural [that is, rational] construct a ladder by which to rise to the contemplation of things supernatural; they build a path to theology through philosophy and the liberal arts, which this man condemns as secular. . . .[9]

Utopia may be seen as just such a ladder, one by which men can rise to the contemplation of supernatural things, and from which they obtain a standard to judge natural things.

The Two Ideals of Utopia

The two ideals portrayed in More's Utopia are the absence of pride and the enjoyment of pleasure. More depicts pride as a social vice resulting from men's unnatural desire to distinguish themselves artificially from their fellows. Social arrangements in Utopia are devised to prevent such distinctions and free men to pursue the pleasure that truly satisfies them. The pleasure More has in mind comes much closer to what today might be called a form of religious altruism compatible with rational speculation.

Before attempting to understand More's concept of pleasure, which transcends Utopia's social arrangements, it is useful to investigate his handling of pride, which is so intimately bound up with those very arrangements.

In the middle of a description of Utopia's marketplace and food storage arrangements, Hythlodaeus interjects:

No doubt about it, avarice and greed are aroused in every kind of living creature by the fear of want, but only in man are they motivated by pride alone—pride which counts it a personal glory to excel others by superfluous display of possession. The latter vice can have no place at all in the Utopian scheme of things.[10]

The Utopian social organization is designed in such a way that neither animal fear of want nor human desire for superfluous display is possible. The prevention of want is no problem in a society in which work is allotted according to the needs and conveniences required by "nature." (In this context More seems to be using "nature" to mean what is necessary to maintain life with ease and comfort.)[11]

The main occupation of the Utopians is agriculture, at which all

[9]*St. Thomas More: Selected Letters*, p. 99.
[10]More, *Works*, IV, 139.
[11]Nature in this context implies a norm of social organization or conduct, although More seems to be using the word to indicate a limit rather than a norm.

citizens work for periods of at least two years at a time. The only other occupations mentioned (aside from religious and governmental offices) are the crafts of woolworking, linenmaking, masonry, metalworking, and carpentry, one of which is required practice for every Utopian in addition to agriculture.

With grain stocked two years in advance in case of crop failure, six hours of required daily work, and any spare time devoted to crafts, More considers that his Utopia provides most generously for all genuine wants. By allowing only for genuine wants and by requiring an equivalent work day from all, Utopian arrangements are designed to eliminate idleness, conspicuous display, and the vicious, corrupting pride that inevitably accompanies them.

Idleness is not permitted the Utopians, who, constantly supervised by their fellows, must either be performing their usual labor or be making intelligent use of their leisure. Conspicuous display is further eliminated by a few simple, even obvious, devices. Citizens dress alike, either in leather, linen of natural color, or in white. There is no reason for anyone to desire colored silks or fine workmanship in his garments, More observes, for he would not be better protected against the cold, nor would he appear better dressed in Utopian eyes. As further precautions against superfluous show, Utopians exchange their homes every ten years by lot, eat the same fare at meals taken together, and draw their household goods from a common stock. The Utopian economy is one in which the goods produced by all are held in common. Where men cannot distinguish themselves from each other by occupation, dress, lodging, riches, or use of free time, there is little opportunity for ostentation, the most common form of pride.

The most telling example of Utopian simplicity is found in the humorous description of the visit of the Anemolian ambassadors.[12] The ambassadors arrive dressed in gorgeous apparel and golden ornaments, and because of their adornments the Utopians take them to be either slaves or clowns. When the ambassadors discover in what contempt they are held by the plain-living Utopians, they hastily abandon their conspicuous finery. The vignette is significant, for it indicates that in Utopia pride is to be treated as a social vice. Pride has little to do with original sin; it is a form of vanity which depends on public honor for both its existence and its perpetuation. For More, pride would not be possible on a desert island. It depends upon difference's being recognized by others and upon the admiration and envy,

[12]Anemolian means "windy," that is, a vain, conceited, inconstant people.

no matter how grudgingly, accorded to the difference. Like gold, which the Utopians use to make chains for their prisoners and chamberpots for themselves, pride depends on the arbitrary scarcity of the item displayed. If nature had made those materials abundant and necessary for human survival, they would be too commonly seen or used to be an occasion for pride.

A commonwealth without pride, More comments proudly, is like a single, united family. The family is not only a community in which all goods are shared in common but also a form of social organization in which intimacy and interdependence preclude pride. If pride is at the root of a disordered commonwealth, it is because it feeds upon others' misfortunes and grows fat upon their miseries.

Pride measures prosperity not by her own advantages but by others' disadvantages. Pride would not consent to be made even a goddess if no poor wretches were left for her to domineer over and scoff at, if her good fortune might not dazzle by comparison with their miseries, if the display of her riches did not torment and intensify their poverty.[13]

The extirpation of pride comes from rearing and educating human beings in a society that scorns unreal distinctions, and, More adds, such a commonwealth never decays, except through the vices arising from wrong attitudes. Lack of pride serves two functions: it helps to ensure the stability of a commonwealth, and by preventing artificial distinctions, it clears the way for the expression of natural differences.[14]

The abolition of pride, however, is only part of what More wanted to depict in his ideal commonwealth. Merely to eliminate pride, an unnatural and artificial pleasure, would be to leave the Utopians without a raison d'être, for well-regulated, harmonious social relations are not an end in themselves. In the place of a sterile pride More tries to develop his readers' understanding of a pleasure that is both natural and congenial to man and is grounded in a reality that transcends him. The subject is broached in a way that is designed to both beguile the reader and lure him into a truer comprehension of pleasure. Pleasure is initially presented in its most easily accessible form, physical enjoyment. It is only as the discussion develops that the reader becomes aware that this pleasure has been modified out of all recognition and finally transmuted into a spiritual good.

Prior to describing his vision of pleasure, More makes sure that the

[13]More, *Works*, IV, p. 243.
[14]Hexter, who stresses the importance of social arrangements, considers the abolition of pride to be the main purpose of More's *Utopia*. Ibid., pp. ci–cii.

Utopians have a generous fund of leisure in which to enjoy it. They are not required to work once the needs of the commonwealth have been supplied, and thus the time required is not onerous.

For the authorities do not keep the citizens against their will at superfluous labor since the constitution of their commonwealth looks in the first place to this sole object: that for all the citizens, as far as the public needs permit, as much time as possible should be withdrawn from the service of the body and devoted to the freedom and culture of the mind. It is in the latter that they deem the happiness of life to consist.[15]

When More speaks of a "decent leisure," he does not mean free time for each to use according to his private whim; leisure is intended for the freedom and culture of the mind.

The chief debate that consumes the Utopians during leisure is whether happiness consists in one or several things, whether it applies to the soul alone or also to the body and to external gifts. When they consider the nature of happiness, the Utopians lean to the view that it is, at least in part, made up of pleasure. Hythlodaeus, in a personal interjection, registers his sharp distaste for any such identification of happiness with pleasure, particularly when religion is used to support it. Hythlodaeus' disapproval is explained by More's choice of language. The word used to denote pleasure is *voluptas,* which is associated with the hedonism of Epicurus and would be understood by More's readers to mean bodily pleasure.

As More describes what pleasures the Utopians consider "genuine" ones, it becomes evident that genuine pleasures are synonymous with freedom and culture of the mind. Genuine pleasures are first divided into pleasures of the body and of the soul. Bodily pleasures are (1) restorative (food and drink) and (2) a calm and harmonious state of health (lack of bodily disorder). The restorative pleasures are then equated with the maintenance of a state of stable and tranquil health. The pleasures of the soul are divided into (1) contemplation of the truth, (2) the practice of the virtues, and (3) the recollection of a well-spent life and the hope of happiness to come. More leaves no doubt that the Utopians value pleasures of the soul above all others.

Once the notion of pleasure has been purged of its coarser associations, More is prepared to discuss the relation of pleasures of the soul to virtue. Virtue is living according to nature, to which end man was created by God. To live according to nature (the dictates of reason) entails helping

[15]Ibid., p. 135.

others to a pleasurable life; to do this is an act of humanity, the virtue most typical of man. (*Iucunditas,* used to denote pleasure in this passage, means that which is pleasant or agreeable without implying the satisfaction or gratification of *voluptas,* and can be applied to either the body or the soul.) The pleasure gained by such humane activity, More says, "gives the mind a greater amount of pleasure than the bodily pleasure . . . forgone would have afforded."[16] This greater pleasure is the consciousness of good deeds and the love of those who have been benefited. Thus the practice of virtue is almost identical to the pleasure that the soul obtains from the recollection of a well-spent life.

Finally, More notes that God repays such acts of humanity with immense and never-ending "gladness." (*Gaudium* is restricted to mental or spiritual pleasure; theologically the term is almost always reserved for the gladness of the beatific vision.) Such gladness is experienced in this life as well as the next one. It leads the Utopians to see the pleasures of the soul as a unity no longer distinguishable from each other. In this unity virtue is merged with pleasure; both consist in the recollection of a well-spent life and the hope of happiness to come, guaranteed by a God whom the Utopians approach rationally, through the contemplation of the truth.[17]

As the Utopians have come to understand pleasure, it is very closely connected with the insights of religion.

They never have a discussion of philosophy without uniting certain principles taken from religion as well as from philosophy, which uses rational arguments. Without these principles they think reason insufficient and weak by itself for the investigation of true happiness.[18]

The principles in question are the immortality of the soul, which is born for happiness, and the belief in rewards and punishment after death. Unlike their philosophy, which is natural, Utopian religion is supernatural; its truths are confirmed but not ascertained by reason.

When legislating for his commonwealth, More recounts, King Utopus maintained an open mind about variations in religious belief. He did, however, require that all citizens believe in the two religious truths that by their "own natural force . . . stand forth conspicuously": the aforemen-

---

[16]Ibid., pp. 165–167.
[17]Contemplation of the truth can be approached variously. More recognizes intellectual pursuits such as exploring the secrets of nature as a use of reason pleasing to God and a form of divine worship. For such pursuits the Utopians may even be excused from required work.
[18]More, *Works,* IV, 161.

tioned immortality of the soul and the existence of rewards and punishments in the next life.

> . . . and if anyone thinks otherwise, they do not regard him even as a member of mankind, seeing that he has lowered the lofty nature of his soul to the level of a beast's miserable body. . . .[19]

Belief in the immortality of the soul and in rewards and punishments after death is the religious complement to the pleasures of the soul that the Utopians establish by virtue of reason alone: the contemplation of the truth and the recollection of a well-spent life. Indeed, the Utopians count as most holy (if not most sane) those ascetics among them who reject as harmful all pleasures in this life, devote themselves to the service of their fellows, and long for the happiness of a future life. This ascetic sect is called "Buthrescae," meaning "extraordinarily religious." The Utopians' claim that a truer view of pleasure than that espoused by the majority among them must wait upon religious inspiration may refer to the Buthrescae. Although their relation to the larger Utopian community is hazy, the Buthrescae are clearly a device by which More reemphasizes the limitations of natural reason.

More's description of pleasure or happiness is, like the Platonic contemplation of the forms, an activity that depends upon a suprasensible reality. The suprasensible reality has revealed to the Utopians the two fundamental tenets of their religion. In contrast to Plato, More restricts quite considerably the capacity of reason, which can ratify but not discover these principles. The raison d'être of Utopia is pleasure-seeking activity based on understanding of a reality that transcends Utopian reasoning powers.

The two ideals that More uses as a basis for his commonwealth are the elimination of pride and the pursuit of spiritual pleasure, or virtue. More's Utopians describe with precision the relation of pride to pleasure:

> . . . whatever things mortals imagine by a futile consensus to be sweet to them in spite of being against nature (as though they have the power to change the nature of things as they do their names) are all so far from making for happiness that they are even a great hindrance to it. The reason is that they possess the minds of persons in whom they have once become deepseated with a false idea of pleasure so that no room is left anywhere for true and genuine delights.[20]

[19]Ibid., p. 221. Utopus varies the formula slightly; he speaks of the belief in divine providence: "that the world is [not] the mere sport of chance. . . ." Ibid. Divine providence appears to mean the same thing as a belief in rewards and punishment after life.
[20]Ibid., p. 167.

There is no doubt that the spurious pleasure More has in mind is pride, for in the passage that follows he attacks those who think themselves better men, the better the coat they wear, and proceeds to excoriate pride of lineage and wealth. The abolition of pride is, then, a prerequisite for true pleasure because, in contrast to pride, pleasure has a fixed nature and a definite content that cannot be changed.

For More, the evil and corruption that are the consequences of pride stem from its variable nature and indefinite content. Pride ignores the true nature of an activity. Its values are based on men's perverse habits and depraved judgments—judgments that vary in content and are arbitrary in nature. Once human nature is cleansed of pride, it is drawn by virtue itself to the supreme good.[21] Once men no longer insist on evaluating both themselves and others on the basis of artificial distinctions, they are free to act as their nature bids them. For More, Nature is not a stern taskmaster; she requires only that men act in such a way as to further their own pleasure by furthering the pleasure of others. Nature's dictates coincide with the virtue More calls most peculiar to man: humanity.

The reason the Utopians experience recognition rather than revelation when Hythlodaeus acquaints them with Christianity is that the "new religion" coincides so well with their previous mode of life. The sharing of goods in common, which Hythlodaeus so admires, marks the limit of what Utopians are legally required to do. They are dissuaded from pride and from a perverse enjoyment of pride by an equal distribution of goods. They are free, if they wish, to be more than just by sacrificing their present pleasure for another's good. The two ideals by which More organizes his commonwealth are interdependent. Knowledge of the true nature of pleasure requires the abolition of pride. The absence of pride is not an end in itself but a prerequisite to man's ability to act rightly. The great common prayer with which Hythlodaeus ends his description of Utopia marks the relation of pleasure to pride with a final solemnity. The Utopians thank God for both the happiest commonwealth and the truest religion. If there is a better religion or commonwealth, the Utopians ask God to make it known to them; if they have the best, they beg God to preserve them in it. In their prayer, the Utopians show that the absence of pride is not merely a prerequisite for religious belief but part of the very core of religion, as they conceive it.

[21]Raphael, which is Hythlodaeus' first name, means "healing of God." Ibid., pp. 301–302.

The Static Character of Utopia

The Utopian society that Hythlodaeus visits is one that does not permit change or development in its essentials. Permanence and immutability, for More as well as Plato, were essential characteristics of truth. The true nature of pleasure is as little open to debate as the immortality of the soul and belief in a divine providence ruling the world, required by King Utopus of all his citizens. The great common prayer of the Utopians allows, in theory, for the possibility of error and, to that degree, makes More's Utopia more open-ended than either Plato's or Andreae's.[22] But as Utopian truths have been established by religious insight and sanctioned first by reason and subsequently by the Christian religion introduced by Hythlodaeus, it is unlikely that More thought that truths so verified would be contradicted either by God or by a continued use of the same reasoning faculty. The possibility of error is more plausibly explained by the initial Utopian ignorance of Christianity, and by the diversity of religious beliefs and practices allowed by King Utopus, in the interests of peace and because

. . . if it should be the case that one single religion is true and all the rest are false . . . provided the matter was handled reasonably and moderately, truth by its own natural force would finally emerge sooner or later and stand forth conspicuously.[23]

Despite some variation in their religious beliefs, the Utopians agree about the true nature of pleasure. By allowing differences of opinion on lesser religious matters among the Utopians, More makes all the more conspicuous the important truths about which there can be no disagreement.

The Utopian good and the Platonic good do differ in emphasis. Platonic contemplation is solitary activity, indifferent to the presence of other human beings, whereas More's concept of pleasure requires that the Utopians add to their concern for their own happiness in the next life a consideration for their fellow citizens in this one and a willingness to defer their own present pleasures for their needs. But Utopian self-denial significantly resembles Platonic contemplation in that it is an activity that varies neither in its nature nor in its effects. Renunciation of present pleasures does not change anything within Utopia; it serves only to reinforce the extirpation of pride and the hope of reward for good deeds in the afterlife.

More notes the commonwealth "never decays, except through the

[22]More, *Utopia*, ed. Surtz (paperback edition), p. xxix.
[23]More, *Works*, IV, 221.

vices arising from wrong attitudes."[24] Utopian education, intended to prevent such vices from ever arising, is entrusted to priests. Consequently education reinforces and in turn is reinforced by religious beliefs. Armed with a powerful educational system, the Utopians need very few laws, and those that do exist have, like education, a religious sanction. Lawyers are not needed in Utopia because the most obvious interpretation of the law always prevails. To enforce compliance with the law, penalties are secondary to the belief that the world is ruled by a divine providence and that the laws reflect that rule. A Utopian who would break the law jeopardizes at the same time his hopes for the future life.

However implausible it may seem, some Utopians do break the law; adultery is given as one example.[25] The penalty, much more severe for Utopians than for foreigners, could hardly be remedial after the melded force of education, religion, and law has proved ineffective. Criminals are punished to provide an object lesson for Utopians that "having had an excellent rearing to a virtuous life, they still could not be restrained from crime."[26] While punishments can be remitted if there are clear signs of repentence, More's stress is much more upon the deterrent effect than the remedial value of punishment.[27]

Punishment clearly serves to maintain the status quo in Utopia. So does war, which is discussed in elaborate and comic detail. More's treatment of war is clearly a satire on contemporary practice and not to be taken seriously. The peace-loving Utopians never initiate aggressive action unless it is to punish a neighboring tyrant in a country friendly to them.[28] But, with

[24]Ibid., p. 229. Cf. p. 245.
[25]More's account of what happens to Utopians who do not believe in the two main tenets of religion appears confused. He says that they are not punished, but only silenced and publicly excluded from office. However, the priests can also exclude from divine service any persons found to be "unusually bad"; if such persons do not speedily repent, they are punished by the Senate for impiety. It is possible that by "unusually bad" More meant bad actions rather than religious disbelief, but the two are not easily separated, as More maintains that without religious belief the laws are sure to be broken. Ibid., pp. 221–223.
[26]Ibid., p. 185.
[27]Crime is dealt with within the family, unless the offense is so serious that the Utopians will benefit by seeing a public punishment. More's criterion for determining the form of punishment is social utility: slavery is more profitable to the Utopians than putting a man to death. More uses social utility as a criterion only in matters that do not directly relate to Utopian values; slavery, for instance, is permitted only for foreigners and is considered a lighter form of punishment than that which is meted out to the Utopians.
[28]The Utopians' use of disaffected factions in their enemies' cities is very similar to the technique used by Plato's rulers.

this one exception, war would seem to belong to the category of "accidents," which originate outside Utopia and to which Utopians respond in order to preserve their way of life. (More mentions only one other type of accident, "a fierce pestilence," which forced the Utopians to replenish their cities with citizens from Utopian colonies.)[29]

In Utopia, politics exists only in the weakest sense of consciously maintaining the existing arrangements of society. The Utopians are ruled by syphogrants (meaning either wise or silly old men) who are elected to their office by the populace, grouped into families of thirty. The syphogrants in turn elect a governor who holds office for life. All officials are selected from among scholars who have been excused from manual labor in order to pursue their studies. Any consultation between officials must take place within the senate "to prevent . . . a conspiracy between the governor and the tranibors . . . to change the order of the commonwealth."[30]

The primary function of Utopian officials is to prevent idleness and to settle disputes. Hythlodaeus remarks that

. . . there is no danger of trouble from domestic discord, which has been the only cause of ruin to the well-established prosperity of many cities. As long as harmony is preserved at home . . . not all the envy of neighboring rulers, though it has rather often attempted it and has always been repelled, can avail to shatter or shake that nation.[31]

In fact, if any innovation ever took place in Utopia, it occurred when that rather shadowy figure, King Utopus, founded the city. Once having conquered the territory, Utopus proceeded to make Utopia into an isolated island by digging a channel the length of the land that had connected Utopia to the mainland. He then established the present layout of the city and arranged the religious settlement to put an end to the incessant religious wrangling that preceded his reign.

Like the Platonic legislator, More-Utopus is not a part of the commonwealth he has created. While he was waiting for *Utopia* to be published, More wrote Erasmus a letter in which he imagined himself as king of Utopia, crowned with a diadem of wheat, and wearing a Franciscan habit.[32] But the author of Utopia, once he has established good and stable laws in his city, has no more work to do. He remains outside the unchanging common-

[29]More, *Works*, IV, 201 and 137.
[30]Ibid., p. 125. The tranibors are intermediate officials who make up the Senate. The meaning of "tranibors" (also called protophylarchs) is not established.
[31]Ibid., p. 245.
[32]*St. Thomas More: Selected Letters*, p. 85.

wealth that he has established and in which permanent values are expressed in such stable forms that their legislator-creator is no longer needed.

Utopia as a Standard of Judgment

In Book I of *Utopia,* Hythlodaeus compares the ideal commonwealth he has visited to Plato's *Republic* and to the teachings of Christ. The undoubted superiority of all three are contrasted to contemporary practice:

But preachers, crafty men that they are, finding that men grievously disliked to have their morals adjusted to the rule of Christ . . . accommodated His teaching to men's morals as if it were a rule of soft lead that at least in some way or other the two might be made to correspond.[33]

The discrepancy between a standard by which men are judged and one they bend to fit already established practice is the central problem of Book I of *Utopia.* The same problem, in another form, constitutes the substance of the dispute between More and Hythlodaeus: the extent to which true knowledge of how to order a commonwealth implies responsibility to share that knowledge with those in power who are likely to ridicule or at best ignore it.

It is the argument between the two men is worth examining in some detail for the light it throws upon the concept of a standard of judgment. At the outset of the discussion Hythlodaeus imagines the advice he would give, were he a member of the privy council of the French king. He would suggest to a monarch intent on expansion that he would have quite enough to do if he governed one kingdom well. To the king's desire to raise more revenue by using the royal prerogative, Hythlodaeus would reply that impoverishing one's subjects would be a poor way to maintain peace and safeguard the realm against rebellion; the king would be better advised if he considered himself the servant of his people, not their master. Finally, Hythlodaeus would warn the king to look to his own indolence and arrogance; once these were attended to, he would find himself content to live on his own revenues and within his own territories.

It is noteworthy that Hythlodaeus does not describe his own advice as requiring any radical innovation in the commonwealth. Rather, it is the

---

[33]More, *Works,* IV, 101–103. The editors quote Erasmus' explanation: "We speak of a Lesbian rule . . . when law is adapted to morals, and morals are not mended according to laws. . . ." Ibid., p. 376 (from Erasmus' *Adagia*). Cf. Aristotle: "For when the thing is indefinite the rule also is indefinite, like the leaden rule used in making the Lesbian moulding; the rule adapts itself to the shape of the stone and is not rigid. . . ." Aristotle *Ethics* v. 10. 1137b.

monarch who is accused of rashness: "To persons who have made up their
minds to go headlong by the opposite road, the man who beckons them
back and points out dangers ahead can hardly be welcome."[34] Hythlodaeus
is concerned to arrest developments he judges dangerous to the commonwealth, and the cause of such developments is in good part pride, in this
case expressed in the arrogance and indolence of monarchs. His quarrel
with the men who normally counsel a king is that they carelessly advise him
to abandon the good institutions of his ancestors while perversely clinging
to the bad ones.

The same desire to arrest dangerous developments characterizes
Hythlodaeus' criticism of enclosure. The sheep are devouring the land
because the nobility, not content with merely being idle, do positive harm
to the country in an attempt to increase their revenue. Hythlodaeus advo-
cates laws that would restore the land to the tenants and restrict the number
of the wealthy able to be brought up in idleness. Similarly, he criticizes the
laws against thievery for being too harsh; such men have had no other
choice but to become thieves, being either the unemployed soldiers or the
dispossessed tenants and dismissed retainers of the idle nobility.

More agrees with Hythlodaeus that his ideas are "novel" and would
be coldly received in the councils of kings. What is novel about Hythlodaeus' advice? Not the proposals themselves, but the form in which they
are tendered. Instead of a rule of soft lead to be accommodated to the
demands of a given situation, Hythlodaeus offers a series of absolute injunc-
tions, which, like the doctrine of Christ, may appear to be folly when compared to the perverse morals of men, but are meant to be preached openly
from the rooftops. It is the fixed and absolute standard of judgment Hythlodaeus employs which makes him appear so intransigent and makes his
advice appear so novel. The extirpation of pride, in monarchs no less than in
their subjects, is a prerequisite for the acceptance and understanding of his
advice.

The standard Hythlodaeus uses is different in kind from the reality
he judges because it is part of a body of immutable truths: Christ's doctrine
in Book I of *Utopia,* and the required religious beliefs of the Utopians in
Book II. The standard of judgment, which More offers in the form of Utopia,
is immutable; it derives from normative requirements of man's nature that,
when they are allowed their proper expression, are always and everywhere
the same. These requirements, which I have called the utopian ideals, are

[34]More, *Works,* IV, 101.

the principles by which nonutopian activities and institutions are judged and found wanting.

William Budé, in his prefatory letter to *Utopia*, uses Utopian ideals as just such a standard of judgment. He contrasts the pliability of his contemporaries with the standard offered by the Gospels and the Utopians. "But suppose we were to estimate laws by the standard of truth and by the command of the Gospel to be simple." Budé's speculations became, as his own language indicates, increasingly improbable. He suggests, rather wryly, that if Christ's law were fixed in the mind of mortals "by the beam-spikes of a strong and settled conviction," vice and avarice would vanish and the golden age of Saturn would return."[35]

In Book I Hythlodaeus exhibits a similar skepticism. He uses the examples of the Polylerites (people of much nonsense) and the Macarians (happy, blessed ones) to argue for a monarch who will live on his own income and avoid military adventures abroad. By such half whimsical and half caustic examples Hythlodaeus suggests the improbability of reforms. But at the same time he prepares his listeners to understand Utopia as a standard of judgment which both measures the tendency or direction of change in the present and suggests what elements of the present are worth preserving.[36]

Utopia as a Thought Experiment

Both Plato and More introduce their ideal commonwealths with a discussion that ends in an impasse: neither Socrates nor More is able to convince or to be convinced by Thrasymachus or Hythlodaeus.[37] The utopias that follow such unsuccessful theoretical debates are another way of continuing dialogues that have broken down into irresolvable confrontations of opinions.

Book I of More's *Utopia* is a series of dialogues, many of which are abortive. An early discussion of laws and land enclosure between Hyth-

[35]Ibid., pp. 7 and 11.
[36]Busleyden, in his prefatory letter to *Utopia*, acknowledges that More has laid the world under an obligation:

. . .by holding up before reasonable mortals themselves that ideal of a commonwealth, that pattern and perfect model of morality, whose equal has never been seen anywhere in the world for the soundness of its constitution, for its perfection, and for its desirability.

Ibid., p. 35.
[37]Surtz comments that More's humanist readers would see the adoption of the dialogue form as an imitation of Plato, while also noting a difference: More's dialogue is narrative in form, whereas Plato's is dialectic. More, *Utopia*, ed. Surtz (paperback edition), p. xvii.

lodaeus and a lawyer at Cardinal Morton's residence in England is cut off by the Cardinal because the lawyer is so intent on his own rebuttal that he cannot make the effort to understand Hythlodaeus.

This vignette, in which scholastic methods of disputation are satirized, allows More to show one way in which a dialogue breaks down. It also enables him to give a concrete example of the type of flattery which characterizes the councils of monarchs and to which Hythlodaeus so vehemently objects. It is only when Cardinal Morton gives qualified approval to Hythlodaeus' proposals that the rest of the company is willing to risk their assent. There follows an acrimonious dispute between a "hanger-on" at the Cardinal's court and a friar, in which the Cardinal again is forced to intervene. Hythlodaeus calls these conversations typical of what he would expect to occur in the council of the French king, were he to offer his proposals there. At best his advice would be greeted with incomprehension, and more probably with ridicule and disdain.

The most striking disagreement in Book I arises between More and Hythlodaeus. The argument is not about the content of Hythlodaeus' advice to the king but centers rather on the form in which advice should be given in order to be effective. Hythlodaeus will not allow his proposals to be compromised or moderated in any particular. More's answer is to call Hythlodaeus' advice an academic philosophy that claims everything is suitable to every place.

More proposes, in his turn, the use of an "indirect approach," more adapted to the councils of statesmen. "What you cannot turn to good you must make as little bad as you can."[38] Hythlodaeus interprets More's suggestion as one of diplomatic accommodation to the status quo. What More wants to make him understand, however, is the advantage of a gradual approach that attempts to change a situation by working patiently at specific problems within it. Hythlodaeus' attitude will lead to his abandoning the commonwealth entirely, because he cannot pluck up all its vices by the root. More's quarrel with Hythlodaeus' approach is that it assumes men will turn into saints, capable of accepting and willing to act on every item of criticism. Hythlodaeus answers him by using the very absolutist terms that are at issue, claiming that if his opinion were different from the Council's, it would amount to having none at all; if his opinions were the same, it would be because he was sharing in their madness. At worst he would be cor-

[38]More, *Works*, IV, 99–101.

rupted, at best he would be a screen for the wickedness of others.[39] In a deliberate evocation of his predecessor, Hythlodaeus compares himself to Plato's philosophers who would not even try to govern existing commonwealths. They observe people rushing into the streets only to be soaked by rain and, unable to reason with such madmen, they are content to remain secluded indoors.

The argument that has begun as a quarrel about method changes at this point into an argument about substance. Hythlodaeus includes community of property in his requirements for a total cure of the commonwealth. More's objections are traditional ones: men are motivated by a desire for gain and will only work for profit; authority, in order to be respected, requires that differences of station be observed.[40] While Hythlodaeus could reply by repeating his criticism of idle nobles and rapacious kings, he does not choose to do so: " 'I do not wonder' he rejoined, 'that it looks this way to you, being a person who has no picture at all, or else a false one, of the situation I mean.' "[41]

He prefers instead to shift the terms of the debate by trying an indirect approach of his own.[42] He will attempt to make More see what his absolute values really are by showing him how they would work in an environment perfectly suited to receive them, and this new method of debate is what has been described as a thought experiment. By treating his ideals as if they were fully actualized (in his picture of a society successfully based upon community of goods), Hythlodaeus attempts to convince More (and perhaps himself also) that his ideals will permit no compromise. He is aided in this endeavor because there are practically no indifferent elements in

[39]Giles's tetrastich, which prefaced the *Utopia,* emphasizes the absence of Hythlodaeus' type of abstract theory and general principle in Utopia. "Utopus, my ruler, converted me, formerly not an island, into an island. Alone of all lands, without the aid of abstract philosophy, I have represented for mortals the philosophical city." Ibid., p. 19.

[40]Hexter calls the arguments against community of property commonplaces at More's time and believes that by placing these arguments before the description of Utopia, More intended his reader to understand them as criticisms of contemporary Europe, rather than of Utopia. Hexter *More's Utopia*, pp. 39–42.

[41]More, *Works*, IV, 107.

[42]The editors note that were Hythlodaeus interested only in philosophic debate, he should have answered More's objection on a theoretical level. Later, when he is well launched into his explanation of Utopia, Hythlodaeus says: "We have taken upon ourselves only to *describe* their principles, and not also to *defend* them." Ibid., p. 179 (my italics). The statement needs qualification, for Hythlodaeus' description, if convincing, does become an indirect defense of his principles.

Utopia. The Utopian ideal controls entirely the Utopian reality, which itself becomes value-charged as the ideal is specified in concrete institutions and mores. The exploration of ideals in thought serves to renew and reinforce Hythlodaeus' own conviction that these ideals are desirable. And in the process of making the ideals comprehensive and coherent to himself by organizing a reality in their service, Hythlodaeus creates a moral and aesthetic picture intended to persuade his readers.

Unlike modern utopian authors, however, Hythlodaeus has the great advantage of describing ideals that are "public." Hythlodaeus can assume that his listener (or More can assume that his reader) pays at least lip service to the values Utopia embodies. If, as Hythlodaeus claims, men have grown so presumptuous as to decide for themselves how far they will obey God's law, they still recognize that it is God's law they interpret for their own purposes.[43] Not only can Utopian values be described as having an existence independent of Utopia, but man's nature is also formed in such a way that he can be brought to recognize values that he already knows but is not willing to acknowledge.

Hythlodaeus paints a picture of Utopia in order to show what his values are and why he will not accommodate them to the exigencies of the present. Since he does not intend Utopia as a practical proposal to be brought into existence, the listener-reader is not told that history will necessarily develop in the direction of Utopia. When Hythlodaeus' audience has understood that Utopian values correspond to the fundamental requirements of their nature, and of human nature in general, Utopia will have served its purpose.

Utopian values function so as to give men a critical perspective on social reality. More makes immediate use of this critical distance in his ironic conclusion to Hythlodaeus' vision. He calls the Utopian religion, method of waging war, and community of goods absurd.[44]

[43]At the end of his description of Utopia, Hythlodaeus charges that Europeans have "distorted and debased the right and, finally, by making laws, have palmed it off as justice." Ibid., p. 241. The editors comment that Hytholdaeus' statement represents the traditional view that no authority could make *lex* into *ius* by a mere act of the will. Ibid., p. 562.

[44]As if to underline the impractical or impossible character of Utopia, More included in the prefaces to *Utopia* an ironic letter to Peter Giles, in which he professes regret at not knowing where Utopia is, as he has encountered a theologian "burning with an extraordinary desire to visit Utopia." Ibid., p. 43. In another letter to Giles, Hythlodaeus is described as quite inaccessible—he is off on another voyage. Ibid., pp. 251–253.

This latter [community of goods] alone utterly overthrows all the nobility, magnificence, splendor, and majesty which are, in the estimation of the common people, the true glories and ornaments of the commonwealth.[45]

Thus More ironically undercuts his own previous objections to community of property in Book I by observing that it results in nobility and magnificence (both forms of pride) being esteemed. "The estimation of the common people" is certainly not More's standard of judgment, but it leads him to underline the disparity between the real and the ideal and to admit that "there are very many features in the Utopian commonwealth which it is easier for me to wish for in our countries than to have any hope of seeing realized."[46]

[45]Ibid., p. 245.
[46]Ibid., pp. 245–247.

The *Christianopolis* of Johann Valentin Andreae

5

The *Reipublicae Christianopolitanae Descriptio* was published in 1619. Andreas Voigt, one of Andreae's commentators, doubts whether Christianopolis was intended to represent a practical execution of an ideal, suggesting rather that it be taken in a purely allegorical sense.[1]

It is true that Andreae uses much more abstract and moralistic language than either Plato or More. He offers very little detail or concrete imagery in describing his ideal city, the favored comparisons being those between lightness and darkness, sin and virtue, wisdom and ignorance. Nor does he show himself capable of the irony of Plato or the wit of More. The sustained seriousness of his tone, coupled with his tendency to personify vice and virtue and to draw frequent lessons from his personifications may account for the closer resemblance of Andreae's utopia to allegory. There is, however, an adequate description of the activities and institutions needed for an organized social group to maintain itself in existence; thus for the purposes of this study *Christianopolis* qualifies as a utopia.

Christianopolis was chosen to complete the study of classical utopias because it contains a Preface that offers valuable information about the relation of the ideal to the actual world and permits comparisons with Plato and More. In fact, *Christianopolis* was chosen instead of the more imaginative work of Campanella partly because of the indications Andreae gives to the reader of how he should approach the utopia. While the Preface will serve primarily as a basis for discussing *Christianopolis* as a standard of judgment and thought experiment, the utopia proper, in which the author's visit to Christianopolis is described, will be used to identify the ideals by which Andreae constructs his utopia and renders it impervious to change.

The Two Ideals of Christianopolis
The two ideals of Andreae's utopia are the worship of God through the cultivation of Christian virtue and the pursuit of knowledge.[2] The cultivation

[1]Andreas Voigt, *Die Sozialen Utopien* (Leipzig: n.n., 1906), p. 75, quoted in Johann Valentin Andreae, *Christianopolis: An Ideal State of the Seventeenth Century,* trans. Felix E. Held (New York: Oxford University Press, 1916), p. 25. Unless otherwise noted, subsequent references to Andreae are to the Held translation and will be cited as "Held."
[2]The Latin for "natural science" is *physica.* Johann V. Andreae, *Reipublicae Christianopolitanae descriptio* (Argentorati: Sumptibus Laeredum Lazari Zetneri, 1619), p. 147. See pp. 105, 107 for similar usage. "Nature" is frequently *natura rerum* in the original. Ibid., p. 107. *Scire* is used to refer to both knowledge of God (ibid., pp. 88, 93, 143) and knowledge of science (ibid., pp. 148, 197).

of Christian virtue is a continual endeavor, for the possibility of backsliding is always present, even to the most disciplined. The secondary ideal, the pursuit of knowledge, is described by the organization of the various disciplines through which learning is acquired. Although such knowledge has practical benefits for society, in the eyes of the author its justification is that it affords another way of knowing and venerating the creator. "The citizens . . . while they measure various things, first of all make an especial effort to measure and weigh themselves. . . ."[3] Men are not allowed to engage in the acquisition of knowledge until they have achieved a near perfect discipline in Christian virtue, and as both pursuits impress upon them the limits of reason and the grandeur of God, the acquisition of knowledge becomes as much an exercise in humility as an intellectual investigation.

The Preface to *Christianopolis*, entitled "Hail, Christian Reader," does not leave the reader in any doubt about the lesson he is expected to learn from a visit to utopia. Christianopolis is a city dedicated to the worship of God and to the practice of a Christian life based on His law. The religion is Lutheran, but Andreae says "they avoid the names of sects especially . . . and though they love to hear the name of Lutheran, yet they strive first of all to be Christians."[4] The city, located on a triangular island called Caphar Salama (village of peace), recognizes "no prerogative except of virtue," the greatest of which is devotion to God.[5] The citizens express their devotion to God by living impeccably Christian lives. The chief aim of the state is

. . . that after divine reverence has been inculcated and the foulness of sin exposed we learn earlier [in life] to be unwilling to sin, than not to dare to; but if we do dare then that we be not able; and if we break through absolutely, that we be compelled to atone for our acts and cleanse ourselves.[6]

The ideal of Chrisitanopolis is contained in divine law: the fear of God and love of one's neighbor. Andreae's unwearied reiteration of these precepts seems to express a certain bafflement at the controversy and confusion within contemporary Christian society. For the author, both the Gospels and the law of God point to a single evident truth, which precludes any confusion or conflicting interpretations about its meaning.

[3]Held, p. 221.
[4]Ibid., p. 241.
[5]Ibid., p. 163. Andreae's frequent use of the numbers 3, 4, and 7 and the figures of the triangle, square, and circle to describe Christianopolis most probably is intended as religious symbolism.
[6]Ibid., pp. 257–258.

The physical arrangement of Christianopolis reflects its author's certainty and precision about matters both human and divine. The city is in the form of a square, each side of which is seven hundred feet long and bounded by walls. A tower at each corner looks to the four quarters of the earth. At the exact center of Andreae's geometrical city is its innermost shrine, the college, in which are two tablets with writing in letters of gold. Each tablet contains ten commandments spelling out the rules of religion and of daily life in Christianopolis.[7] The first tablet presents the essentials of Lutheranism, and the second one translates these tenets into precepts for right living.

The tablets permit no distinction between the administration of the city and its religious life. The city is governed by a triumvirate rather than a monarch, a division of authority which Andreae justifies by noting that the monarchical dignity is reserved for Christ, who "does not tolerate too absolute a representative."[8] The duties of two of the three rulers bear witness to the inseparability of Christian life and Christian belief. Abialdon is the chief priest; his time is spent in holy meditation and zealous preaching of the word of God.[9] Abiefer is a judge, skilled in methods of taming the passions and administering the "specific proportion of things," including measures, weights, and numbers.[10] He believes that the best commonwealth is one modeled on God's plan, and he is assisted in forwarding his belief by a most pious wife called Understanding.[11]

The governors are at the same time teachers of the youth, who are raised by the state after the age of six. The children are taught the worship of God and the practice of Christian ethics; only after these have taken root is any attention paid to their mental development. Andreae describes this

[7]Ibid., pp. 175–178. Held believes that Christianopolis is modeled on Geneva, which Andreae visited in 1610. Cf. pp. 27–28.

[8]Ibid., p. 174. Andreae's emphasis on God as the monarchical ruler of men and author of their law (rather than God as the suffering and loving redeemer) is a part of his Lutheranism. See Edwin A. Burtt, *Types of Religious Philosophy* (revised ed., New York: Harper and Brothers, 1951), pp. 72 ff.

[9]Abialdon means "father of strength." II Sam. 23:31. Abiefer may be intended as a reference to Abiezer, "father of help." Josh. 17:2.

[10]Held, p. 183.

[11]Understanding appears to be the most human of the inhabitants of Christianopolis because of her tendency to be overcurious, for which fault her husband judiciously reproves her. Andreae has some rather pointed remarks to make on the virtue of silence in women. Ibid., p. 185. Cf. p. 260. Chapter XXXIV, translated as "Understanding," (ibid., p. 184) is "De Ratione" in the original (Andreae, *Republicae*, p. 83).

procedure to be the building of a miniature republic as a successor to the greater one. The functions of governing and teaching are considered inseparable, as either task requires the talent and experience of the other.

Andreae attempts to model most of the activities that take place in Christianopolis on God's plan for human governance. The example of the patriarchs is cited to justify the care with which land is cultivated and livestock is bred. The closer the work is to God's plan, the more the results are deemed satisfactory. Commerce is used to demonstrate the generosity of God in endowing the earth so richly. The crafts are practiced not only from necessity but also in order that the spark of divinity in man may show in his handiwork.

It is difficult to discuss Andreae's ideal of a Christian commonwealth in any detail because the language the author uses in portraying it is exceedingly abstract and he does not give many illustrations. Like More, Andreae allows a minority within his utopia to live like monks, in poverty and imitation of Christ. Having already learned all there is to know about human affairs, these ascetics prefer to live in ignorance of the world, simplicity, and silence. But unlike More's ascetics, who are given to cheerful labor and in some cases marry so as not to deprive the commonwealth of children, Andreae's zealots are not allowed any particular activity by which to express themselves. They do not, for instance, renounce present pleasures for future rewards but appear content merely to exist in a state of holiness. Andreae seems to consider it sufficient that he can point to this minority as an example of extreme holiness. But though we are told that this group's collective virtue is "beyond human excellence," they do not differ much from the average citizen, except in their rejection of learning and modest comforts. Within Christianopolis their function is most probably exemplary: they serve as a constant reminder of the frivolity of creature comforts and the vanity of human knowledge when it is not a path to the deity.

Fritz Brüggemann has remarked that the citizens of Christianopolis seem to be entirely a product of the laws under which they live, and are influenced neither by the behavior of others nor by their relations to them.[12] This reliance on law rather than human interaction to regulate conduct is most probably explained by Andreae's Lutheran beliefs:

Everyone carries within him domestic, rustic, or even paternal and inborn evil and wickedness, and communicates these to his comrades, with so

[12]Fritz Brüggemann, *Utopie und Robinsonade* (Weimar: A. Duncker, 1914), p. 150.

poisonous a contagion that it spares not even those who ought to be con-
secrated entirely to God. . . .[13]

The struggle toward godliness is, presumably, an internal one against a
nature corrupted by sin, and virtuous conduct is merely a sign that the battle
is being waged on another, more spiritual, level.

    The activity to which Andreae devotes most attention within his city
is the pursuit of knowledge.[14] The third triumvir, Abida, is in charge of
human learning.[15] There are eight departments of learning; those not directly dealing with religious learning are devoted to research. Logic, for
one, is allowed to serve knowledge as long as it is understood that its proper
subject matter is things human, not divine. Metaphysics, another department of knowledge, includes the study of the universe in its original perfection; a third department is given over to arithmetic, geometry, and mystic
numbers, in the belief that the "supreme Architect did not make this mighty
mechanism haphazard, but He completed it most wisely by measures, numbers, and proportions. . . ."[16] There is also a department of astronomy and
astrology, and one of natural science in which men investigate the purpose
of plants and animals, the use of metals, and the constitution of material
things.

    The pursuit of knowledge takes place in the College of Christian-
opolis, which also houses religion and justice, the concern of the other two
members of the triumvirate. The part of the College given over to knowledge includes a laboratory for chemical science, in which the properties of
mineral, vegetable, and animal life are investigated in order to discover
those that might serve to further human health. There is also a pharmacy
where the results of the laboratory investigations are meticulously
classified. The halls of anatomy and physics are described in terms of the
elegance of their practical as well as theoretical results.

[13]Held, p. 248.
[14]Held attempts to show that Andreae's College was the model for Bacon's House of Salomon
and for the founders of the Royal Society. He stresses Andreae's and Bacon's common interest
in the practical application of scientific knowledge. But a central feature of the House of
Salomon, cooperative research, is lacking in Andreae's College. The scientific research Bacon
proposes is a cooperative enterprise in which the results of experiments performed by one
group of men become the subject matter for further experimentation or systematization by
another group. For Andreae, any one researcher, with sufficient knowledge, is capable of
understanding the design of nature and the uses to which it can be put. See Held introduction
to *Christianopolis*, pp. 41–74.
[15]Abidah means "father of knowledge." Gen. 25:4.
[16]Held, pp. 221–222.

Andreae's description of knowledge supports his claim that it has practical utility and need not be practiced as an entirely theoretical discipline. But it is because such knowledge is a method of knowing God, rather than because it is an aid to man, that Andreae expects all his citizens to be learned in one or another of these disciplines.

All these, forsooth, are very beautiful things, and it is below his dignity for man not to know them, after the faithful investigations of so many men. For we have not been sent into this world, even the most splendid theater of God, that as beasts we should merely devour the pastures of the earth; but that we might walk about observing His wonders, distributing His gifts, and valuing His works.[17]

Without knowledge men are, in Andreae's words, little better than swineherds, and he drives his point home by distributing honors according to the contribution men make to the various disciplines.

Andreae's concept of knowledge, to the extent it includes what would now be called the natural sciences, does not emphasize the interdependence of the various branches of scientific research. While both the classification and the practical use of scientific findings would seem to require some form of communication between the different disciplines devoted to investigating nature, the author does not indicate how this might occur. The explanation for this omission is found in Andreae's assumptions about the natural world. As he conceives nature to be the single harmonious creation of God, it is logical for him to assume that nature's products are interdependent. Once known, they can be displayed and classified in an orderly fashion because they bear the imprint of God's purpose and order in creating them. It is not necessary for men to cooperate with one another in the pursuit of scientific knowledge, because God has already arranged nature in a coherent and intelligible manner for them.

The relation between Andreae's two ideals is close. Knowledge, together with the practical uses to which it can be put, attests to the existence of a wise Creator, and is another means of venerating him. Andreae's priorities are never in doubt; the worship of God and cultivation of virtue are of greater value than any development of mental powers. The ascetics who choose holy ignorance over knowledge serve as a warning against overreliance on intellect, for previously they were the most learned men in the city, conversant with "the slipperiness of wisdom, the windings of

[17]Ibid., p. 231.

knowledge. . . ."[18] Theosophy (the study of sacred mysteries) always takes precedence over metaphysics. Moreover, all forms of knowledge lead of themselves to God not only because the coherence of the natural world depends on its being God's artifact but also because knowledge leads to humility, which is an awareness of the limitations of natural knowledge.

The ideal Andreae offers for Christianopolis may be said to transcend the limits both of his utopia and of man's reason. This ideal is obedience to a God who makes himself known primarily through miracles and commandments and only secondarily through reason. It is "because they do not want a purely imaginative treasure" that the citizens of Christianopolis recognize and believe in Christ.[19] The main concern of Andreae's utopians is to live a disciplined and virtuous life, in which sin and its fruits are brought under strict control, though never entirely vanquished. Only when this discipline is achieved are men allowed to investigate nature and use its benefits to improve human life. While such investigations may have practical results that improve life within the city, Andreae is careful, whenever he admits this benefit, to refer it to God. *Christianopolis* may be said to express one truth, the existence of God and His plan for men, which is the standard by which all other activities, including knowledge, are finally judged.

The Static Character of Christianopolis

The narrator of Andreae's utopia is closely questioned by the magistrates of Christianopolis about his occupation, character, and state of knowledge before he is admitted into that pure abode of truth and goodness. His entry is permitted because he experiences a pressing desire to correct his errors and to become fit to experience those "better, truer, more fixed, and more stable conditions . . . which the world promises, but never and nowhere produces."[20] In contrast to other societies, utopia appears to the visitor to be invincible, for unless its citizens were to become lax in combating the old Adam within them, no evil can ever endanger Christianopolis.[21]

Despite man's sinful and wayward nature, Andreae finds no need of lawyers in Christianopolis. Such disputes as may occur are always settled informally. Punishments are administered in order to reform the malefac-

[18]Ibid., p. 239.
[19]Ibid., p. 236.
[20]Ibid., p. 145.
[21]"Hence the city is invincible, unless it yield first to its own vices." Ibid., p. 183. Cf. More, *Works*, IV, 229. "The latter [the commonwealth] never decays except through vices which arise from wrong attitudes."

tor; crimes against God are most severely dealt with, then crimes against men, and finally crimes against property. Penalties include fasting, labor, whipping, and, in very rare cases, imprisonment. The only crime that is described in detail, however, is the denial of God, which is called an intolerable horror to the state. After repeated warnings to the offender, the priestly governor pronounces on him the "wrath of God, ban of the church, disgust of the state, and the abhorrence of every good man. . . ."[22] Exile, considered worse than death, is used in such cases as a last resort.

Punishment is one way of ensuring the stability of Christianopolis. War and commercial relationships are barely mentioned, the author having described his utopia as geographically isolated and self-sufficient. The armory is a museum, and although the citizens have weapons in case of an emergency, Andreae offers no description of what he would consider such an emergency to be.

Political activity also attests to the stability of utopia; it is indistinguishable from religious concerns. The councilors meet in a Senate, where they discuss (in order) the truths of Christianity, cultivation of virtues, methods of improving the mind, and the need for any treaties, wars, negotiations, buildings, or supplies. All debate is public: "Since all things in the Christian Republic are referred to God, there is no need of secrets and councils of state, in which Satan in his kingdom rejoices."[23] As unanimity exists about matters concerning God and natural knowledge, such public debates are really another form of education.

Andreae devotes some attention to history and includes a room for archives in his College. No inhabitant is permitted to be ignorant of the past history of Christianopolis, although the author admits that "the latter so strongly reechoes every age, that they think they have lived in almost any age." Virtue, it may be said, has no history, but it does offer "champions of God" outstanding examples of holiness to contemplate and imitate.[24] Church history is of most concern to the author; he calls it the only ark of salvation against the waters of the universal flood. Andreae begins and ends his case for church history with divine providence. Where religion flourishes, it is not by chance but by the favor of heaven guiding the church throughout time and teaching by prophecies and miracles.

Christianopolis is protected from change above all by being a Chris-

---

[22]Held, p. 257.
[23]Ibid., p. 167.
[24]Ibid., pp. 193, 233.

tian state, obedient to God's unswerving will. Its history and its laws reinforce that will by precept and punishment. The only true political act that
can be said to occur in that holy city is the examination of the author-
narrator before he is permitted to enter. The thick walls that gird the city,
with a tower at each corner, appear to be quite superfluous protection to
citizens so armed against change.

Christianopolis as a Standard of Judgment

When Andreae describes worldly history, he contrasts it with the peace and
contentment of Christianopolis. Worldly history is "a rehearsal of the events
of human tragedy. . . ."[25] Among the catastrophes that characterize life
outside utopia are hideous wars, horrible massacres, boastful conceit,
arrogant wealth, the confusion of ranks, secrets, and wickedness. It is
rather startling to find that Andreae's dismal view of the nonutopian present does not entail any urgent proposals for change in the direction of
Christianopolis.

In the Preface to *Christianopolis,* the author distinguishes two
classes of men in exisiting commonwealths: those who adamantly defend
the status quo, causing conflict and dissent in the process, and those who
are silent and tolerant, enduring human affairs while wishing for moderate
change. The defenders of the status quo may, Andreae suggests, be part of
the plan of Antichrist. These are the men who frustrate any attempt to
remedy even the worst abuses of society. Either from ambition and greed or
from mental dullness, they prosecute the proponents of moderate change,
depriving them of the protection of the law and driving them out of
society.[26] But when he comes to deal with moderate change, Andreae gives
no indication that he hopes for more than "a correction of . . . terrible
disgraces in the most temperate way. . . ." Even temperate reform has its
difficulties, for "excellent laws stand out to the view; but if anyone would
urge their enforcement, he would be ridiculed."[27] Andreae would like to
see a reform of the churches, courts, and universities, along with the abolition of the vices that characterize these institutions—ambition, greed,
license, and jealousy. But to reform the court, were it possible, is not to
prepare the way for Christianopolis, a city that has no rulers, only magis-

[25]Ibid., p. 232.
[26]The change Andreae has in mind is the maintenance and extension of Lutheranism, as he
makes clear when he speaks of the "boldness with which we ourselves oppose the most
evident truth. . . ." Ibid., p. 134.
[27]Ibid., pp. 133, 237.

trates. Rather, Christianopolis embodies a "most evident truth" that would
serve men as the standard by which to measure the abuses of existing
society, were they only to turn their minds toward it.[28]

By describing an ideal society, Andreae is offering Christians a standard of judgment different from the one prevailing in existing societies.
Using such a standard, they will be able to conduct their own lives in such a
way as to avoid the superstition, dishonesty, and immorality that are the
prevailing norms. Andreae is much less sanguine—and much less
concerned—about worldly cities, which in any case in good time can be
expected to wither away because of their wickedness; Satan also is a part of
God's plan.

In one of his many enumerations of the foolishness of this world,
Andreae remarks: "What utterly absurd things are done in a republic because the WHY is neither known nor tolerated."[29] The author offers utopia
as a means of better understanding the "why" of worldly cities by constructing a fictive society based on the evident truths of Christianity. Even within
Christianopolis, where the "why" is better understood than in the real
world, councilmen continually "examine the present according to models,
and if they find they are deteriorating a single bit, they repair the matter."[30]
Andreae's ideal society is not perfect, only as nearly perfect as human volition can contrive.

As the narrator prepares to leave Christianopolis, the Chancellor
reminds him that the republic he has been shown is a pattern and begs him
to be a gentle and moderate interpreter of it. The model or pattern that
Andreae offers is to be used primarily to judge existing societies, although it
can be used to judge Christianopolis as well because the truth portrayed in
utopia transcends both societies—the real and the fictive one. The model is
a standard different in kind from the reality it measures. Andreae warns that
it is not with the tools of human philosophy that one can measure the New
Jerusalem. The Chancellor's farewell to his visitor includes the following
significant exhortation: "No one will be a better friend to us than he who
shall make our state conform more nearly to the kingdom of heaven, or
(what is the same) remove it farther from the world."[31]

Like the formal, unchanging structure of utopia, the standard of
judgment derived from it is fixed and immutable and offers a contrast to the

[28]Ibid., p. 134. For a similar description, see pp. 237–238.
[29]Ibid., p. 185 (Andreae's emphasis).
[30]Ibid., p. 267.
[31]Ibid., p. 279.

flux and uncertainty that characterize the affairs of the world, where "intrigue, avarice, gluttony, vice, and wrath, yea even stupidity and rashness, have no measure and will tolerate none."[32] When the word of God is accepted, Andreae notes, a measure is available, and one need no longer look to the society of men for approval. Andreae states that the standard should be used, not to bring Christianopolis into being, but to prevent men who wish to live as Christians from becoming identical with men of the world. If there is to be any transformation, Andreae will look for it in the hearts of men:

. . . the world is not so sure of its affairs as it would like to seem, nor is it so steadfast in its views that it cannot be turned aside; not yet . . . are all so far from Christ that no one would be willing to admit His rules of life, and then regulate his own life according to them, if the opportunity were given.[33]

Christianopolis as a Thought Experiment
As he indicates in his Preface, Andreae is addressing himself to the Christian reader. To the extent that both the author and his audience hold basic assumptions in common, Andreae's utopia differs from Plato's and More's, where irreconcilably different judgments about the nature of reality or the means of changing it precede the joint exploration of utopia. Consequently, Andreae does not show us, as do Plato and More, the point at which dialogue breaks down or when different means of communication are needed to reestablish it. But Andreae does refer, in his Preface, to the number of idle disputes in which men indulge, and he speaks of his strong desire for an "intermittent silence."[34] In *Christianopolis* Andreae offers a picture of a society in harmony and at peace with itself and indicates by his picture that Christian ideals, rightly understood, will eliminate the incessant disputes and the fanaticism that accompany them in contemporary societies.[35]

Andreae's educational scheme in *Christianopolis* includes the use of pictures and illustrations as a means of instructing the youth. In describing the department of ethics he comments that "we seek or shun respectively,

---

[32]Ibid., p. 221.
[33]Ibid., p. 138.
[34]Ibid., p. 135.
[35]Ibid., p. 175. Cf. pp. 138–139. In Andreae's words, "the cause of Christianity lay near my heart, and I desired to advance that cause by all means. As I could not do this directly, I tried a roundabout method. . . ." J. V. Andreae, *Vita ab ipso conscripta* (Berlin: F. H. Rheinwald, 1849), p. 46, cited in Held, introduction to *Christianopolis*, p. 26.

what we picture good or bad for ourselves."[36] Andreae's utopia, like More's
and Plato's, can be seen as an attempt to paint a picture of the ideal society.
As theological dispute has degenerated into dogmatism, Andreae uses
another form of persuasion to convince the reader to accept the validity of
certain truths and values.[37] He does this by shifting the level of discourse:

. . . I have determined not to praise my citizens, but to describe them. . . . I
could not speak to you about different things more frankly or freely, I could
not give you facts with less restriction, nor draw forth your opinion more
unreservedly than in this manner. . . . If you find our state attractive, nothing
shall be denied you; if you decline it, nothing shall be thrust upon you.[38]

The investigation of ideals in thought is an exercise in persuasion, an
attempt to convince the reader to suspend his judgment until he has been
presented with the whole, and can see what a society would be like in which
the author's values have become reality. The utopian fiction of discovery
and exploration of another society is more than a fiction. It suggests that
both author and reader put aside their previous positions and agree tem-
porarily to suspend their judgment: ". . . it is not my business here to teach
what I think right, but to rehearse what I saw." Furthermore, "Our laws
compel or constrain no one, they do persuade—standing forth with the
Word of God. . . ."[39]

The visitor to Andreae's utopia, no less than Plato's or More's, must
be unprejudiced. The author, in the role of visitor-narrator, is congratulated
by the examiners when he is admitted into the city: "You are ours . . . you
who bring to us an unsullied slate, washed clean, as it were by the sea
itself."[40] Having shown his own willingness to approach utopia with an open
mind, Andreae warns the reader that he must do the same:

Whether you approve or disapprove of this matter I shall praise you, provided you answer with like candor. But if you answer me with some soph-
ism, nothing will be easier for me than to . . . ignore you.[41]

[36]Held, p. 235. *Civitas Solis* also uses pictures to educate the youth, and it is possible that
Andreae may have seen Campanella's manuscript before he published *Christianopolis*. See
Held, introduction to *Christianopolis*, pp. 21–22.
[37]Andreae's writings include a fable in which Truth wanders about, neglected and abused by
those she wants to help. She is told by Aesop to "Clothe your form in fable and fairytale, and
you will be able to do your duty to God and man." J. V. Andreae, *Apologorum Christianorum
Manipuli Sex et Alethea Exul.* ("Mythologiae Christianae Libri Tres"; n.p., n.n., n.d.), cited in
Held, introduction to *Christianopolis*, p. 25.
[38]Held, p. 140.
[39]Ibid., pp. 250, 279.
[40]Ibid., p. 148.
[41]Ibid., p. 140.

The first chapter of *Christianopolis*, which is allegorical, continues this warning. The author sets sail on the Academic Sea in the good ship *Phantasy*. Envy and calumny stir up the Ethiopian Sea (probably the "Sea of Stupidity," according to Held) into which the ship has voyaged. The author is shipwrecked and then thrown up on the island of Caphar Salama.

For the author, who is at the same time legislator of Christianopolis and visitor to it, the attempt to understand ideals by drawing out their implications in thought permits him to test their adequacy by an exercise of reason in which accident and chance have no place: "For inasmuch as other people (and I myself also) do not like to be corrected, I have built this city for myself where I may exercise the dictatorship."[42] And as he leaves the island of Caphar Salama, Andreae offers his excuses to the reader for any inadequacies in his construction. Citing More as precedent, he remarks that *Christianopolis* is written for his friends, with whom he can joke, and not for "eminent men." He expects that, among friends, its many imperfections will be overlooked, for he knows he has overestimated important matters, undervalued greater ones, and described his beautiful Republic in reverse order. Such exercises of reason cannot help but be somewhat haphazard in their construction. But an element of the arbitrary is not a great handicap when the author can assume that the reader is Christian, capable of understanding utopian truths because he is created with a nature that requires these truths for its completion and equipped to recognize these truths when they are displayed in their full beauty. When the utopian ideal is seen as having an objective existence independent of the city in which it is discovered, the inadequacies of the utopian city are not so important. The utopian ideal is not dependent on the existence of utopia for its own existence. Consequently, both the author and his Christian reader need not be too concerned if their voyage of exploration is unsuccessful. The truth they set out to discover remains true independent of their attempt to grasp it more fully by articulating it in thought.

[42]Ibid.

The Changing Nature of Utopian Assumptions

6

Classical and Modern Utopias

Classical utopias, as I have attempted to describe them, are efforts to explore the implications of first principles by specifying them in thought. The principles thus investigated are not themselves believed to need justification, because classical utopias are predicated on the notion, found in Plato and surviving in the Christian concept of God the Creator, that the phenomenal world is the expression of an intelligible or noumenal reality. In the classical utopia, characteristics of the phenomenal world are molded so that, to the degree possible, they are representative of the intelligible world and point beyond themselves to it.

If realization is not a fundamental concern of classical utopias, it is because they are predicated on an intelligible reality that stands in continuing tension to existing reality. In a sense classical utopias can be understood as descriptive models for the fundamental character of being. Like a superbly executed line drawing, they suggest just enough to make the viewer uneasy with his habitual vision of reality.

In the three utopias examined, the highest activity is contemplative: unobstructed knowledge, appreciation of, and in More's and Andreae's cases, obedience to, a reality that transcends utopia. Among the assumptions that led to and sustained such contemplative activity is a concept of causality as the movement from potentiality to actuality. The medieval Christian conceived himself to be maintained in existence by the permanent and indivisible act of creation-conservation of God. This condition was reflected, however weakly, in man's own nature as a tendency toward the first cause. Change was seen, not primarily as a temporal occurrence, but as change from a potential to an actual state of being. Temporality was conceived as a defect, expressed as a resistance or obstruction in matter that prevented a plenitude of being.[1] It is in their rejection of time that classical utopias become fit objects of contemplation. They are vehicles for the type of change that Poulet describes—change that need not issue in action or insert itself in a temporal sequence.

The modern utopias to be examined next place a very different valuation on change and on time. Carl Becker cites as peculiar to the modern mind

The disposition and the determination to regard ideas and concepts, the truth of things as well as the things themselves, as changing entities, the character and significance of which at any given time can be fully grasped

[1]Georges Poulet, *Études sur le temps humain* (Paris: Librairie Plon, 1949), pp. ii–iii.

only by regarding them as points in an endless process of differentiation, of unfolding. . . .[2]

Modern utopias view change as a temporal process. Utopia itself is something that can be attained, and therefore carries with it the corollary that change is desirable. The attainment of utopia is conceived, not as putting an end to the process of change, but as marking that stage of society's development at which man's environment has ceased to impede or thwart whatever forms of change the author considers desirable. Both Bellamy and Wells maintain that human nature does not change in utopia. But by this they mean simply that the desire for change, which is to bring utopia into being, will continue to make itself felt in other forms than social improvement once utopia is established. One of the central questions this study asks is whether the modern utopia can convincingly portray this continual change and development.

The differences between classical and modern utopias may well be expressed by saying that in modern utopias transcendence becomes temporal. Modern utopias find their meaning by portraying a future state in which the inadequacies of present social arrangements are overcome. Their meaning derives in part from a knowledge of the preutopian conditions that have been superseded. Not only do modern utopias rely on the past as their raison d'être; they also make claims on the postutopian future, for they maintain that human nature will be able to express itself more adequately and fully once utopian conditions are brought into existence.

Indicative of the different attitude toward change in classical and modern utopian thought is the shift from spatial to temporal utopias. Louis Sébastien Mercier's eighteenth-century utopia is entitled *Memoirs of the Year 2500,* and on the title page Mercier quotes Leibnitz: "The present is pregnant with the future."[3] The classical utopia, located in the present, implies the real existence of the utopian ideal—the coexistence in time of the standard of judgment and that which it judges. Instead of a standard of judgment by which all societies can be measured, the modern utopia offers

[2]Carl Becker, *The Heavenly City of the Eighteenth-Century Philosophers* (New Haven: Yale University Press, 1932), p. 19.
[3]"Le présent est gros de l'avenir." Louis Sébastien Mercier, *L'An Deux Mille Quatre Cent Quarante. Rêve s'il en fût jamais; suivi De L'Homme De Fer, Songe* (3 vols.; n.p., n.n., 1791). (W. Hooper, who prepared the first English version in 1772, added sixty years to the date.) Spatial utopias, of course, continue to be written, even when utopias located in the past and future become commonplace. Cabet, Hertzka, Howells, and Skinner all locate their utopias in the present.

a specific critique of an existing society and itself as an alternative to it. Its location in the future emphasizes that what is important is, not to judge, but to change. Mercier gives a good example of how flexible a critique can be, compared to the classical utopia's universal standard of judgment. Addressing himself to other social critics, Mercier says that it is not contradictory for a writer wishing to improve government to praise a republic in France and a monarchy in England. The justification for such tactics is that England suffers from an excess of liberty and France from an excess of arbitrary power; both conditions require different sorts of changes and are criticized accordingly.

As utopias become time-oriented, they also tend to become universal states. This tendency reflects technological developments, as well as the absence of unoccupied geographical space that might act as a shield for the modern utopia.[4] A state that wishes to preserve itself inviolate in the modern world must have the power to control other states, but such control implies the responsibility of ruling over the subject state and thus leads to the establishment of a universal state. If utopia is to be achieved by the conscious efforts of men, it cannot ignore the existence of nonutopian society. To do so would leave utopia open to the charge of egoism or narrow humanity. When what is valuable becomes the *attainment* of a better social organization, it appears criminal not to help less fortunate societies progress toward utopia. As Harrington observes,

. . . to ask whether it be lawful for a commonwealth to aspire to the empire of the world, . . . is to ask whether it be lawful for it to do its duty, or to put the world into a better condition than it was before.[5]

Modern utopias that are universal in scope thus avoid the charge of self-satisfied indifference in the presence of the less fortunate.

Classical utopias would be open to the same charge, were they conceived primarily as societies to be brought into being. But if classical utopias are better seen as ideal constructions by which to measure existing reality than as models for change, their isolation from other societies offers no grounds for a moral indictment; it merely indicates the lack of concern of classical utopian authors for concrete social action.

[4]In *The New Atlantis* Bacon already found it necessary to explain how his utopia could have remained undiscovered and at the same time be able to have access to Western knowledge. Francis Bacon, *The New Atlantis,* in *Ideal Commonwealths,* ed. Henry Morley (New York: The Colonial Press, 1901), p. 113.
[5]James Harrington, *The Commonwealth of Oceana* (reprint of the 1771 London edition) in *Works: The Oceana and Other Works* (Darmstadt: Scientia Verlag Aalen, 1963), p. 185.

When they locate their ideal states in the future, modern utopian authors not only implicitly change the relation of utopia to existing states but also change the content of utopia itself. The ideal state acquires a history. Instead of the rather vague references to a founder or a wise monarch reminiscent of the Greek legislator, modern utopias offer a detailed description of how they developed from the author's own world.[6] This history usually takes the form of an explanation to the visitor from the past of what has happened in the intervening years. History becomes a device by which the modern utopian author comments explicitly both on the evils of the past and on the change that permitted progress to a better state. Mercier's ideal state, for example, resulted from a bloodless revolution, under the aegis of a philosophic monarch. The explanation of how the transformation occurred allows the author to criticize in detail the defects of his own society and at the same time to encourage his countrymen to desire and plan for change.

Paralleling the change in historical awareness is the treatment accorded to the visitor-narrator of utopia. The classical visitor-narrator is ahistorical. Hythlodaeus describes what he has observed or has been shown; he does not continually interject comparisons between Utopia and sixteenth-century Europe. And Andreae's comparisons are highly abstract treatments of vice and virtue, good and bad, which do not refer to a particular time or place. The sailors who visit Bacon's and Campanella's utopias could as well be Everyman; their own pasts are not brought into the narration, and they do not leave utopia bent on reform. The modern utopian visitor is, of course, a much more historical animal. His description of what he observes in utopia frequently takes the form of a dialogue with his utopian guide in which both questions and answers are made to refer directly to the visitor's preutopian experiences. Or if utopia is presented as a dream and the dreamer is rudely awakened, he finds the nonutopian present intolerable and looks avidly for impending signs of the change he has witnessed. The ending of Campanella's utopia is instructive in the careful balance it maintains between the classical and the modern positions. The Grandmaster of the Knights Hospittalers [sic], to whom the Genoese Sea Captain has been

---

[6]Bacon, *Ideal Commonwealths*, pp. 117–119. The figure of the legislator also takes on a historical dimension. In Étienne Cabet's utopia, for instance, it is the lack of a single directive intelligence that is made responsible for the "viciousness" of preutopian history. Icarie is the creation of a benevolent dictator who selflessly agreed to take in hand the chaos of history and direct it to the creation of utopia. Étienne Cabet, *Voyage en Icarie* (Paris: Au Bureau du Populaire, Rue Jean-Jacques-Rousseau, 14, 1848).

telling his adventures, says that astrologers predict that the next 100 years will contain more history than the last 4,000. The captain replies: "Ah well! God gives all in His good time. They astrologize too much."[7]

In sum, modern utopias define themselves in terms of their mythical past as well as their utopian present. But when utopia acquires a history, the author acquires a problem foreign to classical utopian authors: namely, the attitude that utopia should take toward its own history. This is the same problem, in a different form, that would confront a modern utopian author were he to situate his utopia geographically in the present. To ask what should be the utopians' attitude toward nonutopians is really to question what function, if any, a knowledge of preutopian misfortune, egoism, or evil will have in utopia. Mercier's utopians, for instance, consider history to offer lessons by example, but as most of the examples are unedifying, very little history is considered worthwhile. What history is taught celebrates the benefactors of humanity: the men who invented the shuttle, plow, and pulley. The nineteenth-century utopias are even more selective. They treat history as leading to and justifying utopia, but because they are less certain what human nature is than were their eighteenth-century predecessors, the nineteenth-century utopians tend to draw from history only cautionary examples of what to avoid, rather than illustrations of exemplary men to be imitated.

Transitional Utopias: Seventeenth Century
In the transition period from the ahistorical classical utopia to the historically self-conscious modern utopia a number of new characteristics appear in utopian writing.[8] Bodin foreshadows the more action-oriented attitude toward utopias which was to become very prevalent by the eighteenth century:

Not that we intend to describe a purely ideal and unrealizable commonwealth such as that imagined by Plato, or Thomas More the Chancellor of England. We intend to confine ourselves as far as possible to those political forms that are practicable.[9]

[7]Thomas Campanella, *City of the Sun*, in *Ideal Commonwealths*, p. 179.
[8]See Glenn Negley and J. Max Patrick, *The Quest for Utopia* (New York: Doubleday & Co., 1962), pp. 283–294, for a discussion of "ideal" and "practical" utopias. The authors treat model constitutions such as Harrington's as paradigm "practical" utopias, whereas the emphasis of this study is on the increased attention given to history within utopia itself.
[9]Jean Bodin, *The Six Books of the Commonwealth*, abridged and translated by M. J. Tooley (Oxford: Basil Blackwell, n.d.), p. 2.

His emphasis on what is practicable, reinforced by his study of the variety of different legal systems and character types, leads him to regard classical utopias as counsels of perfection, inadequate to answer the specific problems of French politics. But the increased awareness that every society, both past and present, has its own special and different characteristics did not immediately lead to a recognition of historical development such as is characteristic of modern utopias. Rather, historical writing, using natural philosophy as its model, began increasingly to treat society as subject to fixed causal laws, having their basis in human nature.[10]

A good example of this type of historical writing is Francis Bacon's *History of Henry VII*. While he is careful to pay lip service to divine providence, Bacon's interest lies in connecting events with their immediate causes. By distinguishing primary from secondary causes and writing history in which the latter predominates, Bacon attempts to provide men with the systematic and coherently connected knowledge they needed to improve, not merely understand, their world.[11]

The distinction between primary and secondary causes reappears in *The New Atlantis* where Bacon's society of savants is given two names: Salomon's House, in honor of the Hebrew king to whom Bacon attributes the authorship of a natural history of plants; and the College of the Six Days' Works, so that God may have the glory of man's workmanship.[12]

The distinction is indirectly reinforced by the way Bacon presents his utopia. The inhabitants live in a city called Bensalem (Son of Peace or Salvation) on the island of New Atlantis. They receive their knowledge of the Old and New Testaments by a miracle. A pillar of light is seen floating on the ocean, and as the inhabitants attempt to approach it, they are held at a distance of sixty yards, until one of their number recognizes in prayer that the pillar of light is a "true miracle," its occurrence signaling that God has broken his own laws of nature for a greater end.[13] The description is important because it shows Bacon carefully distinguishing primary causes (in this case revealed knowledge) and placing them in a separate province where reason cannot operate.

Reason comes clearly into its own when Bacon describes the House of

---

[10]Stephen Toulmin and June Goodfield, *The Discovery of Time* (New York: Harper and Row, Publishers, Torchbook paperback, 1965), pp. 113–115.
[11]Ibid., pp. 107–108; J. R. Hale, ed., *The Evolution of British Historiography from Bacon to Namier* (New York: The World Publishing Company, Meridian paperback, 1964), pp. 16–18.
[12]Bacon, *Ideal Commonwealths*, p. 119.
[13]Ibid., p. 111.

Salomon: "The end of our foundation is the knowledge of causes, and secret motions of things; and the enlarging of the bounds of human empire, to the effecting of all things possible."[14] Nature, rightly studied, yields knowledge, and knowledge leads to action that is the ability to produce new natures.[15] Nature is no longer an object of contemplation in Bacon's writings but is rather a body of material to be overcome. His science is based on a logic of discovery, not a logic of intelligibility, because the natural world is no longer the intelligible counterpart to man's intelligence. For Bacon, human error (the "idols") is a social and psychological phenomenon capable of being overcome; its remedy lies in a new method to guide reason in scientific research and in a novel form of social organization in which scientific activity is carried on in isolation from society.[16]

Within the utopian tradition, Bacon's originality consists in his treatment of science as an independent and autonomous enterprise, symbolized in utopia by the physical distance and lack of communication between the college and the city. The isolation and autonomy of Bacon's scientists is in striking contrast to the integration and subordination of scientific research to other values in Campanella's and Andreae's utopias.[17] And in contrast to the classical utopias, Bacon's has only one ideal: the discovery and elaboration of secondary causes as a means of furthering scientific knowledge.

The ideal of Bacon's utopia, the discovery, classification, and use of scientific knowledge, is a cooperative enterprise, achieved by breaking down into its constituent parts the research necessary to know and to use nature. His description of scientific activity differs from both the primary and secondary ideals of classical utopias. Unlike the Platonic contemplation of transcendent forms, Bacon's program of scientific research depends *directly* upon an appropriate division of labor, reflecting the new understanding of science, such as is exemplified by the House of Salomon. The House of Salomon is, in turn, isolated from the city of Bensalem, where the religious, economic, and family activities of society take place. In Plato's *Republic* a just social organization was a necessary but not a sufficient condition for the occurrence of contemplative activity. In *The New Atlantis*, by contrast, Bacon describes two

[14]Ibid., p. 129.
[15]John Herman Randall, Jr., *The Career of Philosophy*, Vol. I: *From the Middle Ages to the Enlightenment* (New York: Columbia University Press, 1962), p. 250. Cf. Bacon, *Ideal Commonwealths*, p. 131.
[16]Randall, *The Career of Philosophy*, I, 243–249.
[17]Judah Bierman, "Science and Society in the *New Atlantis* and Other Renaissance Utopias," *PMLA*, LXXVIII (December 1963), 495 ff.

ypes of activity: scientific research and religious and social life. The two activities are as distinct and unrelated to each other as the two societies in which hey occur, the House of Salomon and the city of Bensalem.[18]

Bacon's program of scientific research resembles the ideal of modern utopias in its dependence on both a certain form of organization and on the activities of other men. But in his description of the nature of scientific research Bacon remains partially within the classical tradition. The purpose of such research is to discover the form, essence, or quiddity in any natural phenomenon. The form is the general quality or genus found in a particular nature which, together with its specific difference, allows it to be classified with others of a like nature.[19] Although nature is no longer immediately intelligible to man, it still has an objective guarantee. Men do not impose arbitrary categories on nature; they discover forms or essences that have an independent and unchanging existence in nature. The purpose of scientific research is knowledge of nature as well as control over it, and what one knows (although not the uses to which it is put) has an objective validation; its existence is independent of the mind that attempts to know it.

New Atlantis is, Bacon says, a "mirror in the world, worthy to hold men's eye. . . ."[20] Unlike modern utopias, Bacon's mirror reflects an activity the purpose of which cannot be adequately described in terms of the institutional organization that makes it possible. The knowledge obtained by scientific research is objective knowledge, which reflects accurately the nature of the universe. Despite Bacon's effort to distinguish between primary and secondary causes, his knowledge of secondary causes depends in the long run on a primary cause that guarantees their objective and unchanging nature.

The New Atlantis also deals with a question that greatly exercised Bacon's contemporaries: men's relation to their past, expressed in the controversy over whether the ancients had a monopoly of knowledge. Bacon maintained the superiority of his own age, not because of any doctrine of progress or of limitless improvement, but because of the incremental way in which knowledge grows in the sciences. Those who come later in time fall heir to more knowledge, much as an old man may be expected to have riper judgment than a young one.

While sanguine about the increase of knowledge in his own age,

---

[18]Ibid., p. 495.
[19]Randall, *The Career of Philosophy*, I, 247–249.
[20]Bacon, *Ideal Commonwealths*, p. 120.

Bacon was cautious in his expectations of seeing the House of Salomon actually brought into existence. He hoped for a monarch who would supply the
necessary monetary backing, and he counted on himself to direct the enterprise, but he was much less certain that he could find men able and willing to
cooperate in scientific research.

> For the last, touching impossibility, I take it that all these things are to be held
> possible and performable, which may be done by some persons, though not
> by one alone; and which may be done in the succession of ages, though not
> in one man's life. . . .[21]

It might be said that Bacon expected his utopia to come into being in the full-
ness of time, rather than as a result of any concerted effort in the present.

The New Atlantis is a curiously ambivalent utopia. It is isolated in
space, as were the classical utopias, but its ideal activity depends on time, on
the "succession of ages," for its achievement. The objects of knowledge may
be independent of man, but the process of knowing is not, like the Platonic
contemplation of the forms, independent of the efforts of other men. Bacon's
utopian ideal was a new proposal for the acquisition and organization of
knowledge; by implication it was also a criticism of the way men studied the
natural world in seventeenth-century Europe.[22] Yet, the New Atlantis cannot
be said to be a standard by which to judge society, for apart from the reform of
science it offers no systematic comment on the existing social organization.
To the contrary, Bacon's care in separating the House of Salomon from Bensalem indicates a desire to reassure his reader that the effects of scientific
knowledge will not change the nature of a godly society. Rather, the aids science can offer, "the divinations of diseases, plagues, . . . scarcity, tempests,
[and] earthquakes . . . ," serve to secure that society all the more certainly
from accident and disease.[23]

It is only Bacon's ideal of scientific activity that should be understood
as a blueprint for future change. Part of that ideal, the amount of knowledge
to be acquired and the uses to be made of it, depends upon the cooperation
of other men and is contingent upon change in the future. Because the type
of knowledge Bacon describes is not self-contained and satisfactory in itself

[21] Bacon, *Works*, IV, quoted in Richard Foster Jones, *Ancients and Moderns: A Study of the Rise
of the Scientific Movement in Seventeenth-Century England* (Berkeley: University of California
Press, 1965), p. 55. Jones notes that in the first half of the century there was a tendency to
consider Bacon's utopia, like Plato's and More's, unrealizable. During the Puritan revolution
Bacon's proposal began to be seriously considered. Ibid., pp. 171, 317 n. 86.
[22] Randall, *The Career of Philosophy*, I, 249–254.
[23] Bacon, *Ideal Commonwealths*, p. 137.

to the knower, its vindication depends upon utopia coming into existence and proving the adequacy of such knowledge by the results it will obtain over a period of time.

It is probably no accident that Bacon stopped writing *The New Atlantis* after he finished his description of the House of Salomon, for short of his vision of a newly organized science, Bacon's utopia is neither critical nor innovative. Bacon's alter ego, King Salomana, was a lawgiver who ruled over New Atlantis 1,900 years ago and who was responsible for its present organization. He considered his land such a happy one that "it might be a thousand ways altered to the worse, but scarce any one way to the better. . . ."[24] To preserve the kingdom in its prosperous state, he forbade any contact with foreigners. Significantly, *The New Atlantis* breaks off with a governor of the House of Salomon giving the visitor 2,000 ducats, and the latter leaving to tell the world what he has seen. Isolated by its past from the European world, Bacon's utopia appears to be groping for contact with that world, and hoping for a future which would be identical for both.

Action-minded utopias, as Judith Shklar has called them, begin to appear with frequency in the seventeenth century.[25] *Oceana* is dedicated to Oliver Cromwell with the hope that the Lord Protector would use this model commonwealth as a guide when he established a new government to succeed the Protectorate.[26] Its title page carries a quotation in Latin from the *Satires* of Horace, designed to remind the reader that Oceana could be England in the future: ". . . why do you smile? but change the name and it is of you that the tale is told."[27]

Harrington wrote *Oceana* with English conditions in mind, intending his commonwealth to be established first of all in that country. What permitted Harrington to be so confident about Oceana's prospects for realization? One answer, suggested by J. G. A. Pocock, rests on the difference between Harrington's theory of history and that of his master, Machiavelli. Machiavelli held that it was in the nature of all things, including systems of government, to decline. The forces impelling degeneration are "an innate tendency for things to perish by the mere excess of their own being, for each virtue to pro-

[24]Ibid., p. 117.
[25]Judith N. Shklar, "The Political Theory of Utopia," in *Utopias and Utopian Thought,* ed. Frank E. Manuel (Boston: Houghton Mifflin Company, 1966), p. 373. Shklar cites Hartlib, Harrington, and Winstanley as examples.
[26]Charles Blitzer, *An Immortal Commonwealth: The Political Thought of James Harrington* (New Haven: Yale University Press, 1960), p. xxii.
[27]Ibid., p. 32.

duce its corresponding vice and for the latter in the end to prevail, for fortune to throw down what it had built up."[28] A wise legislator could at best retard, but certainly not eliminate, the instability inherent in the nature of all terrestrial things.

But in Harrington's view, if commonwealths decline, it is because men have not understood and taken into account an important law derived from the study of history: constitutions at variance with the distribution of land cause instability in government. According to Pocock, degeneration had ceased to be essential and had become accidental for Harrington.[29] This change of attitude was possible because Harrington located the cause of degeneration, not in man's nature, but in the social structure. Harrington's comment on Machiavelli's notion that a corrupt people are not capable of a commonwealth makes clear the difference in approach:

. . . nor can I otherwise com out of the labyrinth, than by saying, the balance altering a people . . . [that is] government, must of necessity be corrupt: but corruption in this sense signifys no more than that the corruption of one government . . . is the generation of another.[30]

Changed social conditions, no doubt, account in good part for Harrington's way of explaining history. To paraphrase Pocock, Harrington lived in a territorial and agrarian community, where law, justice, custom, and tenure were more important than the logic of the individual's conduct in politics; where institutions, rather than actions, determined the nature of political life. History lent itself to interpretation in terms of the changing structure of society.[31] Harrington could claim that the agrarian law upon which Oceana was based would eliminate the instability that had characterized previous English governments because historical processes, once understood, could be controlled.

By making the goal of his ideal commonwealth stability, or the elimination of undesirable change, Harrington remains within the classical utopian framework. But Oceana is modern in the attention it gives to historical

[28]J. G. A. Pocock, The Ancient Constitution and the Feudal Law: A Study of English Historical Thought in the Seventeenth Century (Cambridge: At the University Press, 1957), p. 145.
[29]Ibid., p. 146. By "essential" Pocock must be understood to mean irremediable. To the extent that Harrington thought he had discovered necessary laws of political change, degeneration would not be "accidental." For a discussion of Harrington's attempt to apply the techniques of the natural sciences to politics, see James Harrington, The Political Writings of James Harrington: Representative Selections, ed. Charles Blitzer (New York: The Liberal Arts Press, 1955), pp. xxvi–xxxi.
[30]Harrington, Works, p. 68; see also pp. 178–179.
[31]Pocock, The Ancient Constitution, p. 146.

development. To the extent that Oceana is designed as a solution to a pattern of political instability that history has made evident, one can argue that the rationale of Harrington's utopia is located in preutopian problems. While More's Utopia also offers remedies for "preutopian" social problems, Utopia can be understood independently of these problems, which are only particular expressions of a fundamental vice in man's nature—pride. Realization is not, for More, a fundamental category. To understand Oceana, on the other hand, one must have in mind the particular set of problems it was designed to meet: the dissolution of the Gothic balance and the resulting governmental instability.

The changed emphasis on realization can be pinpointed by comparing the classical utopian paradox to what may be called the modern paradox. The classical paradox is the Platonic one. The conditions under which a philosopher might become a king, or a king a philosopher, already presuppose the existence of the utopia that the philosopher-king is to bring into being. In other words, the classical utopia is based on principles so different from those that are operative in contemporary society that it is difficult to find a basis in contemporary society that can lead to utopia.

By contrast, the modern utopian paradox might be called a historical paradox. The modern utopia is based on principles formulated as a corrective to problems of preutopian society. The raison d'être of modern utopias, extrinsic to the utopia itself, is located in preutopian problems that require change. The modern utopia is designed to expedite change by providing a definite solution to preutopian problems, but once utopia is brought into existence, it eliminates the preutopian conditions that constitute its raison d'être. By solving these preutopian problems, modern utopias eliminate, at the same time, their major source of justification.[32]

Transitional Utopias: Eighteenth Century
Model constitutions continued to be written, and in much greater number, in the eighteenth century. Both Thomas Spence's Constitution of Spensonia and Jean-Claude Chappuis's Plan Social are predicated on an increasing confidence in man's ability to handle social change.[33] Where Harrington had

[32]See the discussion of nineteenth-century utopias later in this chapter.
[33]See Thomas Spence, The Constitution of Spensonia: A Country in Fairyland Situated between Utopia and Oceana, Brought from Thence by Captain Swallow (London: n.n., 1803), cited in Negley and Patrick, The Quest for Utopia, pp. 489–502; Anon., Histoire du Grand et Admirable Royaume d'Antangil (Saumur: Thomas Maire, 1616), summarized in Frédéric Lachèvre, Les Sucesseurs de Cyrano de Bergerac (Paris: Librairie Ancienne Honoré Champion, 1922), pp.

attempted to understand the causes of political change in order to arrest them (Oceana is designed to prevent the decisive shifts in the ownership of property which cause instability), the new attitude of the eighteenth century tries to use and control change in order to direct it toward deliberately chosen ends. In fact, one purpose for which eighteenth-century model constitutions were written was to make change rational and amenable to control by giving it a goal of the same nature.

However, neither Spence nor Chappuis, any more than Harrington, considered change to be good in itself. Henry Vyverberg observes that in eighteenth-century France both the theorists of progress and the theorists of decadence thought that the criteria by which they measured change were of absolute and eternal validity. Theories of progress did not lead their authors to adopt positions of ethical relativism as long as progress was seen primarily as a method or means to the attainment of a preestablished goal.[34]

The ends toward which most eighteenth-century thinkers believed social change should be directed retained an objective status, and reason remained the faculty that identified those ends—justice, truth, and virtue —which were valid for all ages and nations.[35] Chappuis, for instance, proposed that his society be established on the basis of universal equality: "The Supreme Being imprints everywhere a mark for man to lead him to a happiness as perfect and long-lasting as his existence. *This mark is equality.* It is present in all of Nature."[36] He expected Louis XIV to read his plan, be convinced, and put it forthwith into effect. How his century was able to do justice to such truths when all previous ages had failed was not a problem. Either those who lived in previous ages, Chappuis explained, were victims of an initial ignorance that then solidified into custom, or they simply did not think or, having thought, did not know how to do better.

In the first chapter of Mercier's utopia, ignorance is also offered as an explanation of how wrongs, once recognized, could have remained so long uncorrected. At times this form of reasoning leads Mercier to claim that a sure sign that something is true is its suppression by the established authorities (the latter are either the victims or the perpetrators of ignorance

261–269; Jean-Claude Chappuis, *Le Plan Social de Jean-Claude Chappuis: Une Utopie Socialiste au XVIIIᵉ Siècle*, ed. Jacques Tout (Paris: Librairie du Recueil Sirey, 1942).
[34]Henry Vyverberg, *Historical Pessimism in the French Enlightenment* (Cambridge, Mass.: Harvard University Press, 1958), pp. 71–76, 79.
[35]Ibid., pp. 82–84.
[36]Chappuis, *Le Plan Social*, p. 66 (my translation; Chappuis's italics).

and custom). Once men are freed from abstract theorizing, from the useless system building of a metaphysics inherited from the past, they can turn their attention to physics (in which Mercier includes technology) the goal of which is the happiness of men. When he abandons traditional physics, Mercier also eliminates one of its key assumptions: that there exists a right reason common to all men. He is then forced to consider the possibility that ignorance is so rooted in some men's natures that it may prevent them from ever recognizing or acting upon the self-evident truths expressed in his utopia.

To illustrate this dilemma, Mercier attaches to the end of *L'An Deux Mille Quatre Cent Quarante* a brief description of another dream, called *L'Homme de Fer*.[37] The narrator has been changed into a man of iron capable of imposing his will upon his countrymen by brute force. He roves the streets of Paris, battling abuses and rectifying injustices, until he is captured in an iron vise, especially invented for the purpose, and dismembered. The attempt to use force rather than reason to change men is a short-lived one. Mercier identifies his man of iron, brought low by the forces of ignorance. He is Justice and will be freed from his chains only by the sovereign who is virtuous enough to become his first subject.

It may have been the very pessimism so evident in *L'Homme de Fer* which led Mercier to replace God with posterity as final judge (and justifier) of his utopian vision. Mercier's vision, like that of Condorcet, opens onto a vista of illimitable progress. His utopia is dedicated, not to the present, but to the year 2440. In a comment that echoes the controversy between the ancients and the moderns, Mercier declares that future generations will extend the sway of the present so far into antiquity that not even the memory of the latter will remain. The inhabitants of the year 2440 are no less forward-looking. They picture the soul of man, which is always susceptible to change, ascending a chain of being that reaches to the stars and inhabited planets, and increasing in perfection at every stage of its ascent. Progress, as Mercier describes it, appears to be its own goal—a vision of the future, in this one respect, startlingly near that of H. G. Wells. But Mercier lacks Wells's self-conscious individualism. Faithful to his Enlightenment upbringing, he does not conceive any tension between the individual and society or any distinction between altruistic and self-regarding motives.

[37]Mercier, *L'An Deux Mille*, III, 127–182. The complete title is *L'Homme de Fer, Songe. Rendormons-nous.*

Nineteenth-Century Utopias

Frank Manuel has suggested that a new term be coined for the open-ended
nineteenth-century utopia: "euchronia"—good place becomes good time.[38]
Although eighteenth-century utopian authors had come to believe in the
possibility of utopia coming into existence, for the most part they continued
to construct static and timeless societies that imitated the natural order of the
Newtonian universe. Change within utopia could only be a derogation of its
own perfection and of man's nature, which would ultimately find in utopia a
suitable environment in which to display itself. The author-legislator of the
eighteenth-century utopia, once having constructed and brought into being
his ideal state, needed only to provide for its maintenance against a natural
tendency to corruption.[39]

By the nineteenth century the last link between perfection and stability had eroded, and utopias become much more profoundly historical. Condorcet and Mercier, to the extent that the latter does not fix an absolute term
to man's development, foreshadow the nineteenth-century utopian vision
found in a Saint-Simon, a Fourier, or a Comte. These men were reformers
whose critique of contemporary society was inseparable from an explanation
of historical change intended to show that utopia would inevitably come into
being.[40] Nor was history itself thought to come to an end in utopia. In
Condorcet's vision of the future, progress had already become a self-
nourishing process in which new techniques and new intellectual achieve-
ments opened up further possibilities of advancement and invited even
further achievement. So limitless were the possibilities that beyond a certain
point the mind could only posit an indefinite progress; it was incapable of
grasping its substance.[41]

Both Saint-Simon and Comte were inheritors of Condorcet's belief in
a dynamic future, one that they modified by placing greater emphasis on the
value of individual personality. They adopted a psychology, derived from
Bichat, which stressed the ineradicable differences between men; and by this
new emphasis on the value of the unique individual, they transformed earlier
utopian forms of egalitarianism (condemned for having ignored individuality

[38]Frank Manuel, "Toward a Psychological History of Utopias," Utopias and Utopian Thought,
pp. 79–80.
[39]Frank E. and Fritzie P. Manuel, French Utopias (New York: The Free Press, 1966), pp. 8, 10.
[40]Ibid., p. 10.
[41]Marquis de Condorcet, Esquisse d'un tableau historique des progrès de l'esprit humain
(posthumous work; Paris: Chez Agasse, L'An III de la République), pp. 358, 381.

and prevented the growth of the unique) into equality of self-realization.[42] For the eighteenth century, progress was a rational necessity; for the nineteenth it was an organic growth in history or a biological necessity.[43] To take the place of a universal human nature guaranteed by a creative act of which God alone was capable, the nineteenth century endowed individual passion and energy with creative force and allowed men the hope of eternal self-transcendence.[44]

With increasing attention being paid to personality, nineteenth-century utopias no longer assume that the happiness of the individual and that of the race are identical. One indicator of happiness is the degree of individual difference and self-expression which utopia can accommodate; the corollary of such values is a dynamic society without much interest in the present or in the character types who made or maintained it. Whereas for Plato the despot whose desires are limitless leads the most miserable of lives, for modern utopians limitless desire comes to be a guarantee of the indefinite perfectibility of man.[45]

Mannheim's definition of utopias as reality-transcending doctrines is a good characterization of modern utopian writing.[46] Classical utopias reflected a reality that transcended both existing societies and utopia itself. For the modern writer, however, transcendence is a function of utopia's relation to the present. Or better, when authors such as Bellamy stress the inevitability of utopia, they conceive utopia to be immanent in the present. Mannheim's use of transcendence is typical. It is a temporal category used to make historical rather than ontological distinctions. In Mannheim's language "transcend" means to have not yet come into being; a utopia that has been incorporated in the real world becomes an ideology. Iris Murdoch has remarked upon another facet of the same phenomenon. She observes that in

[42]Manuel, *Utopians and Utopian Thought,* pp. 82–83. See also Judith Shklar, *After Utopia: The Decline of Political Faith* (Princeton: Princeton University Press, 1957), pp. 82–98, for a discussion of the emergence of nineteenth-century individualism.

[43]Shklar, *After Utopia,* p. 72.

[44]Manuel, *Utopias and Utopian Thought,* p. 82, Cf. Shklar, *After Utopia,* pp. 123–128.

[45]Louis Bredvold suggests that the beginnings of moral relativism are to be found in the new emphasis on sensibility. That the virtuous life is a happy one was a commonplace notion, but in reformulations such as Diderot's (a happy life is a virtuous one) each individual knows best for himself whether he is achieving happiness. Louis I. Bredvold, *The Natural History of Sensibility* (Detroit: Wayne State University Press, paperback, 1962), p. 44.

[46]Karl Mannheim, *Ideology and Utopia: An Introduction to the Sociology of Knowledge* (New York: Harcourt, Brace and Company, Harvest paperback, 1957), pp. 193–200.

modern philosophy the image by which morality is understood is movement, not vision. Instead of being an object of contemplation, good is an attribute of the will.[47] Modern utopias conform to this pattern, for they are rooted in the inadequacies of a particular historical situation which they are designed to overcome and are programs for action rather than objects of contempla tion. The utopian writings of Cabet, Bellamy, Wells, and Hertzka all illustrate this activist bent; their ideal states are designed to come into being within the lifetime of the authors.

The new character of modern utopias also accounts for the number of revisions to which utopian projects are subject. Spence, Chappuis, and Bellamy all produced several versions of their ideal societies, for if utopia is to initiate change, large numbers of men must find it persuasive. If one version of utopia does not move men to action, the fault may be in too detailed or too simplified a description, and another version may be more successful. Already in Mercier's writing, the need for such persuasion is explicitly recognized: "And truth is truth only when it becomes as a new-bridge; it must be put into couplets of song . . . it must descend from our books to be clothed in comic opera or in vaudeville."[48] And De Jouvenel does Mercier one better in treating utopias as forms for popularizing long-term planning for the masses. Utopias are useful because they allow one to look at a picture of the future and then decide whether the picture is both "likable" and "likely."[49]

In sum, modern utopias offer a critique of the wrongs of contemporary society, the purpose of which is to foster change in the present. Unlike classical utopias, they do not propose a universal standard of judgment by which to measure the inadequacies of any society. They may be said to offer moral judgments, if moral judgments are thought to issue in activities in which change is both desirable and possible, but they do not provide value judgments in the classical sense.

Often the writing of a modern utopia becomes itself an attempt to stabilize the terms of moral discourse. While the classical utopia assumes the existence of objective values recognized or recognizable by all men, the modern utopia tries to convince men to believe in certain values and to act in terms of them. Indeed, one of the most serious problems a modern utopian author faces is that of justifying the values on which his critique is based. To

[47]Iris Murdoch, "The Idea of Perfection," The Yale Review, Vol. 53 (Spring 1964), pp. 344–345.
[48]Mercier, L'An Deux Mille, III, 123 (my translation; Mercier's italics).
[49]Bertrand de Jouvenel, "Utopia for Practical Purposes," in Utopias and Utopian Thought, pp. 222–223, 226.

be able to draw universal rules of morality solely from history, one must pre-suppose that history has a rational and necessary end that is, in some sense, beneficial to the men who bend their purposes to conform with it.[50] If the modern author, for whom utopia itself is the rational end or highest foresee-able stage of historical development, tries to justify utopia by history alone, he assumes the validity of the very values in question. The visitor to utopia, who represents contemporary misconceptions and prejudices, and who be-comes convinced of the desirability of utopia after a short sojourn in it, is an alternate device by which modern utopians attempt to justify their values. But because the visitor to utopia is, finally, as much the author's creation as the utopia he visits, this stratagem is not a very convincing one.

In the following chapters it is argued that modern utopian authors, in their attempt to describe what man may become rather than what he most fundamentally is, locate man's substance in the past—in what men were and should not continue to be. Consequently, modern utopian authors give value, not to what man *is* in the ideal society, but rather to the *absence* of certain social arrangements and character traits identified with the preutopian past. In other words, the justification for modern utopias is extrinsic to the utopia itself.

Because the modern utopia's raison d'être is in a past that has been superseded, its relation to contemporary society is best described as imma-nent. In Bellamy the immanence is historical: a better future will necessarily develop out of the present. In Wells the future is immanent in men's longing and aspirations for a more orderly and decent world than the one they pres-ently inhabit.

Whether or not modern utopias are thought to offer an adequate justification of the values upon which they are constructed is closely tied to the problem of utopia's realization. While classical utopias remain valuable as thought experiments irrespective of their realization, modern utopias derive almost all their meaning from their immanence: the premises from which modern utopias make sense is that change in the direction of utopia can occur. Unlike its classical counterpart, however, the modern utopia offers only one ideal: a better set of social arrangements. If the reader accepts the author's version of improved social arrangements, the modern utopian "ideal" remains an ideal from the perspective of the nonutopian present. But if the reader were to imagine himself living in utopia, the ideal would no longer be a value to be achieved or defended but would be an established and

[50]See Shklar, *After Utopia*, p. 71.

unquestioned fact. For the modern author, values no longer have an existence and validity independent of man; values are "recognized" as valuable when they are seen in terms of or in contrast to the undesirable state they are designed to remedy. The utopian citizen accordingly would have no way of knowing that his society is valuable because he would have nothing with which to contrast it. He could not understand his past, which would appear to him, in the best eighteenth-century tradition, to be a record of the follies and perversities of his ancestors.

Despite the authors' efforts to make their societies dynamic, the modern citizen of utopia, living in a world that has solved all its problems, has no purposes or goals beyond his own satisfaction. Consequently he does not have a future that differs in substance from his present and that might give him grounds for considering whether man may not sometimes be the victim as well as the maker of history. The activity that takes place in the modern utopia can be explained as activity necessary to keep utopia functioning, but if utopians have no past or future, such activity becomes shorn of the temporal dimensions through which the moderns confer significance.

For Christianity the ideal future might be called the substance of the present: the kingdom of God is within you. Were this attitude to stand for that of classical utopias, the modern reformulation might be: the kingdom of God is in the utopian future, justified by the preutopian past—it is not of the present.

Edward Bellamy's *Looking Backward* and *Equality*

7

Edward Bellamy wrote *Looking Backward: 2000–1887* in 1884 and *Equality* in 1897. The latter was Bellamy's last book, part of which was written during illness.[1] *Equality* is a much longer and more detailed account of the utopia presented in *Looking Backward,* but, apart from the later volume's increased attention to religion and its place in society, the argument of the two books is similar.

Reared in the Calvinist faith by his father, a mildly evangelical Baptist minister, Bellamy later rejected orthodox religion and traditional Emersonian self-reliance in favor of his own "religion of solidarity." The new religion was to result from the psychic development of new levels of consciousness; during this development men would slough off the constraints of a self-enclosed personality for the freedom of an impersonal cosmic awareness.

Comte's solidaristic concept of living for others in the past and in the future was important in Bellamy's development, as was the Civil War, which, in the author's image of a cohesive array of marching men, stood for the surrender and submergence of the personality to an ideal of freedom greater than itself.[2]

In the year 2000 Bellamy imagines that all countries of any importance will have adopted the economic reforms pioneered by the United States. Nations will have become autonomous within a federal system. With scarcity no longer an incentive for aggression, international relations will have become harmonious, and the eventual unification of the world into one nation can be expected in the near future.[3]

Bellamy's spokesman in this paradise is a physician, Dr. Leete, who is also the host of Julian West, the inadvertent visitor from the nineteenth century. West is transported to utopia very simply: the well-to-do Bostonian has trouble sleeping and summons a mesmerist. When he awakens, 113 years have elapsed, and, finding himself in a Boston he no longer recognizes, West reies on Dr. Leete for guidance and for explanation. A tedious romance between the visitor and Dr. Leete's daughter serves, in Bellamy's

[1] Edward Bellamy, *Selected Writings on Religion and Society,* ed. Joseph Schiffman (New York: The Liberal Arts Press, 1955), p. xlii.
[2] Ibid., pp. xi ff. For an excellent discussion of Bellamy's religious development, see the introduction by John L. Thomas to *Looking Backward: 2000–1887* (Cambridge, Mass.: The Belknap Press of Harvard University Press, 1967).
[3] Edward Bellamy, *Looking Backward: 2000–1887* (New York: Grosset and Dunlap, n.d. [ca. 1909]), pp. 140–143.

words, "to alleviate the instructive quality of the book. . . ."[4] It has been suggested that Julian West is meant to be an example of the greater psychic development toward altruism that Bellamy wanted to portray as normal in utopia.[5] While it is true that West does develop a new sense of values, this change is obligatory for any visitor to utopia. West is primarily a device for explaining utopia to the reader, and in utopia he reserves his greatest admiration, not for any increase in spiritual awareness, but for the new economic arrangements. In contrast to Howells, who tried to portray a spontaneous, direct, and active altruism in his utopia, Bellamy's utopians express their "altruism" through their economic arrangements, which, by eliminating poverty and class distinctions, have fostered the growth of equality.

In its emphasis on economic arrangements as both the source of present injustices and the means of remedying them, Bellamy's utopia is typical of much of nineteenth-century utopian thought. He shares with other utopian visionaries, such as Etienne Cabet and Theodor Hertzka, both the belief that utopia should and can be brought about and the encouragement of active efforts to hasten its arrival. Hertzka, in his eagerness to distinguish himself from such an "unpractical enthusiast" as Sir Thomas More, speaks for many activist reformers of Bellamy's bent.

For this book is not the idle creation of an uncontrolled imagination, but the outcome . . . of profound scientific investigation. . . . Thoughtlessness and inaction are, in truth, at present the only props of the existing economic and social order. What was formerly necessary, and therefore inevitable, has become injurious and superfluous; there is no longer anything to compel us to endure the misery of an obsolete system. . . .[6]

The major concern of this study is with the ways in which Bellamy's portrayal of the utopian ideal and its relation to the present differ from those of his classical predecessors. In its static character and its ability to serve as a thought experiment, the modern utopia still resembles its classical counterpart. But even these commonalities do not remain stable because the implications of an immobile society change during the process of bringing utopia into existence, and the result of a thought experiment is not quite the same

---

[4]Bellamy, *Looking Backward*, p. xx.
[5]Joseph Schiffman, "Edward Bellamy's Altruistic Man," *American Quarterly*, VI (Fall 1954), 195–209.
[6]Theodor Hertzka, *Freeland: A Social Anticipation*, trans. Arthur Ransom (London: Chatto and Windus, 1891), pp. 442–443. Cf. Etienne Cabet, *Voyage en Icarie* (Paris: Au Bureau du Populaire, Rue Jean-Jacques-Rousseau, 14, 1848), pp. i–v.

when the differences in men's natures become more important than what they have in common.

The Ideal of <u>Looking Backward</u> and <u>Equality</u>

The single ideal of Bellamy's utopia, the prerequisite for a rightly ordered society, is economic equality. In the introduction to *Equality*, Bellamy reminisces:

. . . it was in the fall or winter of 1886 that I sat down to my desk with the definite purpose of trying to reason out a method of economic organization by which the republic might guarantee the livelihood and material welfare of its citizens on a basis of equality corresponding to and supplementing their political equality.[7]

The equal division of wealth among all members of society recommends itself to Bellamy on both economic and moral grounds. It is the most efficient way to run an economy because it creates a vastly increased consumer demand, which in turn is a continual stimulus to the economy to increase its productive capacity. The fair distribution of wealth also follows the golden rule of Christ, for it embodies the ethical ideal of equal treatment for all.

Nothing can be in the long run or on a large scale sound economics which is not sound ethics. It is not, therefore, a mere coincidence, but a logical necessity, that the supreme word of both ethics and economics should be one and the same equality.[8]

Bellamy's utopia is based on the ideal of economic equality, which has the advantage of being, at the same time, morally right and the most efficient way to organize society. The work that Bellamy's citizens perform can be explained in terms of the utopian social organization, and, from the point of view of an inhabitant of utopia, there seems to be no other basis upon which it can be explained. In contrast to the ideal activity of classical utopias, which is based on a reality that transcends utopian society, the explanation for modern utopian activity is found in the organization of utopia and, for those acquainted with the past, in its contrast to a ruder age. Bellamy's claim that economic equality is both efficient and moral is one example of this justification in terms of the past, for the measure of both efficiency and morality is the waste and inhumanity of nineteenth-century society.

[7]As cited in Vernon Louis Parrington, Jr., *American Dreams: A Study of American Utopias* (New York: Russell & Russell, 1964), p. 72.
[8]Edward Bellamy, *Equality* (New York: D. Appleton and Company, 1897), p. 195.

Economic activity in the year 2000 takes the form of an industrial army, which Bellamy claims is the most rational and efficient way of organizing work. The industrial army is a concept that repays exploration, for how its members are selected, their motives for joining, how different types of work are classified, and the reasons for such classifications are all indicators of the degree to which activity and organization are really inseparable in utopia. All young citizens in Bellamy's future society are evaluated on the basis of their school and early work habits, and their rank among those ready to enter the labor market is determined according to the intelligence, efficiency, and devotion to duty that they have shown. Those with the highest rating obtain first choice of job and locality. The administration equalizes the labor conditions, as much as possible, by providing shorter hours for more arduous labor; the control of working hours permits, at the same time, the regulation of supply and demand.

The beginning worker serves for three years in a general unclassified grade of common laborers, then as an apprentice. After these preliminary stages, he becomes a regular laborer, classed in one of three grades according to his ability and industry. Regradings, which occur regularly, allow a worker to rise or descend in the rank list. Both permission to specialize and ability to choose the area of specialization depend on getting and keeping a certain grade. Bellamy, not afraid of explicit categorizations, remarks that those who remain at the lowest grade are "likely to be as deficient in sensibility to their position as in ability to better it."[9]

Although technically no greater honor is assigned to one job than to another, and although emulation is dismissed as an incentive for inferior natures, it is difficult to see what other motive serves to keep the economic system functioning.[10] Bellamy's own preference is clearly for the nobler type of worker who measures his duties by his endowments. But this preference begs the question, as endowments have already been graded and classed (presumably with accuracy) by the industrial army and, in addition, any worker inclined to shirk his duties is punished by a regime of bread and water. Moreover, promotion from one rank to another is considered a public

---

[9]Bellamy, *Looking Backward*, p. 127.
[10]Bellamy is never clear whether he means by emulation the desire to be esteemed by others or the desire for self-esteem or the desire for superiority. See Arthur O. Lovejoy, *Reflections on Human Nature* (Baltimore: The Johns Hopkins Press, 1961), pp. 87–127. Probably the first and third senses, which reflect aspects of the capitalistic competition that Bellamy deplored, are nearest to his meaning. (The relation of emulation to capitalist competition will be discussed in more detail later in this chapter.)

distinction marked by the wearing of an iron, silver, or gilt badge—a custom that blurs even more the initial differentiaton attempted between those inferior natures motivated by emulation and the superior ones motivated by their duty to fulfill their natural abilities.[11]

His distaste for emulation leads Bellamy to maintain that in utopia the coarse motive of gain, typical of nineteenth-century individualism, has been replaced by patriotism, service to the nation, and a passion for humanity. Yet these abstractions are given no content that would allow one to picture their functioning as actual motives. Consequently, emulation and natural endowments come to seem indistinguishable, since the only method that Bellamy offers to determine natural endowment is the rank and badge system, which must also serve as the goal for those motivated by emulation.

It is not surprising to find that Bellamy has portrayed economic activity as almost entirely the result of the way in which the industrial army is organized. The fact that economic activity in utopia is pictured in terms of a rather rigid social organization is indicative of Bellamy's desire to subdue the potential anarchy it is capable of generating; the alternative, "each man for himself," or what theorists have called the state of nature, is condemned as being demonstrably destructive of human dignity and equality. But at the same time, at the level of individual motivation, nothing other than emulation is available to explain the functioning of the industrial army. Emulation appears to express either the desire of inferior types to advance in the industrial army or the desire of superior persons for honor. In both cases the reason for emulation is to be found in the already existing economic organization and therefore cannot serve as a basis for calling economic activity more than social.

Further evidence for the social character of Bellamy's ideal is found in his treatment of education. In classical utopias, education strengthened those preexisting traits in human nature that the author judged desirable, and inhibited those he thought harmful. In the modern utopia, in which a better environment is much more instrumental in determining the way in which men act, one might expect the formative powers of education to be stressed

[11]Bellamy's use of badges is reminiscent of Plato's use of different metals to represent differences in the activities of the three classes in the Republic (the contemplative activity of the philosophers being represented by gold). But Plato's ordering of activities involved judgments that Bellamy does not seem prepared to make. Plato's rank order is based on the value and on the perishable nature of both the metals and the activity typical of each class. Bellamy's use of three metals indicates only a numerical ranking. It is not even possible to suggest on what basis one is allotted a badge, since the grounds for promotion, beyond unanimity, are not described.

even more. But in Bellamy's treatment, education is merged with the economic system, rather than being given a broadly formative influence apart from it. In the year 2000 the nation guarantees the nurture, education, and maintenance of every citizen from the cradle to the grave. For those who enter the industrial army the line between education and nurture-maintenance is a thin one because school performance is merged with the first three years of unclassified labor in order to determine the rank of candidates for the industrial army.

The role of education is more clearly delineated for those who choose professions after finishing their term of general labor (brain workers as opposed to hand workers) and therefore must continue their studies in schools of technology, medicine, art, and higher liberal learning. The professions are organized as a counterpart to the industrial army, and a definite choice of occupation must be made before the age of thirty, six years after entering the industrial army; otherwise there would remain too brief a period in which the state could profit from the professional talent it has educated.

Apart from determining the citizens' natural aptitude for future occupations that allow them to serve the nation, what do the schools do? Manual training, Bellamy states, is not allowed to encroach upon general culture, but beyond that brief comment he tells us next to nothing about what general culture might be. A theoretical knowledge of industry and tools, reinforced by frequent visits to the workshop, is explicitly mentioned as a part of education, as is further training in postgraduate schools; both take place during the working as well as the retirement years (retirement occurs after twenty-four years of industrial service). But despite the author's emphasis upon the freedom of mind that comes with economic security (he calls it a "moral atmosphere of serenity"), Bellamy gives no intimation why his citizens would continue their studies other than to suggest that the intellect matures late in life.[12] "Late blooming" is hardly a sufficient motive for education unless one ascribes to the intellect an active thirst for knowledge, which in any case Bellamy does not do.

A long and detailed critique of nineteenth-century education is phrased entirely in economic terms and provides a partial explanation of the continued close relation between the two in Bellamy's utopia.

The basis of education is economic, requiring as it does the maintenance of the pupil without economic return during the educational period. If the edu-

---

[12]Bellamy, *Equality*, p. 249.

cation is to amount to anything, that period must cover the years of childhood and adolescence to the age of at least twenty. That involves a very large expenditure, which not one parent in a thousand was able to support in your day. The state might have assumed it, of course, but that would have amounted to the rich supporting the children of the poor, and naturally they would not hear to that, at least beyond the primary grades of education.[13]

Aside from exposing and reforming nineteenth-century malpractices, the treatment of education if astonishingly scant when one considers what a fertile field malleable human nature offers an enterprising utopian author. In Bellamy's case the most probable explanation for this omission is his belief that human nature has not changed in utopia; only the conditions of human life have changed, and with them the motives of human action. It should be remarked that Bellamy's claim that human nature has not changed in utopia is quite different from the classical utopian view that human nature is fundamentally the same. The classical view assumed that the basic requirements of men's natures are identical and that therefore one value or good is capable of satisfying their nature. The modern claim that human nature has not changed considers diversity a fundamental characteristic of men's nature. The similar nature of preutopian and utopian men refers to a temporal rather than an essential similarity.

Bellamy's view that human nature has not changed in utopia, put in temporal perspective, means that once the deleterious motive of competitive economic gain is removed, human nature is freed—is no longer impeded, so to speak—in the event that it wishes an education. But Bellamy suggests no specific, concrete motives for desiring knowledge, such as curiosity about the nature of the universe or a desire to explore the past or predict the future. He seems to rest his case for education firmly upon economics when he says that "the greater efficiency which education gives to all sorts of labor, except the rudest, makes up in a short period for the time lost in acquiring it."[14]

Both economic and educational activity, to the extent that the two are distinguishable, can thus be described as social activity, which can be justified only in the already existing utopian social organization. In addition to being social, the modern utopian ideal has been described as "pervasive," to indicate that one ideal determines the nature of all other activities in utopia. The pervasive principle is reductionist in its operation: in Bellamy's society all utopian activities in which independent motives or purposes might

[13]Ibid., pp. 247–248.
[14]Bellamy, *Looking Backward*, p. 217.

operate are reduced to the social ideal of economic equality. One example of the pervasive character of the ideal has already been provided in the virtual identity that Bellamy establishes between education and economics. Two other apparently independent activities, the arts and criminality, upon examination appear derivative from economic equality and thus offer additional evidence of the pervasiveness of the social ideal.

Bellamy is typical of his century in regarding the arts as an autonomous area of activity:

I would call attention to the fact that sentimental love of the beautiful and sublime in nature, the charm which mountains, sea, and landscape so potently exercise upon the modern mind through a subtle sense of sympathy, is a comparatively modern and recent growth of the human mind. . . . If culture can add such a province as this to human nature within a century, it is surely not visionary to count on a still more complete future development of the same group of subtle psychical faculties.[15]

But within utopia the autonomy of the arts is not maintained. Intellectual sympathy, now available to a vastly increased proportion of individuals, is the faculty that permits the appreciation of the arts, among which Bellamy includes cleanliness. This appreciation is said to make the conditions of life pleasanter by eliminating the inconvenience (odor is cited as an example) that often resulted, in preutopian times, from association with the uncouth.

Although Bellamy is frequently vague about the difference, he does distinguish the pleasant environment created by the arts from universal education, which is necessary for the citizen's full enjoyment of aesthetic matters. (And, of course, the level of hygiene was much more closely related to the level of education in Bellamy's day than it is now.) Education is claimed to have produced an era of unparalleled intellectual splendor, of which the preutopian renaissance offered only a faint suggestion. An aspiring author, in this second renaissance, can exempt himself from service to the industrial army—if he is able to secure sufficient public popularity and remuneration. Every author has an equal chance to try to obtain recognition from the public, whose verdict is deemed conclusive.

Bellamy's treatment of the arts, then, assumes that quality is identified by an almost unanimous public opinion. He bases this unanimity

[15]Edward Bellamy, *The Religion of Solidarity*, ed. Arthur Morgan (Yellow Springs, Ohio: Antioch Bookplate Company, 1940), pp. 22–23. In a comment added in 1887 to the original manuscript (written in 1874) Bellamy says that the thoughts expressed in it represent the germ of his philosophy of life, which he later expanded but never substantially altered. Ibid., p. 43.

on universal education of a high level. But education, as Bellamy treats it, is almost identical to the desire for economic equality, the social ideal. The unanimity that supports the arts would thus appear to be merely another facet of the social ideal.

The same problem recurs when Bellamy tries to show why the artist should want to obtain such honors. The only explanation offered is that such honors are fair: all participants start from the same basis. But the sense and significance of fairness is never given, and the reader is left to suspect that it is again economic equality expressed in another form. Similarly, when Bellamy describes a feeling of pleasure that the reader may experience over a book, the feeling is not shown as part of a distinctive mode of activity or way of perceiving. Public opinion, fairness, the feeling of pleasure—all seem to lack referents other than the all-pervasive one of economic equality.

In an article written in 1889, William Morris criticizes Bellamy's utopia for offering inadequate scope to the artistic impulse:

[Bellamy's] temperament may be called the unmixed modern one, unhistoric and unartistic; it makes its owner (if a socialist) perfectly satisfied with modern civilization, if only the injustice, misery, and waste of class society could be got rid of; which half change seems possible to him. The only ideal of life which such a man can see is that of the industrious *professional* middle class man of today, purified from their crime of complicity with the monopolist class, and become independent instead of being, as they are now, parasitical. . . .[16]

Morris suggests, in contrast to Bellamy, that art is not a mere adjunct to equality of condition but the necessary and indispensable instrument of both variety in life and human happiness. His criticism of *Looking Backward* is, finally, that it offers only one ideal—economic equality.[17]

In view of Bellamy's assertion that human nature has not changed by living in utopia, his treatment of crime may offer grounds for modifying Morris's criticism. In apparent contradiction to his claim for the continuity

[16]William Morris, *The Commonweal* (January 22, 1889), quoted in A. L. Morton, *The English Utopia* (London: Lawrence and Wishart, 1952), p. 154 (Morris's italics; Morton's interpolation).
[17]Despite Morris's perception of the weakness of Bellamy's utopia, *News From Nowhere* also offers but one ideal (pleasurable work in natural surroundings) which is both social and pervasive in nature. These characteristics of the ideal are difficult for modern utopias to avoid insofar as their ideal is derived from a critique of the present, whose multiple defects are explained as resulting from one cause. The relation of the pervasive to the social character of the ideal is discussed later in this chapter.

of human nature, Bellamy observes that nineteenth-century crime was due almost entirely to inequality of possession. When the nation became the sole trustee of wealth, he says, "We cut this root, and the passion tree that overshadowed your society withered, like Jonah's gourd, in a day."[18] Crimes of violence, attributed to ignorance and bestiality, have almost disappeared in Bellamy's utopia. What crime remains is treated as an outcropping of ancestral traits (atavism), and the criminal is sent to the hospital, not to jail. This procedure has a certain logic, for if all motives for crime have been abolished and crime continues to exist, what explanation other than atavism or hereditary disorder is possible?

In *Erewhon* and *Erewhon Revisited*, Butler, with satiric intent, pushes assumptions about criminality such as those Bellamy was prone to make to their logical and ludicrous extreme. Butler describes a society in which illness is a crime and crime is an illness to be cured by hospitalization or a "straightener." The point is well taken, for if crime can be explained entirely in terms of attendant circumstances or events, one is no more responsible for crime than for a disease or accident. (Indeed, one could argue that contagion is a much more serious risk than corruption for an onlooker.) If immorality is not dealt with on its own terms, almost any other terms such as societal conditions or aesthetic displeasure can be shown to have some relevance.[19]

Bellamy's difficulty, seen in his treatment of education and the arts as well as crime, comes in separating indicators (badges, ranks, public acclaim) from causes. He is reluctant to attribute preutopian evil to constant characteristics in human nature, but unless he can supply other plausible justifications for the various activities within utopia, the reader may fill in the lack himself by mistaking the indicators for the causes of such activity.

In other words, it seems that Bellamy is able to maintain that human nature has remained the same by reducing human motives to the desire for economic equality or variants thereof, such as fairness in artistic competition. In this process he has separated motive from its basis in human nature and is then free to assimilate motive into varying forms of economic organization. But if Bellamy is to be taken seriously when he asserts that human nature has not changed in utopia (although economic organization has), then what is left as a permanent part of human nature are only those traits

[18]Bellamy, *Looking Backward*, p. 201.
[19]Samuel Butler, *Erewhon and Erewhon Revisited* (New York: Random House, 1927), pp. 88 ff. (See also the chapter on W. D. Howells for a discussion of morality in aesthetic terms.)

that were *thwarted* in the old capitalistic system but are *fully expressed* in the new economic organization. Those characteristics are, of course, various forms of the desire for equality, which are indistinguishable from Bellamy's economic organization because they find unique expression through and as a result of that economic organization. Bellamy's ideal is therefore pervasive, eliminating or reducing all motives to the social one of economic equality.

The different motives accounting for activities in preutopian and utopian society vary according to the different forms of economic organization in the two societies. Bellamy's economic arrangements were previously called social because of the lack of any other motives that would have suggested the presence of nonsocial forms of behavior. But it is now possible to call these economic arrangements, as well as the activity that takes place through them, social in a much stronger sense. Such social activities are the unique and adequate receptacle of a *constant* trait in human nature—the desire for equality. Social activity is thus the sole and adequate expression of man's nature in Bellamy's utopia. When the new era was inaugurated, Bellamy says:

There was, of course, a large residuum too hopelessly perverted, too congenitally deformed, to have the power of leading a good life, however assisted. Toward these the new society, strong in the perfect justice of its attitude, proceeded with merciful firmness . . . the new order, guaranteeing an equality of plenty to all, left no plea for the thief and robber, no excuse for the beggar, no provocation for the violent. . . . With a good conscience, therefore, the new society proceeded to deal with all vicious and criminal persons as morally insane, and to segregate them . . . wholly secluded from the world—and absolutely prevented from continuing their kind. By this means the race, in the first generation after the Revolution, was able to leave behind itself forever a load of inherited depravity and base congenital instincts, and so ever since it has gone on from generation to generation, purging itself of its uncleanness.[20]

There is, in short, no excuse for an old human nature in a new social order. Atavism does not, any more than the rubric "morally insane," answer the problem of continued criminality. It merely poses the question at one remove: why do people continue to act in a manner that reflects circumstances and causes no longer in existence? Bellamy might have used as an explanation something approximating Bagehot's "cake of custom," or he might have suggested a lag in human nature's ability to respond to changed

[20]Bellamy, *Equality*, pp. 363–364.

social conditions. But in so doing Bellamy would also have had to allow for the possibility that outmoded habits or basic, slow-changing human appetites would affect the functioning of the economic system. Such retarding elements, in any case, are incompatible with the utopian citizen's awareness of the near-perfect rationality of his economic system in comparison with nineteenth-century private capitalism. Once the root is cut, the gourd should, according to Bellamy's logic, wither. If reason is at fault, those in whom reason is defective—those who are no longer capable of being considered fully human—must be isolated and eliminated.

For Bellamy, then, whatever has not changed in human nature finds sole and adequate expression in social activity. But he does not describe the constant factor in human nature—the desire for equality—as capable of supporting any other value or ideal than the economic. Equality in the economic realm does not serve as the basis for the occurrence of other and different activities. It is this lack that makes it tempting to describe Bellamy's equality in terms of similarity: like human natures produce like actions.

By distinguishing a level of activity not used in this analysis (biological necessity), Herbert Marcuse suggests *how* the pervasive character of the utopian ideal derives from its social nature. Marcuse distinguishes two levels within the historical structure: a phylogenetic-biological level (scarcity), at which animal man develops in a struggle with nature, and a sociological level (hierarchical distribution of scarcity), at which socialized individuals and groups struggle among themselves and with their environment.[21] Marcuse notes that the two levels are in constant interaction, but social phenomena generated at the second level (the division of labor, law, government) are exogenous to the first. These phenomena are more malleable and are capable of faster change without altering the first, more fundamental instinctual level.

In Bellamy's utopia the two levels appear to have become entirely separated. The sociological level—society organized to ensure economic equality—appears able to alter entirely, or even make superfluous, the phylogenetic-biological level. In utopia the basic appetites, such as sex and hunger, which are expressed at the phylogenetic-biological level, no longer appear in any form as motives for activity at the sociological level. This is perhaps the most striking instance of the capacity of the social ideal to imprint its nature on motives that are not in themselves social.

[21] Herbert Marcuse, *Eros and Civilization: A Philosophical Inquiry into Freud* (New York: Alfred A. Knopf, Inc., and Random House, Vintage paperback, 1962), p. 120.

Morris comments on Bellamy's difficulty in handling the delicate problem of motivation in terms that parallel Marcuse's analysis. He criticizes Bellamy for assuming, within utopia, the same drive to provide for such needs as hunger as characterized nineteenth-century Boston, needs that utopia was supposed to eliminate.

The underlying vice in it [Bellamy's utopia] is that the author cannot conceive . . . anything else than the *machinery* of society, and that, doubtless naturally, he reads into the future of society, which he tells us is unwastefully conducted, that terror of starvation which is the necessary accompaniment of a society in which two-thirds or more of its labour-power *is* wasted. . . .[22]

Either Bellamy assumed such drives and could not explain them in terms of his utopia, or he eliminated them. In Morris's explanation the motive for activity within utopia is preutopian fear of starvation. In the terms of this study it is the existence of a social organization designed to produce economic equality. And in both cases utopian activity appears equally incomprehensible.

The Static Character of <u>Looking Backward</u> and <u>Equality</u>
The modern utopian author who intends that his ideal society be brought into being may be held to account for the way that society would function if it existed. The classical utopias discussed earlier in this study were perfect societies that deliberately excluded change as incompatible with perfection. Immobility was one of the characteristics that made them effective standards of judgment—points of stability by which to measure the flux of existing reality.

Most modern utopian authors deny that their societies should contain any such static perfection. For utopia to be a fit place in which men can live and develop their capacities, the modern utopian author must design a system that accommodates, even encourages, change. Bellamy and Wells are emphatic in their insistence that utopia must have a future as well as a past. That the past is capable of important development is established, for it has resulted in utopia. But such development is seen as a mere foretaste of what will occur in the utopian future. Bellamy's statement, referred to earlier, that Boston in the year 2000 is enjoying a renaissance of such brilliance as to make the sixteenth-century Renaissance pale into insignificance is typical of the

[22]Morris, *Commonweal*, quoted in Morton, *English Utopia*, pp. 154–155 (Morris's italics).

claims made for modern utopias. In the Preface to *Looking Backward,* the author declares his confidence in utopia's future:

The almost universal theme of the writers and orators who have celebrated this bimillennial epoch has been the future rather than the past, not the advance that has been made, but the progress that shall be made, ever onward and upward, till the race shall achieve its ineffable destiny. This is well, wholly well, but it seems to me that nowhere can we find more solid ground for daring anticipations of human development during the next one thousand years, than by "Looking Backward" upon the progress of the last one hundred.[23]

Bellamy suggests that a "solid ground" for future development was laid in the progress of the last century. Of what does this "solid ground" consist? The changes in nineteenth-century capitalist society were accomplished through peaceful industrial evolution. Capital became concentrated in large monopolies and trusts that absorbed or eliminated all but a few small business firms. Although initially a hardship to individuals, the consolidation resulted in a vast increase in productive efficiency and wealth, and after a period of time the public, which had resisted consolidation, came to see that it was the source of the material well-being and progress they enjoyed. Still later the remaining monopolies merged into a single syndicate, and the people themselves assumed control of their economic affairs, just as a century before they had taken over the conduct of their political affairs.

Bellamy maintains that the development of monopoly capitalism into state or national capitalism was inevitable.

The solution came as the result of a process of industrial development which could not have terminated otherwise. All that society had to do was to recognize and cooperate with that evolution, when its tendency had become unmistakable.[24]

Yet if progress in the past was inevitable and a necessary development of the logic inherent in economic forces, these forces afford little scope for change in the future. The logical last step, the unification of nations separate only in name into a world state, is already anticipated, and Bellamy does not foresee any further political-economic development beyond it. To be sure, the economy will continue to produce an ever-increasing abundance of goods and products, but Bellamy to the contrary, such productivity is not really progress, only more of what already exists.

In *Equality,* Bellamy seems to acknowledge implicitly that ever-

[23]Bellamy, *Looking Backward,* p. xxi.
[24]Ibid., p. 49. Cf. *Equality,* p. 385.

increasing abundance is too weak a vehicle of change, for he devotes greater attention to the change of opinion that, he claims, accompanies economic evolution. Within this new emphasis, he attributes the inevitability of the revolution to the increase of intelligence among the masses since the sixteenth century. In this more voluntaristic version of events, all the evils of the capitalist system were necessary in order for men to gain a clear conception of what was at stake (the irresponsible power of private capitalism) and to establish a "wholly new economic system . . . based upon public control. . . ."[25]

But increased intelligence provides no better solution to the problem of future change than economic productivity. The increase of intelligence came about because of a specific set of conditions: men were able to contrast the rationality of a consolidated economic enterprise with the remaining irrationality of uncoordinated management and to draw the appropriate lesson. But once the lesson has been learned, economic enterprise within utopia is fully rational. To the extent that the increase of intelligence depends upon the contrast between rational and irrational social arrangements, utopia offers limited possibilities for continued progress in that realm as well.

As has been noted, Bellamy maintains that within utopia human nature has not changed; only human motives have changed with the new environment. He does not say what human nature is apart from its motives, but it seems apparent that the new environment has eliminated one important motive for change, that which depends on the contrast of reason and unreason. In describing a sermon (piped into the home) Bellamy indicates that he is aware of the problem. He has the minister say that "it is not now in this happy age that humanity is proving the divinity within it. It was rather in those evil days when not even . . . the struggle for existence . . . could wholly banish generosity and kindness from the earth."[26] Bellamy gives very few such indications of unease; in Wells's and Howells's utopias the signs of discomfort are much more explicit.

When Bellamy is not propounding economic developments as a motive for future change in utopia, he favors the notion that progress will be based on the continual development of men's spiritual capability. He says that "the first full and clear revelation of the natural and inherent varieties in human endowments" dates from the introduction of economic equality.[27] In

[25]Bellamy, *Equality*, p. 330.
[26]Bellamy, *Looking Backward*, p. 278.
[27]Bellamy, *Equality*, p. 392. (Variety in human nature and the value of innovation are the bases on which Wells builds his utopia; this point will be discussed more fully in the chapter on Wells.)

Bellamy's reading of future history, once men were no longer crippled by an inadequate material environment, they were able to concentrate their energies on spiritual evolution. The twentieth century, accordingly, has seen the most progress in the science of the soul and its relation to the Eternal and the Infinite. Men have eaten, in Bellamy's language, the fruit of the tree of love and the mutuality that resulted has permitted them to develop an entirely new phase of civilization the motto of which is: Ye Shall Be As Gods.[28]

Among Bellamy's unpublished papers there is a description of the new epoch:

These intense emotions, whether of pain or of pleasure, these ravishments, we do not want them. . . . We look for a placid race that shall not alternate between honey and vinegar, but live on mild ambrosia ever. To love unwisely is to dread direfully. We will have no dread.[29]

But when love's object is men as spiritual and as like-minded as oneself, it amounts to little more than self-congratulaton. As a basis for progress in utopia love based on homogeneity is not convincing, and in their mild enjoyment this "placid race" does not appear capable of being agents of the progress Bellamy wishes to see in utopia.

Bellamy's utopia cannot accommodate change as novelty, if novelty is understood to mean the development of men or institutions into something different from what they are when they attain utopia. A minimum condition of novelty—the need or the will to devise something better than what exists at present—is lacking in utopia. But if the utopian environment cannot support developmental change, then change of a weaker sort may still occur as a response to accidents or factors beyond men's control. There are, however, difficulties even in imagining this lesser type of change. Utopia is, to all intents and purposes, a world state, precluding change in reaction to threats from hostile neighbors. The economy is too rationalized to allow any unanticipated side effects such as depletion of resources or overabundance of production. The natural environment presents no threat, as men have made themselves largely independent of it by machines.[30]

[28]Ibid., pp. 267–268.
[29]Bellamy's unpublished papers, quoted in Arthur Morgan, *The Philosophy of Edward Bellamy* (New York: King's Crown Press, 1945), p. 72.
[30]In a story called "The Machine Stops," E. M. Forster takes Bellamy's position to one possible conclusion. He imagines a society in which a machine *is* the environment. As the automatic self-repair mechanisms with which the machine is equipped fall into disrepair, the machine grinds to a halt. The citizens have long since forgotten how to service the machines upon which they are totally dependent. E. M. Forster, *The Eternal Moment and Other Stories* (New York: Grosset and Dunlap, Universal Library paperback, 1964).

Indeed, the only source of change that seems plausible in Bellamy's utopia is the one his citizens are busy eliminating—atavism. It may not be accidental that the standard determining atavism is the present level of development of utopian citizens, for atavism, so defined, permits "change" to take place without the need to innovate. If one looks at its origin, atavism is the final irrational threat to Bellamy's utopians. It is change whose source is "outside" the utopian system, an accident with no explanation at all. "Progress," then, might be said to consist in eliminating this last source of unwelcome change.[31]

Change as novelty or as a reaction to change initiated from outside the utopian environment is not provided for in Bellamy's ideal society. The type of change that remains possible to utopia is change in its weakest form—the elaboration and consolidation of the status quo. New goods will continue to be produced by new machines, which will, at the same time, improve the environment. In their activities the utopians appear to be busy maintaining the status quo; when atavism has been eliminated, the status quo will, presumably, maintain itself.

Politics, the method by which the arrangements of society are deliberately maintained or changed, has almost disappeared from Bellamy's utopia. The author notes that "most of the purposes for which government formerly existed no longer remain to be subserved."[32] Law became obsolete when the relations between men were simplified. Lying has gone out of fashion, as Julian West remarks, leaving very little work for judges in either civil or criminal cases. The remaining governmental functions have been merged with the economic plant. Bellamy concedes that "a government in the sense of a coordinating directory of . . . associated industries we shall always need, but that is practically all the government we have now."[33]

The past is no guarantor of the future, and despite Bellamy's claim, his utopians do not appear capable of having a history more splendid than any known to the past. Moreover, their own past, as well as the tradition of change it represents, no longer makes sense to the inhabitants of utopia. Dr.

[31]To justify eliminating atavism, Bellamy speaks of "the right of the unborn to be guaranteed an intelligent and refined parentage." Bellamy, *Looking Backward*, p. 222. This type of claim on the future is, no doubt, what Butler had in mind when he required newborn children in Erewhon to sign a deed releasing their parents from any responsibility for their birth or physical defects. (Physical defects constitute a crime in Erewhon.) Butler, *Erewhon*, pp. 174–176.
[32]Bellamy, *Looking Backward*, p. 207.
[33]Bellamy, *Equality*, p. 409.

Leete's daughter tells Julian West that she knows nothing about nineteenth-century conditions and the revolution that emerged from them.

You have no idea how hard I have been trying to post myself on the subject so as to be able to talk intelligently with you, but I fear it is of no use. . . . Since you have been telling me how the old world appeared to you in that dream, your talk has brought those days so terribly near that I can almost see them, and yet I cannot say that they seem a bit more intelligible than before.[34]

Dr. Leete's daughter is not unique. Bellamy says that after the revolution such were the joy and contentment of the populace that they would willingly have forgotten about the past. However, a historian, "moved by a certain crabbed sense of justice," decided to make a record of past events, which he called *Kenloe's Book of the Blind*.[35] The contents of the book are a recapitulation of Bellamy's two utopias, describing the miseries of capitalism and contrasting them to the superior rationality achieved in utopia.[36] The *Book of the Blind* has become irrelevant to the utopians not only because they have sight but also because they have diagnosed the few remaining cases of blindness among themselves and know that their cause is atavism. To remain interested in a disease that is fast disappearing and in any case cannot be cured is to indulge a degree of morbid curiosity of which Bellamy's utopians are quite innocent.

Atavism is all the more irrational if, as Bellamy seems at times to believe, history as well as the personality that tries to base itself in history is discontinuous. In a novel written in 1884 the protagonist says: "In their eyes the past was good or bad for itself, and an evil past could no more shadow a virtuous present than a virtuous present could retroact to brighten or redeem an ugly past."[37] And in *Doctor Heidenhoff's Process* one of the characters remarks that the ancients had a beautiful fable about the waters of Lethe. He goes on to conjecture: "Just think how blessed a thing for men it would be . . . if their memories could be cleansed and disinfected. . . . Then the most disgraced and ashamed might live good and happy lives again."[38] Bellamy forgets that Plato's souls drank the waters of Lethe only *after* they had chosen their lots for the next life.

[34] Ibid., p. 4.
[35] Ibid., p. 382.
[36] The only other historian in utopia is Julian West, who experienced, for the first time in his life, a sudden desire to work. Bellamy attributes the authorship of *Looking Backward* to him, a book addressed in all but name to the nineteenth century, whose history is still to be made.
[37] Edward Bellamy, *Miss Ludington's Sister*, quoted in Morgan, *The Philosophy*, p. 61.
[38] Edward Bellamy, *Doctor Heidenhoff's Process* (London: William Reeves, n.d.), p. 13.

Even Julian West, with direct experience of utopia's past, professes amazement that a nation of rational human beings could have ever consented to live under capitalist conditions. His astonishment is, no doubt, genuine, for it is the function of the visitor to utopia to become convinced of its superiority. But inasmuch as the visitor is merely the means of explaining utopian organization, he quickly falls victim to the utopian citizens' inability to comprehend any reality other than their own.

It is not surprising that utopians cannot understand preutopian society. In Bellamy's twenty-first-century Boston, almost all the activities described are explained in terms of economic equality, the desire for which Bellamy considered a fundamental characteristic of all men. However, because the static character of utopian reality prevents serious change from being described, it tends to make such a character trait appear absolute, even if the author had intended it to be understood as a condition for, or relative to, other traits that the utopians would develop in the future. And when an occurrence cannot be directly related to this economic justification, such as the feeling of pleasure Bellamy's utopians experience when reading a book, the unrelated description appears both inadequate and irrelevant. It accords with no known mode of activity within utopia and appears as an unexplained quirk or as a fetish held over from a prior time without any meaning. Similarly, any activity whose description is omitted in utopia (such as liberal education in all but name) must appear to the reader to be banished from utopia. Because utopia is an artificial construct that claims to be complete, it cannot admit to having overlooked some activities. The author can leave no corner of utopia uncoordinated by omission—only by deliberate design.

What seems to have occurred is that the organization of utopian activities and Bellamy's ideal of economic equality are so dovetailed that to question any given activity becomes tantamount to questioning utopia in its entirety. To ask *how* pleasure justifies the existence of artistic activity, for instance, would be to introduce into utopia another possible principle of determining reality, and to do so would require the entire reorganization of utopia. Utopian society and its ideal appear to be perfectly congruent, so that to ask why a liberal arts education is not described in Bellamy's Boston is to question the adequacy of the author's view of men's nature and the organization of society through which their natures are to find expression.

It might be argued that, were another ideal introduced into utopia, some reorganization might be required, but that the entire utopian reality would hardly be jeopardized. This would be the case if the author were able to show the method or explain the reasons for specifying his ideal in one particular set of institutions and not another. Were then the ideal to be altered or another ideal introduced, the method could be used to make changes in utopian institutions. However, the author does not and cannot show why his ideal results in just this type of organization and no other. The reason is extrinsic to utopia and therefore to any explanation that can be offered within utopia: the author's experience of his own social reality and the extent of his imaginative ingenuity in reconstructing it.

Without a necessary connection of ideal and institution, though the principle and its concrete exemplification appear adequate to each other, within utopia there can be no convincing explanation of the nature of this necessity. If the method by which the ideal is specified into institutions were available within utopia, although ideal and institution would continue to dovetail neatly, it would be possible to suggest alternative ways of specifying the ideal, and change (but not novelty) would be possible within utopia. Without the method, it is as if one were confronted with a jigsaw puzzle —the pieces do indeed fit, but one is at a loss to understand why they were shaped in this particular fashion and no other.

Were the author to explain his reasons for presenting utopian social arrangements as the best exemplification of his ideal, the reader would be dealing no longer with a finished utopia but with the creation of utopia —that is, with the author's attempt at a thought experiment in which his ideal or ideals are displayed as a systematic, coherent, and harmonious whole. Moreover, were the inhabitant of utopia in possession of the author's reasons for specifying his ideal in one particular set of institutions and not another, that ideal would become immanent in utopia. To be able to conceive of an alternative method of embodying the utopian principle is to imply that the ideal is not fully expressed, or not expressed in the only way possible, in utopian reality.

In sum, were Bellamy to give his reasons for embodying his ideal in a specific set of social arrangements, he would be introducing into utopia an awareness of the relativity of his reasoning. And if the author admits that his reasoning is relative, he in effect admits that his ideal society is a possibility rather than a necessity; there are, he would imply, various directions in which existing reality could change other than the one indicated by his utopia.

The modern utopian reality has been described as static, meaning that it is not capable of more than weak change or maintenance of the status quo. Utopia does not appear capable of future development; it lacks any sort of political activity, which is one way in which societies make their own history. In addition, an inhabitant of utopia, if he is conceivable at all, would be unable to understand the history of other nations, which, in Bellamy's utopia, is also the history of his own past.

The utopians in Bellamy's ideal state live in an eternal present in which human nature remains at one with itself, neither changing nor undergoing change.[39] In classical utopias the fixity of human nature reflected an ideal that transcended utopian society and gave it meaning. By contrast, Bellamy's ideal offers no norm for human nature. His ideal addresses itself, not to men's nature, but to the rationalization of economic relations among them. It is a social ideal, and when it is used to organize all of utopian reality, the result is to freeze utopia into one pattern. Human nature is static in Bellamy's future society because the one ideal it expresses is derived from the inadequacies of the past—a past that no longer exists to the extent that it no longer has meaning for the inhabitants of utopia.

Despite the detail with which Bellamy describes Boston in the year 2000, that society appears oversimplified. Its organization is based entirely on the ideal of economic equality, which is fully expressed in utopian institutions. It might be objected that Bellamy's reality is not as simple as it is presented here. After all, he is an absolute dictator while creating his utopia, and he could have avoided some difficulties, such as the continued existence of criminality, either by simply stating that the criminal class no longer exists or by not dealing with the question at all. But Bellamy is no more free than was the classical utopian author in creating his ideal society. The classical utopian author was limited by the transcendence of his ideal—its greater reality that he could express but not create. The modern utopian author is limited by the nature of the nonutopian society he criticizes. If he wishes his utopia to appear as an adequate substitute for existing reality, he is obliged to deal with most of the major social problems of his day. The model would lack even surface plausibility if the author attempted to abolish too many problems by fiat.

---

[39] In another, not-too-dissimilar context, Bellamy put the point succinctly: "There is no way of joining the past with the present, and there is no difference between what is a moment past and what is eternally past." Bellamy, *Doctor Heidenhoff's Process*, p. 124.

Looking Backward and
Equality as a Critique
of the Present

135

Looking Backward and Equality as a Critique of the Present

In *Looking Backward* and in *Equality* the author's presentation of utopian reality appears oversimplified. The reasons for this oversimplification are the social and pervasive character of Bellamy's ideal and the inability of utopian reality to accommodate change. I have suggested that a third characteristic of modern utopias is that they do not afford a standard by which to judge existing reality. The modern utopia is a better critique than a standard. A critique is topical criticism dependent on the conditions it criticizes, and once the conditions that are under attack change, the utopian criticism becomes irrelevant—or at best merely of historical interest. In examining how this occurs, the discussion centers no longer upon the activities that Bellamy describes *in* his utopia but upon utopia as a finished product designed to be a commentary upon the present.

In one of his many critical discussions of nineteenth-century society, Bellamy remarks that even if the capitalists had been moral saints, the economic defects of the system would have remained.[40] Capitalism is compared to husbandry: there are objective conditions that must be fulfilled before either can be expected to work. The conditions necessary to the proper working of capitalism can be summarized as follows:

... the fatal weakness of democracy [has been] that the people, who were the rulers, had individually only an indirect and sentimental interest in the state as a whole ... their real ... and direct interest being concentrated upon their personal fortunes, their private stakes, distinct from and adverse to the general stake. ... the same economic motive—which, while the capital remained in private hands, was a divisive influence ... became the most powerful of cohesive forces [under collective control]. ...[41]

The economic motive that was such a divisive influence in capitalist times is competition. Bellamy gives a number of explanations to account for its prevalence. He suggests that it resulted from the excessive individualism of a laissez-faire economy. He mentions the explanation favored by Morris: ". . . in that wolfish society the struggle for bread borrowed a peculiar desperation . . . a man might not choose, but must plunge into the foul

---

[40]Edward Bellamy, "Talks on Nationalism," *Edward Bellamy Speaks Again: Articles, Public Addresses, Letters* (Kansas City, Mo.: The Peerage Press, 1937), quoted in Bellamy, *Selected Writings*, p. 136.
[41]Bellamy, *Equality*, pp. 28–29.

fight. . . ."[42] Greed for the limited spoils of the capitalist system contributed to competition and resulted in even larger monopolies, which, in turn, widened the gap between the rich and the poor. Another factor was the egoism of the well-to-do, with their desire for the prestige and power that accompanied profits. But most frequently Bellamy blames the social organization itself and cautions the reader that it was not human depravity but the madness of the profits system which caused unbridled competition.

By making the economic system responsible for social injustices, Bellamy put himself at variance with the dominant social philosophers of his day: Spencer, Huxley, and Sumner in the United States. The prevalent view still considered man to be depraved, but it departed from the Christian view of man's destiny by substituting economic rivalry for God as the agent of final judgment. Schiffman has suggested that Bellamy discerned in these social philosophies "the appearance of his old churchly foe, the concept of man's depravity, in secular garb" and reacted with corresponding vehemence.[43]

Whatever the cause, Bellamy rejects those fatalistic explanations that attribute society's malfunctioning to the inherent depravity or inadequacy of man's nature. A competitive system that rewards men, not on the basis of their natural abilities, but for accidents of birth and inheritance is, for Bellamy, immoral, and "the end itself being immoral, the means employed could not possibly make any difference."[44]

In contrast to the ferocious competitive system of the nineteenth century, Bellamy's utopian society is organized to ensure solidarity through economic equality. As has been seen, the difficulty with Bellamy's ideal is that, while it can be used to construct a new form of economic organization, the industrial army, it cannot by itself provide new motivations for economic activity. Morris noted this problem and explained it by suggesting that Bellamy had introduced into his utopia a preutopian motive: fear of starvation. While agreeing with Morris that the motive for utopian activity is very similar to the capitalist motive, this study differs as to what the motive is.

Morris's motive, fear of starvation, wrongly suggests that the author made no attempt to provide any incentives for men to work that would be acceptable by utopian standards. Bellamy does try to provide such incentives, and if the attempt is unsuccessful, it is nonetheless instructive. A

[42]Bellamy, *Looking Backward*, p. 277.
[43]Schiffman, *American Quarterly*, VI, 204.
[44]Bellamy, *Equality*, p. 108.

Looking Backward and   137
Equality as a Critique
of the Present

series of honors, designed to encourage men to achieve their best in the
future Boston, are an important part of the utopian advance from the
nineteenth century. As has been seen, promotion from one rank to another
in the industrial army is designated a public honor and rewarded by an iron,
silver, or gilt badge. Political honors likewise depend on having risen
through the industrial ranks, and as elected officials cannot hope to profit
from their position, their only motive for seeking office is public esteem.
The artist, also, depends on public approval:

An author of much acceptance succeeds in supporting himself by his pen
during the entire period of service [in the industrial army], and the degree of
any writer's literary ability, as determined by the popular voice, is thus the
measure of the opportunity given him to devote his time to literature.[45]

The highest honor in the nation, surpassing even the gilt badge previously
mentioned, is a red badge awarded for "devotion to duty"—mostly to authors, artists, engineers, physicians, and inventors.[46]

    Bellamy's incentives are, on the whole, not very convincing. A man
motivated solely by a red badge is either playing games or not motivated at
all. The badges must be seen merely as a sign of what men desire most in
Bellamy's utopia: public recognition. And as the author does not attempt to
explain *why* men desire public honor, the desire itself must be taken as a
primary irreducible motive for utopian activity.

    The difficulty is that as Bellamy describes public recognition, it is
indistinguishable from emulation, which the author considers to be the
motive of inferior natures and a residue from capitalist times.

Do not imagine, either, because emulation is given free play as an incentive under our system, that we deem it a motive likely to appeal to the nobler
sort of men, or worthy of them. Such as these find their motives within not
without, and measure their duty by their own endowments, not by those
of others. . . . To such natures emulation appears philosophically absurd
by its substitution of envy for admiration, and exultation for regret, in
one's attitude toward the successes and the failures of others.[47]

If the nobler natures in Bellamy's utopia measure their duties by their endowments, public recognition is to that extent superfluous. If, as Bellamy
suggests in the artist's case, public recognition *is* the measure of endowment, the motive for such recognition can hardly be said to be internal.

[45]Bellamy, *Looking Backward*, p. 163.
[46]Ibid., p. 167.
[47]Ibid., pp. 130–131.

Public recognition appears to be indistinguishable from emulation in Bellamy's utopia. Emulation, in turn, seems to be a polite name for competition, the motive of the capitalist era. The difference between emulation and competition is that badges are substituted for monetary rewards. But in a utopia of abundance, with adequate consumer goods for all, the absence of the profit motive is of doubtful significance.

If equality is the condition of men in utopia, emulation appears to be their motive. When utopia is seen in relation to its capitalist past, Morris's criticsm appears valid; Bellamy has surreptitiously smuggled into utopia a most unutopian incentive. When Bellamy's utopia is considered by itself, in isolation from its preutopian past, the "cause" of emulation (or of the desire for public recognition) is, for want of any other sufficient explanation, the already established social organization of utopia.

One reason for calling Bellamy's utopia a critique of nineteenth-century American society rather than a standard by which to judge it is that his utopia is so much more directly related to the conditions it criticizes. Emulation is different only in degree, not in kind, from competition. The difference is that emulation takes place in a social system that does not permit monetary rewards or allow any of its citizens to starve. And to this extent utopia does succeed in being a much more humane society, reflecting its author's concern with the poverty and suffering he saw in his own environment.

But to the extent that Bellamy's ideal society eliminates only the most unpleasant effects of the competitive activity it criticizes, it offers merely a contrast to competitive society. Considered in isolation from its past, utopia makes very little sense. Because its significance lies in the contrast between itself and existing society, utopia remains dependent on the reality it criticizes. Bellamy's utopia is a critique, not a standard, because it makes its criticism of contemporary society by contrast rather than relying on a coherent vision of what human nature needs for its satisfaction.

It is characteristic of modern utopias—and Bellamy's is no exception—that almost as much time is spent delineating the wrongs of the past as is spent describing their solution in utopia. One reason is, of course, that while utopia is not attractive in itself to the modern reader who thinks in terms of change and development, it is attractive as a critique of—or in contrast to—the present. The modern utopia's detailed criticism of the present thus becomes a means of making men dissatisfied with their society and receptive to the utopian future.

Looking Backward and
Equality as a Critique
of the Present

139

Julian West frequently expresses amazement that "a nation of rational beings consented to remain economic serfs . . . after coming into absolute power to change at pleasure all social institutions which inconvenienced them."[48] His amazement is well founded, because the power to change social institutions is not really explained, despite Bellamy's attempts, by any gradual process of economic evolution or necessary development of social institutions. A theory of necessary evolution provides only historical continuity; it cannot by itself explain such novelty as is claimed for utopia. Evolution can account for novelty only in terms of another factor—such as an increased diffusion of intelligence. And unlike a Condorcet, Bellamy does not give substance to his claims for the innovative powers of intelligence by exploring which characteristics of mind might be responsible for novelty and which would maintain continuity with the past.

Evolution, then, does not really explain innovation, and to the extent it were to do so, a utopia designed to encourage change would be superfluous. The power to change social institutions derives from the nonutopian citizen's awareness of utopian possibilities in the future. Utopia seen from outside acts, so to speak, as the catalyst to bring about its own existence.

It has been suggested that the paradox of modern utopias results from the fact that their raison d'être is extrinsic to utopia and is found in preutopian problems that require change. If, as Bellamy thinks, change *is* the expression of man's rationality, utopia can be seen as immanent in the present.

So much for the main, general, and necessary cause and explanation of the great Revolution—namely, the progressive diffusion of intelligence among the masses from the sixteenth to the end of the nineteenth centuries. Given this force of operation, and the revolution of the economic basis of society must sooner or later have been its outcome everywhere: . . . [the timing and manner depending on] the differing conditions of different countries. . . .[49]

Emulation, the motive of utopian activity, is just as necessary to utopian society as competition is to capitalist society. In either case the responsibility for encouraging emulative and competitive activity can be attributed (as Bellamy is willing to do only for competition) to the respective social systems. The crucial difference between utopia and its past is that change, the antidote to competition, is always immanent to preutopian society; whereas

[48]Bellamy, *Equality*, p. 16.
[49]Ibid., p. 307.

once utopia is achieved, change is no longer possible as an antidote to emulation.

    Looking Backward and *Equality* offer a critique of the present rather than a standard by which to judge it. The competitive motive remains in utopia; it is simply expressed in different social arrangements. Utopian society has a different structure from that of the real world. But a different social structure may not be a sufficient motive for desiring utopia to become reality. By refusing to accept the author's version of the future, the reader can, if he wishes, dismiss his critique of the present.

Looking Backward and Equality as a Thought Experiment
In the preface to *Looking Backward* Bellamy tells the reader that his utopia is "a social order at once so simple and logical that it seems but the triumph of common sense. . . ."[50] The triumph of common sense has indeed simplified utopia, but that does not necessarily make utopia more attractive for the reader. From the author's point of view, however, utopia is attractive *because* it is both simple and logical; it has permitted him to imagine a society fully determined by economic equality.

    I have suggested that in the process of constructing a utopia the author tests his ideal by specifying it as concretely as possible, giving to it some of the weight and complexity of the present. While they are being constructed, modern utopias serve the same function as their classical predecessors: the attempt to investigate ideals by means of a thought experiment.

    For the classical utopian author, articulation was a means of knowing ideals or values *more* adequately than he had known them previously. The ideal was already known beforehand in the sense that man's nature required it; without implicitly being guided by it a man would, like Plato's tyrant, be goaded to experience a succession of novel and never satisfying pleasures. But the intellectual conditions that supported such assumptions changed. Under the influence of Cartesian thought, reason was separated from its basis in innate ideas, and ideals were no longer accorded an unquestioned objective status. Reason assumed a more autonomous role, as in Hegel, where it helps determine and not just discover truth. Cassirer describes very well this change in men's attitude toward reason:

The whole eighteenth century understands reason in this sense; not as a found body of knowledge, principles, and truths, but as a kind of energy, a

---

[50]Bellamy, *Looking Backward*, p. xix.

force which is fully comprehensible only in its agency and effects. What reason is, and what it can do, can never be known by its results but only by its function. And its most important function consists in its power to bind and to dissolve. It dissolves everything merely factual, all simple data of experience, and everything believed on the evidence of revelation, tradition and authority; and it does not rest content until it has analyzed all these things into their simplest component parts and into their last elements of belief and opinion.[51]

The modern utopian author is heir to the Enlightment, and reason is for him a concept of agency, not of being. And the modern utopian ideal is derived from a very characteristic activity of modern reason: a critical examination of the present. The ideal results from an appraisal of inadequacies in the present and an attempt to find a remedy for those inadequacies. As Bellamy constructs his utopia, two complementary processes are at work. A criticism of existing society is being made: competitive capitalism is inefficient and immoral; and reason is attempting to provide an alternative: economic equality.

From a nonutopian point of view an ideal such as economic equality may appear subjective and contingent, as part and parcel of the very reality it attempts to criticize. But in the process of constructing a utopia, the ideal derived from criticizing the nature and purpose of preutopian society *becomes* the conditions under which activity in utopia is carried out. The ideal becomes increasingly transparent to reason by being specified and then ordered in a utopian structure. Likewise, by producing this new and detailed order of social arrangements by an act of reasoning, the author succeeds in understanding some of the ramifications and implications of his ideal. If, as in Bellamy's case, there is only one ideal, it serves to organize all aspects of utopian reality.

By investigating the implications of an ideal in thought, reason creates a society ordered according to its own standards of consistency and harmony. The modern like the classical utopian author attempts to test the adequacy of his ideal by making it, in its full specificity, as coherent as possible. Because of this common ordering activity of reason, it is possible to speak of harmony as the goal of classical as well as modern utopias. It is in this rather special sense that utopia is timeless, fulfilling its character of *eu-topos*.

Another similarity between classical and modern utopias is found in the relation of the author to the society he has created. Plato's philosopher-

---

[51]Ernst Cassirer, *The Philosophy of the Enlightenment,* trans. Fritz Koelin and James Pettegrove (Boston: Beacon Press, Beacon paperback, 1955), p. 13.

king legislates for a city-state to which he has only secondary ties. He is separated from the city-state by the superior nature and greater comphrehensiveness of his knowledge, by his position as creator and sustainer of that society. The modern utopian author is similarly separated from his utopia. It is his ability to judge society that makes his knowledge superior to that of the citizens of utopia. His knowledge is more comprehensive because it includes the awareness of a past and future that are different from the present. The modern author's position is, however, only partially parallel to the classical utopian legislator. His desire to see his creation in existence makes the modern author presumably only too aware, as he creates his utopia, of his position outside it.

Both classical and modern utopian authors are dictators; they have total power to decide how to specify their ideals in utopian institutions. The arbitrary character of such decisions was not a problem in classical utopias, to the extent those societies were not intended to come into existence. But with the modern utopias' claim to be a viable reality the arbitrary character of the decision becomes a very serious problem. Utopia may be attractive for its author, whose judgments regarding the nature and purpose of social activity in the real world have become the limits or conditions of activity within utopia. But for the reader who imagines himself in utopia, that reality does not appear viable. Once in utopia he would be unable to understand his own past or to create his own future; he would, consequently, find himself in no position to make judgments about the nature and purpose of social activity within utopia. The future citizen of utopia may envy the author-legislator of utopia, who is acquainted with a preutopian reality in which economic equality was only immanent and not fully expressed. An ideal that is only immanent to reality does, after all, allow criticism of that reality and leaves open the question of change.

For a modern utopia, however, a thought experiment is at best a by-product of its real purpose. The author's primary purpose is to make utopia as real as possible for his reader, a necessity if change is to occur. In a letter to Howells, Bellamy reflects on the problem of presenting a convincing reality:

. . . I think that every writer of fiction, when his fancy seduces him too far from this real life which alone he really knows, has such a cause of weakness and uncertainty as Antaeus might have felt when Hercules lifted him into the air, a weakness to be cured with the novelist as with the giant only by a return to earth. If this be true of the novelist, it is yet more true of the romancer, for it is the undertaking of the latter to give an air of reality even to the unreal. Though he build into the air, he must see to it that he does not seem to build upon the air, for the more airy the pinnacle the more necessary the solidity of the foundation. . . .[52]

The problem is not at all unique to Bellamy; Wells and Howells indicate their awareness of the same difficulty. One explanation for Antaeus' need to touch ground frequently is the nature of modern utopian values. In contrast to the values of classical utopian writers which were held in common, modern authors need to find a common ground that will help make their values acceptable to the publics they address. If the modern ideal is not to be entirely private and subjective, the author needs to build a bridge to the reader. The author and his reader do share one common ground: their social environment. The bridge that the author attempts to build is a shared critical awareness of what is wrong with that social environment. Bellamy indicates that he feels the part of the bridge that rests on the commonly shared past is solid enough. But he is uneasy about the strength of its span and the solidity of the abutment that rests in the future.

Were Bellamy willing to consider his utopia a "mental exercise on . . . the possibilities lateral to reality," as a method of investigating the implications of ideals without intending them to assume reality, he might avoid the risk that his utopia is *only* a critique, a bridge that ends in midair.[53] He could likewise avoid the direct contrast of his ideal with the complexity of the present, which leads to an uneasiness with the former's insubstantiality. If Bellamy were content to justify his utopia by what he learns about his ideal in the process of investigating it, he would be able to acknowledge that his utopians are puppets, or heuristic fictions, not meant to acquire reality, but valuable nonetheless.

The modern utopian critique of existing social arrangements is weakened by offering utopia as a serious alternative to what is criticized. Instead of a standard of judgment the reader is left with a contrast: two pictures juxtaposed one upon the other, with the explanation of why the artist prefers

[52]Bellamy, Letter to William Dean Howells (August 7, 1884), quoted in Bellamy, *Selected Writings*, pp. 137–138. For the distinction between the novelist and the romancer (realism and romance), see William Dean Howells, *European and American Masters*, ed. Clara Marburg Kirk and Rudolf Kirk (New York: New York University Press, 1963), p. 165.
[53]Raymond Ruyer, *L'Utopie et les utopies* (Paris: Presses universitaires de France, 1950), p. 9 (my translation).

the second picture to be found, not in the picture itself, but in the process of painting the picture. For in painting the picture the author *has* made the ideal more objective and universal—for himself.

Bellamy's ideal state is not nearly so convincing to a reader deriving his knowledge from preutopian reality, and for the citizen who lives in utopia but no longer understands its raison d'être its meaning is difficult to imagine. The thought experiment is a basis upon which to criticize existing reality only for the author-legislator and, to a lesser extent, for the reader, depending upon the degree to which he already shares the author's values. If the modern utopian author were willing to abandon the idea of his utopia's coming into existence, his critique would become much stronger. While still differing from a standard of judgment, which contains principles different in kind from those found in existing reality, the critique could point to social arrangements in need of change, leaving somewhat more open the question of the nature of the change required and allowing the reader to consider the utopian solution as a possible, but not a necessary, alternative.

It is interesting to speculate about another alternative that would serve to extricate the modern utopia from the dilemma deriving from its attempt both to criticize and to change reality at the same time. It is possible, for example, for Bellamy to argue that he never intended his utopia to be put into practice. The author could maintain that his utopia is only heuristic: it leads the reader to an awareness that contemporary social arrangements are inadequate, and from that awareness to an appraisal of the viability of the new society presented to him. As the utopian single-factor reality would, if this analysis is convincing, not appear viable, the reader would be stimulated to create a utopia of his own more congenial to his tastes.

By this activity of creation, the reader would place himself in the position from which a modern utopia *can* become an effective critique of existing reality: the position of the author who creates utopia. Although the new utopia the reader might create would most probably continue to be based on a single ideal, a chain reaction could occur, compelling each new reader in turn to go through the same steps. Instead of the complexity of the classical utopian standard of judgment, which offers the reader an independent standpoint from which to criticize existing reality without implying the necessity of changing that reality, one would find that typically modern phenomenon: a subjective judgment, held on personal grounds, but intensely experienced through the effort of creation.

H. G. Wells's
A Modern Utopia

8

In a discussion of H. G. Wells's early writings, Anthony West suggests that "he ultimately did not believe in the ability of the human animal to live up to its ideals."[1] Wells's first image of what the future holds for man, *The Time Machine* (1895), is indeed somber.[2] After a grim description of men degenerated into animals and degraded enough to feed on their own kind, his vision of an even more remote future, when the human species has become extinct and the world is barely warmed by a dying sun, seems more fitting than tragic. Wells's forebodings took another no less pessimistic form in *When the Sleeper Wakes* (1899), which anticipates the types of dictatorships described in *Brave New World* and in *1984*.[3]

By 1901, when *Anticipations* was published, Wells had substituted an "apparent optimism" for his previous "explicit pessimism." According to West, Wells was never at ease with his optimistic appraisal of men's ability to change for the better, and reverted in his later work to the explicit pessimism that characterized his earliest writing.[4] However, when Wells wrote *A Modern Utopia* in 1905, he was still a member of the Fabian Society, confident that men could lead better lives if they could only escape from the deadening restraints of outmoded religious beliefs, moral conventions, and social shibboleths.[5] Whatever uncertainty Wells may have felt about men's capacity to make themselves a better future is not given voice in *A Modern Utopia*. The initial congruence he establishes between earth and utopia appears to be a promising sign. Utopia is situated on a planet exactly like earth, with identical mountains and valleys warmed by a utopian sun. When the author first transports himself, in his imagination, to utopia, he stresses that the resemblance to earth is not merely physical:

From now onward, of course, the fates of these two planets will diverge, men will die here whom wisdom will save there . . . children will be born to them

[1] Anthony West, "H. G. Wells," *Encounter*, VIII (February 1957), 56.
[2] H. G. Wells, *The Time Machine: An Invention* (New York: Random House, 1931).
[3] H. G. Wells, *When the Sleeper Wakes* (London: Harper & Brothers, 1899). West's interpretation of *When the Sleeper Wakes* as a forerunner of Huxley and Orwell diverges from the more widespread view that the novel expresses Wells's naïve and uncritical optimism. See West, *Encounter*, VIII, 55. For the optimistic interpretation, see Bernard Bergonzi, *The Early H. G. Wells: A Study of the Scientific Romances* (Manchester: Manchester University Press, 1961), pp. 140–156.
[4] West, *Encounter*, VIII, 55, 57–58. West finds clear evidence of the retreat from optimism by 1923 when *Men Like Gods* was published. For a similar interpretation, see Antonina Vallentin, *H. G. Wells: Prophet of Our Day* (New York: The John Day Company, 1950), p. 236.
[5] H. G. Wells, *A Modern Utopia* (London: Thomas Nelson and Sons, Ltd., 1905), p. 19. See also Georges Connes, *Étude sur La Pensée de Wells* (n. p.: Librairie Hachette, 1926), pp. 450 ff.; Ingvald Raknem, *H. G. Wells and His Critics* (Oslo: Universitetsforlaget, 1962), pp. 272 ff.

and not to us . . . but this, this moment of reading, is the starting moment, and for the first and last occasion the populations of our planets are abreast.[6]

While Wells is optimistic in *A Modern Utopia*, his optimism is not of a simpleminded science fiction variety; it is tempered by his desire to be plausible. And because he is not convinced that utopia will inevitably come to be, he makes the ideal society seem simple and attainable, partly as a way of goading men to work for its achievement. To imagine a better society is, for Wells, a way of making concrete the vague and ill-defined strivings of the present and, at the same time, a method of channeling these longings in the direction of utopia.

The Ideal of A Modern Utopia

H. G. Wells wanted *A Modern Utopia* to be different in kind from all preceding utopias. Utopias written before Darwin were, he thought, perfect, static states in which change or development was excluded and a balance of happiness won forever. A contemporary utopia, to avoid the tedium of its predecessors, must be dynamic, a hopeful stage rather than a permanent state in mankind's development. Utopia should be visualized as one rung in a long, unending ascent up the ladder of progress. It must be dynamic or, as Wells calls it, kinetic, because of the nature of the ideal embodied in it. The ideal is to be "a flexible common compromise, in which a perpetually novel succession of individualities may converge most effectually upon a comprehensive onward development."[7]

In the last chapter of *A Modern Utopia*, called "Scepticism of the Instrument," Wells mentions his early studies in biology as the source of his conviction that human mental and material equipment is "profoundly provisional."[8] Rejecting Platonic realism for "common sense" nominalism, Wells considers general ideas and classification devices to be the instruments that the mind uses to comprehend and bring order to the otherwise unmanageable uniqueness of reality. It is, Wells thinks, this insistence on individuality and uniqueness which separates modern from classical utopias. In older utopias, he argues, freedom was different from and less important than virtue and happiness, but in the modern utopia it has be-

---

[6]Wells, *A Modern Utopia*, p. 34.

[7]Ibid., p. 17.

[8]Ibid., p. 361. "Scepticism of the Instrument" is an abbreviated version of a paper that Wells gave to the Oxford Philosophical Society in 1903, and that was subsequently printed in *Mind*, XIII (July 1905). For a study of Wells's philosophical affinities to William James and Henri Bergson, see Connes, *Étude sur La Pensée*, pp. 31–56.

come paramount, for the maximum amount of freedom commensurable
with the liberty of others is the prerequisite for a free play of individualities.

The State is to be progressive, it is no longer to be static, and this alters the
general condition of the Utopian problem profoundly; we have to provide
not only for food and clothing . . . but for initiative. The factor that leads the
World State on from one phase of development to the next is the interplay of
individualities; to speak teleologically the world exists for the sake of and
through initiative, and individuality is the method of initiative.[9]

Wells's utopia is deliberately designed to allow maximum expression of individuality. While it may perhaps seem odd to describe the maximum expression of individuality as a social ideal, it is through social arrangements that
Wells encourages and sustains individuality in his utopia.

In criticizing his own society, Wells deplores men's natural disposition to insist on uniformity, a disposition that has increased in measure with
the disruptive effects of scientific innovation upon older and more stable
modes of life. Tolerance and the courteous admission of difference are
necessary if men are to use their present opportunities for innovation successfully, and, he observes, the disposition of the most original and enterprising minds is always toward innovation. In the capacity to innovate, a character
trait of the fortunate minority, lies mankind's hope for a better future. When
he is abruptly plunged back from utopia into the noise, dirt, and jarring misery of nineteenth-century London with its millions of indifferent inhabitants,
Wells notices the face of a young woman student, lighted by the glow of a
setting sun, and with "eyes that dream, surely no sensuous nor personal
dream."[10] She and others like her are the innovators and the material out of
which utopia will be built.

Wells's description of the *samurai,* the order that rules in utopia and
in which most of the innovative types are to be found, makes clear how the
energy of creative persons was wasted in his own time.[11] Under the anarchic
organization of preutopian governments, disinterested feeling was stunted
by self-seeking egoism and narrow-mindedness, vices endemic to such
haphazard forms of social organization. When a group of "disillusioned and
illuminated men" recognized that these conditions were chaotic and became

[9]Wells, *A Modern Utopia,* pp. 92–93.
[10]Ibid., p. 347.
[11]Wells chose the name *samurai* in order to link his elite with the Bushido code, which he
associated with single-minded devotion to a cause. H. G. Wells, *First and Last Things* (2d ed.
rev.; London: Cassell and Company, Ltd., 1917), p. 132.

aware of their cost, they banded together and worked creatively and effectively for a better order.[12] In an earlier sketch of the same development, Wells expected technological advance to create a class of engineers, held together by their scientific education and common understanding of the machines with which they work. They were to form the nucleus around which other constructive minds (doctors, teachers, writers) would group themselves. As the remaining classes in society disintegrate into aimless apathy, power would fall to this elite, who would use it to work for a world state.[13]

By 1905 Wells was much less certain that such an elite would arise of its own accord. But he remained certain that the impetus for their creative activity would be divine discontent, itself a result of the spectacle of wasted possibilities and unnecessary sufferings, consequences of wars and political squabbling, which characterized the conduct of affairs in the nineteenth century.

Within Wells's utopia such criminal waste of talent no longer exists. Its elimination was the purpose for which the *samurai* order was formed, and in the utopia they build men learn from their surroundings and are educated in their youth to appreciate human differences and uniqueness. The utopian governmental unit is the world state, which Wells calls the logical development of locating values in the individual rather than in the race or nation.[14] Within utopia all ways of classifying or pigeonholing men have become provisional; experimentation and innovation are the order of the day. Once barriers are down and impediments are removed, Wells seems to think that continual innovation and development will occur of themselves: "To have free play for one's individuality is, in the modern view, the subjective triumph of existence, as survival in creative work and offspring is its objective triumph."[15]

To the extent that Wells does not explain why the free play of individuality in utopia is to be valued, he leaves the impression that it is, like

[12]Wells, *A Modern Utopia*, pp. 253–255.
[13]H. G. Wells, *Anticipations* (London: Chapman and Hall, 1901), pp. 160 ff. (Wells's elite of engineers and mechanics is, in some respects, similar to Veblen's technological innovators. *The Theory of the Leisure Class* was published in 1899, but there is no indication that Wells knew the book.)
[14]Wells, *A Modern Utopia*, p. 335. Wells's other explanation for the necessity of a world state is that any state powerful enough to remain isolated in the modern world would be powerful enough to rule the world. With such power, tolerance of inferior societies is tantamount to assuming responsibility for such inferiority. Ibid., p. 22.
[15]Ibid., p. 41.

food or sleep, simply a necessity of man's nature, or at least of some men's natures.[16] One lives in a community, Wells suggests, for the sake of meeting other individualities and bettering the interplay between individualities. "The fertilising conflict of individualities is the ultimate meaning of the personal life. . . ."[17]

Individuality, then, is to be valued for itself or for what Wells calls its objective triumph, the future of the species. The human species at any given time is an accumulation of all the successful experiments—material, moral, and intellectual—of its progenitors. Reversing the Hegelian formulation, Wells does not believe that success is the indicator of value but feels that only things that are valuable are successful, at least within utopia. The individual's contribution, if it is valuable, becomes part of the experience of the race. If not, the individual's contribution dies with his memory; his failures leave no mark on posterity. To illustrate, Wells explains that the economic organization of utopia is the happy issue of what was worthwhile in previous economic experiments. The example is, however, somewhat misleading because it is taken from preutopian times when men wanted to achieve utopia. Knowing roughly what they wanted, they had a criterion for success and failure by which to recognize their mistakes. Within utopia Wells does not offer any comparable criterion. If failures really leave no trace and successes are preserved for posterity, the mechanism by which this miracle occurs is never explained.

Wells had great difficulty explaining why innovation and creativity are to be valued in utopia. To call inventiveness a natural human trait does not confer value on it, nor does it explain why Wells constructed a utopia to accommodate innovation rather than food consumption, sexual activity, or some other natural human function. At times he suggests that the future of the human race requires creativity, but he does not insist on this answer, and rightly so, because it poses the same question at one remove: What is the significance of innovation and individuality for future generations?

From another perspective, to value individuality for the future of the species is not far removed from valuing it for its own sake, as can be seen in Susanne Langer's handling of the same issue. She argues that because men are denied an indefinite life-span, they want to experience as much life as possible concentrated in a short period. "If our individuation must be brief,

[16]Wells is inconsistent as to whether individuality is a natural trait, a desirable trait, or both. For a discussion of individuality as Wells's private ideal, see the last section of this chapter.
[17]Wells, *A Modern Utopia*, p. 21.

we want to make it complete. . . ."[18] Wells's attempt to assure that what is valuable will be preserved for posterity is one way of compensating for a brief life-span; the catch is that a sure way to prevent future generations from playing tricks on their forebears is to make them merely replicas of their forebears, stretched out indefinitely in time.

Neither calling creativity a natural human trait nor invoking posterity provides a very good answer to the question of why creativity is valuable. Like the emulation of Bellamy's ideal state, which appeared to be tantamount to competition in tidier surroundings, Wells's individualism seems to be significant primarily when compared with the intolerance and egoism it has replaced.

Wells has very little to say about why men are motivated to develop their individuality in utopia. He does prescribe a penalty for not being creative; it is lack of permission by the state to reproduce. Uncreative persons are called "Dull," according to a fourfold classification that Wells uses to categorize his utopians. Their dullness is measured by their earning only the minimum wage offered by the state for make-work, which is provided to prevent anyone from falling below a decent standard of living and health. Position on the wage scale thus becomes an index of creativity, those at the bottom having so little imagination and innovative ability that they are content to be supplied with the means for a pleasant subsistence. While this broad classification may be used to indicate who does not qualify for such aids to creativity as laboratory equipment and increased leisure, it is too crude to be used for more than an initial elimination. At any rate, Wells does not include his classificatory scheme among incentives for creativity, leaving unresolved the motive for creativity in utopia.

To the extent that the reader is not told why people want or need to be creative in utopia, he explains it either as a brute necessity of man's nature or as the result of the utopian social organization. When the two dovetail so well, as they do in a utopia that has eliminated all irrational impediments to the development of personality, it becomes futile to ask whether man's nature or the social organization is the more basic. Creative activity can equally well be described as the result of an already existing social system designed to encourage it or as the use of a perfectly adapted social system to satisfy a prior demand of human nature for self-expression. In both cases the results are the same, and neither explains why Wells finds

[18]Susanne K. Langer, *Philosophical Sketches* (New York: The New American Library, 1964), p. 101.

creative activity to be valuable. When there is no motive that can be distinguished apart from the activity, and when the results of the activity are said to be significant only for an ill-defined future, the activity can be seen as occurring either for its own sake or for the sake of the social organization that makes that activity possible.

Wells's difficulty in justifying the value he has chosen for utopia is brought into focus in his description of the *samurai*. The *samurai* are an organization made up of men from the two highest of Wells's classes of utopians: the poietic [*sic*] and the kinetic. Poietic men are creative, with imaginations that range beyond the known and accepted. They are likely to be temperamental and erratic, and are contrasted to the more stable kinetic class. The latter are men who, having a more restricted imagination, are comfortable among the known, experienced, and accepted circumstances of life. Kinetic people are ideal administrators of the innovations brought forth by the poietic class, but left to themselves they would not contribute to the growth of the state.

When one looks for a description of creative poietic activity, however, it is disappointing. This voluntary nobility, as Wells calls the *samurai*, is typically engaged in administrative work; its members head colleges, direct the employment of labor, contribute personnel to the medical and legal professions, and legislate. The activity of Wells's double in utopia is equally disappointing. (The author has established the convention that for each person on earth there is a double in utopia.) He is a poietic type, engrossed in devising a better system for dealing with the criminal class than the current one of isolating them upon remote islands. The utopian penal system is a good example of the limitations of both *samurai* activity and of Wells's utopia itself. The author paints a very amusing picture of the bonhomie on the island of drunkards and of the institutionalized swindling on the island of cheats. He does not say how an island of killers or sadists would be organized, although he has included such men among the problems with which a modern utopia must deal.

Wells is adamant that creativity is the preserve of individuals, and not of the state. Because the state represents the average, or the species as a whole, he is wary of any innovation it might undertake. Its end, insofar as Wells gives it one, is to help ensure the continued creative innovation of the species. He pictures the state as establishing limiting conditions or preventing certain occurrences so that individuality can be given more room for development. The limiting conditions are procedural, although they do indicate, by what they exclude, the criteria for creativity. The state, representing the average, cannot, for example, selectively mate humans with a view to innovative offspring. It can, however, prevent certain undesirable types (the Dull and the Base) from having offspring.

Wells's description of the state does not hold up very well under scrutiny. In order to know what is undesirable, one must have some notion, however vague and perfunctory, of what is desirable. The conditions that the state would impose on procreation contain their own implicit goal, the elimination of the noncreative, so that over a period of time utopia would be made up entirely of kinetic and poietic types.[19] Wells's notion of limit would be more plausible were he able to show different and divergent forms of creativity occurring within the space created by such limits. He mentions the arts, philosophy, invention, and discovery but never suggests what characterizes philosophy or discovery as creative enterprises. Because Wells never describes the creative characteristics of these disciplines, it is just as plausible to think of them maintaining the reality established by the limiting conditions as to view them as challenging those limiting conditions or innovating within them.

The minimum content that can be given to Wells's ideal of creativity is a social content; the degree to which innovation can shape or influence the future of the species is the criterion of its success. Although only what is "valuable" will be successful, Wells offers no independent criterion of value, and when he makes posterity the judge of what is valuable in the present, the effort to find a criterion collapses entirely.

Wells's ideal is pervasive as well as social. Every aspect of utopian reality is measured and justified in terms of its contribution to the innovative faculty. Two examples will serve to illustrate the pervasiveness of Wells's ideal: the *samurai* order, which Wells claims has access to some form of transcendence, and the tolerance accorded to the noncreative. In both cases the social nature of the ideal—the fact that no adequate explanation other than existing social arrangements can be found for creative activity —imprints its character on activities that are not necessarily social.

The *samurai* order, designed to encompass the most talented and imaginative men, is easily the most important institution of Wells's utopia. The requirements for entering this elite include passing a college examina-

---

[19]In a later utopia, Wells is more explicit. He imagines a race of people who have used eugenics to eliminate all the character types they consider undesirable. H. G. Wells, *Men Like Gods* (New York: The Macmillan Company, 1923).

tion, control over the emotions, observance of a mild asceticism (no alcohol, tobacco, or indiscriminate sexual indulgence), and the ability to cooperate. Pride is also encouraged as another means of self-control. Once admitted to the order, its members contribute to society by pursuing their own bent—administrative or innovative as the case may be. Once a year the *samurai* interrupt their work to take a journey by themselves of a week's duration. Isolated from the company of men, they are alone with "Nature, necessity, and their own thoughts." The hoped-for effect on the wanderer is to make him see the busy little world dwarfed by "space and eternity, and what one means by God."[20]

Wells says that the *samurai* believe in a transcendental God whose attributes cannot be expressed in a formula because He differs according to every man's individuality. But how Wells's God transcends either the utopian or the preutopian world is not clear. The author rejects terms such as "absolute" (a negative term having no meaning but giving the illusion of positive reality), and this rejection makes God's transcendence somewhat difficult to imagine. What Wells seems to mean by transcendence is something that cannot be measured, that stretches out in time or space beyond the reaches of men's imaginations, and that dwarfs both man and his creations.

The same feeling comes upon Wells as he begins *A Modern Utopia* and imagines the Spirit of Creation (the Infinite) smiling ironically at his attempt to accelerate evolution. This sense of being dwarfed by the unimaginable span of future time is one that Wells experiences frequently; it is most poignantly conveyed in *The Time Machine* when the voyager travels far enough into the future to witness the death of the earth. During one of his annual journeys Wells's double in *A Modern Utopia*, finding himself in the desert surrounded by the vastness of space upon which man has left no mark, gives vent to his sense of smallness and muses on the possibility that God's purposes do not include man. But as his journey continues, he overcomes such doubts and, as ambassador from mankind, tells "the rascal stars how they should not escape us in the end."[21] A sense of insignificance, when Wells does not renege on it, might in some cases be a preparation for self-transcendence, but by itself it can hardly qualify as transcendence. The God of *A Modern Utopia* finally seems to amount to the possibility that the future may not forever include man.

[20]Wells, *A Modern Utopia*, pp. 292, 294.
[21]Ibid., p. 296. Cf. pp. 294–296.

Were Wells's God really a symbol for some form of transcendence, the social and pervasive nature of the utopian ideal would be held in check. Creativity such as the *samurai* exhibit would not appear to be entirely either a characteristic of their nature or a response to institutions designed to encourage creativity. A certain tension, lacking in Wells's notion of creativity because there is no standard by which to measure it, might have been supplied by the existence of a value or ideal either different from the ideal exemplified in utopian institutions or inadequately realized in those institutions.

Wells is nonetheless anxious to assure the reader that utopia has not lost the tension and conflict that characterize the real world. His utopia will be peopled not only with *samurai* but with ordinary cantankerous human beings without particular talents and with their full measure of egocentricity. Soon after his arrival in utopia, Wells encounters an individual of this type, a back-to-nature orator. The orator, who may be intended as a caricature of Rousseau, makes his living copying music (perforating records, in this case). The man is called an ass and a *poseur,* but Wells claims he has a place in utopia designed to include dissent and idiosyncrasy. "Irrelevance is not irrelevant to such a scheme, and our blond-haired friend is exactly just where he ought to be here."[22] The difficulty is that irrelevance is just that; the orator's dissatisfaction with utopia has no other basis than his own vanity, and Wells attributes no other value to it. The orator's criticism cannot be taken seriously when it is only idiosyncratic and at best reminiscent of the self-satisfied complacency and narrow egotism that Wells ascribes to preutopian society. The difference is that in utopia the orator's eccentricity is harmless and, like the Dull, to be tolerated for a time.

To illustrate even more vividly utopia's catholicity, Wells has his double accompanied in his explorations by a love-sick botanist who is so absorbed in a personal romance from the past that he is unable to appreciate the rightness and beauty of what he sees of utopia. When he becomes sufficiently acquainted with utopian thinking to make such a judgment, Wells classifies the botanist at the bottom of the kinetic class (unoriginal and emotional). But when the scientist is not being used as a foil to Wells's personality, he is characterized as passive, ineffectual, and incapable of action or clear thought, terms that clearly put him in the class of the Dull.

Wells tries, rather pointedly, to include in utopia men who are not

[22]Ibid., p. 125.

innovators. But his utopia is based on only one value, creativity, the benefits of which are to be enjoyed by posterity. This ideal society does not really have room for uncreative types, whose only significance in utopia is to show that that society is a tolerant one. The toleration is, moreover, only of a temporary nature. The two lower classes, the Dull and the Base, are both expected to eliminate themselves over a period of time. The Dull, who are either in debt to the state or employed by it, come more closely under its control than do the more enterprising classes. They are provided with a comfortable living and allowed to marry with the provision that they do not reproduce. Wells is not clear about whether the Dull ever rise sufficiently above the minimum wage to be allowed to procreate while still remaining classed as Dull. The Base, who threaten public safety, are isolated on islands with criminals of their own sex, who have been convicted of similar offenses. They are, of course, offered remedial treatment by humane administrators before they are sentenced and sent into exile.

Wells explains that utopian policy toward the Dull and the Base is designed to eliminate those who are bound to fail anyway in the competitive struggle for life on which progress depends. The utopian state makes the process more humane by doing away with the unnecessary mental and physical suffering that had previously accompanied the process of elimination. In sum, competitive selection in utopia is based on the ability to innovate creatively for the future of mankind. Wells is aware that the utopian method of selection still remains a crude one. "It is not classification for Truth, but a classification to an end." The end, in Wells's words, is to "maintain a secure, happy, and progressive State beside an unbroken flow of poietic activity."[23] When confronted with a kindly drunkard or a poetic liar, the state will have to classify them by their most obvious trait, assuming, as Wells does, that the traits are not interdependent:

The State, dealing as it does only with nonindividualised affairs, is not only justified in disregarding, but is bound to disregard a man's special distinction, and to provide for him on the strength of his prevalent aspect as being on the whole poietic, kinetic, or whatnot.[24]

The Dull were included in utopia in the first place to make its problems resemble, as much as possible, those of the real world. But what Wells does not notice is that outside utopia the existence of dull and base types occurs independently of men's will, while within utopia their continued exis-

[23]Ibid., pp. 261, 264.
[24]Ibid., p. 261.

tence is due to a deliberate act of the author's will and can be expected to reflect a value that the author has consciously chosen to include in his utopia. But aside from demonstrating the temporary tolerance of which utopians are capable, the Dull and the Base have no value. They appear to be puppets, included in utopia by the arbitrary fiat of their creator and used for purposes they cannot understand.

Wells's ideal of a freely developing, innovative activity is both social and pervasive. It is social, for unless creativity is simply a fact of man's nature, the only other explanation for such activity is the existence of a utopian society designed to produce it. It is quite possible that Wells would claim that the need to innovate and create is an essential part of man's nature, that self-expression is as much a requirement of man's nature as is food or sleep. But within utopia the sequence appears to be circular: self-expression is directed to maintaining or improving utopian arrangements that were intended to serve as the means for self-expression. Innovation does not seem to have any value or goal independent of the utopian structure that permits and encourages it.

The ideal is, in addition, pervasive because it is the only basis for determining what is significant activity in utopia. Persons whose actions cannot be explained in terms of Wells's ideal are tolerated in utopia but have no value—they contribute nothing to it. Like Bellamy, Wells seems to have severed the biological from the social level in utopia. Leaving aside the doubtful position of creativity, which in any case is not a necessity in the sense that all men are subject to its demands, one finds that material and sexual needs are satisfied as a matter of course in utopia and consequently do not appear as motives or purposes for innovative actions. Nor does Wells's deity, whose purpose, if it includes man, is concerned with the future of the race, offer any alternative to the pervasive social reality. Wells's utopia appears to be one-dimensional, expending its creative energies in maintaining and improving the details of a state that is more humane and better organized than its preutopian counterpart.

Both Wells and Bellamy claim that in utopia human nature does not change but is only given a better environment in which to express itself. But the result, in *A Modern Utopia,* is curiously disappointing. While an appreciation of individual difference has displaced the egotism of preutopian intolerance, in the process of constructing his utopia, Wells seems to have reduced human nature to the desire to express the creativity to which preutopian social arrangements were indifferent or hostile. Instead of placing value in nationality or in nations, utopians value the individual. But the significance of developing individuality is unclear. The reader is left with the suspicion that, apart from the indefinable future of the race, one form of egotism may have been substituted for another.

The Static Character of A Modern Utopia

Wells's explicitly stated hope is that the society described in *A Modern Utopia* will come into being. Utopia is both possible and better worth living in than the present: "Our deliberate intention is to be not, indeed, impossible, but most distinctly impracticable, by every scale that reaches only between to-day and to-morrow." Utopia is not a perfect society, and Wells does not intend that it should become one. He calls perfection the "repudiation of that ineluctable marginal inexactitude which is the mysterious inmost quality of Being."[25] The individual who tries for an inhuman perfection risks becoming too conscious of his achievement and in the process may find himself saddled with a personage instead of a freely developing personality. For Wells, both the static elements of character and the study of perfection come very close to a sterile overemphasis on self.[26]

Because he hopes utopia will come into existence, Wells is responsible for its functioning as well as for its structure. He describes utopian political organization as a world unit of interlocking local and central governments in which resources and labor are efficiently coordinated and nature's energy is used to provide for men's material needs. The *samurai* administer the affairs of utopia and when necessary suggest improvements. Any proposed change is submitted to the people for discussion. The legislative assembly is able to draw up to one-half of its members from outside the *samurai* to benefit from the wisdom that comes from laxity and sin.

If political change results from a conflict between the common good and private interest, or from disagreement over what the common good is or what it requires, there are no politics in Wells's utopia. The author sketches an outline for utopia's political structure, but he does not provide for the disagreements or the inadvertent disorders that make a political structure more than a mechanism for recording consensus. The scant attention that the author pays to politics can be explained by its fate in the later utopia, *Men Like Gods*, in which Wells depicts the last politician to be

[25]Ibid., pp. 17, 30.
[26]Van Wyck Brooks, *The World of H. G. Wells* (New York: Mitchell Kennerly, 1915), pp. 90–92, 145–150.

elected to a legislative assembly, a garrulous, eccentric old man who receives only one vote, presumably his own. His perceptions of reality are so out-of-date that he is dealt with as a mental case. What has rendered the last politician obsolete is a vast increase in intelligence which has made politics unnecessary; education and character formation have taken its place.

Despite Wells's claims that poietic men are creative, both poietic and kinetic *samurai* are engaged primarily in maintaining the status quo or tinkering with it so that it will run more smoothly. Wells concedes that while traces of their former militancy remain, the *samurai* class directs its energy no longer against specific disorders but against "universal human weaknesses, and the inanimate forces that trouble man. . . ."[27] By "human weaknesses," he probably meant the uncreative classes, whose eventual disappearance would leave the utopian population made up entirely of kinetic and poietic types. To make Wells's admission more explicit: change occurs in utopia only as a response to accidents beyond the control of men, such as natural catastrophes, or for the purpose of reinforcing the existing social organization. Wells does not describe any natural catastrophes actually occurring, but he does mention certain seasons, diseases, and inimical beasts and vermin as possibilities.

The *samurai* are responsible for coordinating utopian activities in the hope that energy will not be wasted in political misunderstandings, and Wells compares their directive function to the role of Plato's Guardians. The comparison may be more apt than Wells suspects, for his description of *samurai* activity leaves the impression that their creative energy is concentrated upon maintaining the already existing utopian organization and remedying its remaining imperfections. Significantly, most of Wells's discussion of the *samurai* is devoted to their past, when they were struggling to achieve utopia:

If we are to have any Utopia at all, we must have a clear common purpose, and a great and steadfast movement of will to override all these incurably egotistical dissentients. . . . Utopia could not come about by chance and anarchy, but by coordinated effort and a community of design. . . .[28]

Wells's faith that the will is stronger than the facts it molds and overcomes may hold true for the epoch that will bring utopia into existence. But within the ideal state Wells cannot show will overcoming facts, for there no longer remain any really stubborn facts to overcome.

[27]Wells, *A Modern Utopia*, p. 254.
[28]Ibid., p. 130. Cf. p. 171.

The difficulty with Wells's *samurai* is in the attempt to make ends of means. The *samurai* represent the character traits necessary to bring about utopia. In utopia, they have no real purpose other than tinkering with the social system, the achievement of which had given them a serious purpose in the past. Interestingly enough, in *First and Last Things* Wells criticized those of his readers who had formed themselves into a *samurai* type of elite for having overemphasized the disciplinary and organizational aspects of the order at the expense of constructive efforts to change society, and he allots part of the responsibility to himself for having paid too much attention to the organization of the order in *A Modern Utopia*.

The issue of whether significant change or novelty can occur within utopia can be seen from another perspective. Because the social ideal of utopia is pervasive, the utopians have no standpoint outside their society, such as might be provided by a deity who transcends utopia, from which they could criticize it and attempt fundamental change. The gamut of known biological needs has been satisfied, with due allowance for personal idiosyncrasy, precluding that area from becoming one where sufficient discomfort could accumulate to give utopians a critical perspective on their society. It is, of course, most likely that the first-generation utopians retain some sense of why their society is valuable. Having experienced preutopian conditions, they can use the contrast between what was and what is to make value judgments about utopia. But for the homebred, second-generation utopian, the history of the past would appear as a tissue of crimes and inexplicable follies.

Novelty and creative innovation, the traits that Wells values, are important if men are to achieve his utopia, but within utopia they cease to have the same value. What change does occur in utopia is weak change —that is, either a response to natural catastrophes that cannot be anticipated or administrative change that elaborates or alters details of existing arrangements without attempting fundamentally to change them. The only example of change Wells mentions which would not fit into these two categories might be called changes in taste or style, as illustrated by the great variation in the ways people dress in utopia; in some cases their clothing is even untidy, tasteless, or foppish. But beyond such suggestions, the author does not venture. And when that not-so-distant point in the future is reached at which the entire population is assimilated into the *samurai* class, it is difficult to imagine how the *samurai* will keep themselves busy, let alone innovate.

His intentions to the contrary, Wells's utopia does not portray change and novelty but rather describes a mopping-up job on the remnants of preutopian disorder. Wells himself is aware that the mainstay of utopia, its prospects for innovation, is precarious. He knows that past utopias have presented themselves as happiness in being and that happy lands have no history. His utopia is to avoid that trap, for it will have to deal with drunkards and idiots, with unimaginative and unteachable types, and therefore it will have a history. But then Wells goes on to show how such failures will be eliminated from utopia, without worrying about what will happen to its ability to make itself a history. He acknowledges that when the kinetic type prevails there will be a problem:

. . . the state ceases to grow, first in this department of activity, and then in that, and so long as its conditions remain the same it remains orderly and efficient. But it has lost its power of initiative and change; its power of adaptation is gone, and with that secular change of conditions which is the law of life, stresses must arise within and without, and bring at last either through revolution or through defeat the release of fresh poietic power.[29]

Wells's discussion lacks any description of how indigenous stresses will arise *within* utopia. And since the state is a world state, it is equally difficult to understand what Wells means by *outside* stresses, unless he has natural change in mind.

Wells's utopian state represents, in its first stage, the average person. As the population becomes assimilated into the *samurai* order, the state will come to represent the creative individual, at which point the utopian ideal will be fully expressed in utopian reality. Of course, as Wells insists, utopian classifications may always remain provisional, but even so it is difficult to imagine what type of change could occur in utopia to challenge the permanency or, better, to maintain the provisionality of the classifications.

A Modern Utopia as a Critique of the Present

A Modern Utopia is best understood as a critique of present reality, rather than a standard by which to judge it, because the utopian ideal differs only in degree, not in kind, from the rationale that sustains existing social organizations. Wells directs his criticism of contemporary society to men's tendency to form aggregates based on occupation, class, religion, nation, and

[29]Ibid., p. 263.

race. His most strenuous objections are reserved for the parochial mind that makes provisional and accidental classifications into absolutes:

> True to the law that all human aggregation involves the development of a spirit of opposition to whatever is external to the aggregation . . . the incompatibility of alien races is being steadily exaggerated.[30]

Wells believes that men's natural tendency toward self-conceit and their dislike of the different or strange were only reinforced by such artificial categories. It was the desire to make such narrow egotism obsolete that led Wells to construct a world state in which difference and innovation were welcome.

The irony of Wells's achievement is that when individual innovation becomes pervasive in utopia, it takes on all the characteristics of self-satisfied egotism, which Wells deplored in its more restricted, preutopian form. It is not that he makes exorbitant claims for life in utopia. He warns that in the new society freedom will not be absolute:

> Perfect human liberty is possible only to a despot who is absolutely and universally obeyed. Then to will would be to command and achieve, and within the limits of natural law we could at any moment do exactly as it pleases us to do.[31]

Despite Wells's warning of utopia's limitations, his ideal of individual innovation appears arbitrary because it is no longer limited by any other reality in tension with it. The backdrop of preutopian intolerance, from which innovation derived its meaning and urgency, is missing. The same problem reappears when Wells criticizes contemporary ideologies. Imperialism is condemned because it leads to the domination of one race over another. Liberalism, somewhat more palatable, is faulted because it offers no more than a policy of international laissez-faire, an unstable compromise that can lead to disorder and war. Utopia has eliminated these demeaning credos of preutopian reality, for creative innovation can flourish only in a society that has overcome self-serving and artificial distinctions. But when the innovative ideal is freed from such impediments and becomes

[30] Ibid., p. 316.
[31] Ibid., p. 41. Wells's perfectly free despot is Plato's perfectly unjust man, but Wells would not, like Plato, call the despot unjust because he is the slave of passions that he has made into absolutes. For Wells, perfect liberty is despotic because it will infringe on the rights of others. Ibid., pp. 41–42. Plato *Republic* ix. 576^b–580^d. Cf. Raknem, *H. G. Wells and His Critics*, pp. 272 ff., for a discussion of Wells's emphasis on the will as power, which Raknem compares to Comte's and Nietzsche's philosophy.

the pervasive organizing principle, it contains as much senseless attention to arbitrary differences of personality or endowment as did the older forms of egotism. Like nationalism, innovation, in the last analysis, appears arbitrary because it has no purpose beyond itself; in circular fashion its value is explained in terms of the social organization that encourages and sustains it.

While a society in which poverty, disease, and other unintended injustices have been eliminated is certainly more humane (and for that reason attractive), Wells cannot claim that his innovative ideal corresponds to a *permanent* quality in human nature and still uphold the restrictions by which the Dull and the Base are gradually eliminated from utopia. And if a more humane society is the incentive to bring about utopia, Bellamy's egalitarian state or Morris's ideal of pleasurable work in natural surroundings appears as attractive as Wells's proposal, for in these ideal societies suffering has also been reduced to its unavoidable minimum. The problem is that Wells cannot establish a necessary relationship between a humane and a creative society as Plato did between knowledge of the Good and the just society. Wells cannot show that creative innovation either requires or results in a more humane society, because the former's nature is not really known—it is a hope for man's future rather than a knowledge of his needs and capacities in the present.

Wells's utopia is a critique, rather than a standard of judgment, because his criticism of preutopian society, no matter how justified, remains topical criticism, significant because of the undesirable conditions it holds up to view and the encouragement it offers men to alter them. Because Wells's utopia is intended to bring about change, he is anxious to identify sources of innovation in the present:

After all, after all, dispersed, hidden, disorganized, undiscovered, unsuspected even by themselves, the *samurai* of Utopia are in this world, the motives that are developed and organized there stir dumbly here and stifle in ten thousand futile hearts. . . .[32]

Utopia is immanent in existing reality. If the contemporary conditions that Wells is anxious to eliminate change and the change is not in the direction anticipated by utopia, Wells's overt criticism, as well as the criticism implicit in the contrast between utopia and the present, is severely undermined. It is possible to imagine, for example, a world in which distinctions are no longer made on the basis of class, nationality, or race, but in which over-

[32]Wells, *A Modern Utopia*, pp. 347–348.

population and inadequate food supplies have become central problems. Wells's utopian ideal is too directly related to the conditions he criticizes to offer an effective alternative once the set of conditions has changed.[33] Or, as the author puts it, "I am just running as hard as I can by the side of the marching facts and pointing to them. . . ."[34]

Wells's utopia is most attractive when it is seen in relation to the time and conditions he was criticizing: ". . . the more important thing about an aggregatory idea from the State maker's point of view is not so much what it explicitly involves as what it implicitly repudiates."[35] When the ideal is shown, not as an end in itself, but in relation to a reality that it measures and attempts to change, it retains much of the quality of disinterestedness, which is an important part of its appeal. In preutopian society, where the ideal is not yet pervasive, it offers men a standpoint from which they can criticize their society, and is itself a meaningful contrast to the present. Wells's *samurai* are quite plausible and attractive as a group of dedicated visionaries, intent on making a better world. But they are no longer attractive—or innovative—once they are imagined to have created a better world, for their ideal then is expressed in institutions that can be neither challenged nor changed.

Wells's ideal society is not a desirable one toward which to work because the explanation of utopia, its raison d'être, is extrinsic to utopia proper. Utopia derives its meaning from the possibilities for change which it suggests. Within utopia, value judgments capable of bringing about further change are no longer possible:

. . . in the world of reality [utopia], which . . . is nothing more nor less than the world of individuality, there are no absolute rights and wrongs, there are no qualitative questions at all, but only quantitative adjustments.[36]

And in *The New Machiavelli,* Wells expands upon the idea, admonishing Michael Angelo to "reject all such ideas as Right, Liberty, Happiness, Duty and Beauty and hold fast to the assertion of the fundamental nature of life as

[33] In *The Future in America* Wells describes the "rule of three" method (which he used to enlarge upon the present in *When the Sleeper Wakes* [1899]) as producing a gigantic caricature of the existing world. H. G. Wells, *The Future in America* (London: Chapman and Hall, 1906), pp. 11–12. The "rule of three" method, which consists in multiplying a contemporary statistic by three for each hundred-year period, is not used in *A Modern Utopia*.
[34] H. G. Wells, *The War that Will End War* (London: Palmer, 1914), quoted in F. H. Doughty, *H. G. Wells Educationist* (London: Jonathan Cape Ltd., 1926), p. 173.
[35] Wells, *A Modern Utopia*, p. 308.
[36] Ibid., p. 45.

a tissue and succession of births.''[37] Such a world would make it difficult to retain any sense of the rationale of utopia. It is tempting to reject Wells's utopia for being meaningless were it to be attained, just as it is tempting to reject his critique of existing society on the grounds that it issues in utopia. Wells comments that "Whatever institution has existed or exists, however irrational, however preposterous, has . . . an effect of realness and rightness no untried thing may share.''[38] The problem is not simply that utopia is untried; it is that we cannot identify within it enough of the characteristics for the sake of which we desire change in the present.

A Modern Utopia as a Thought Experiment

Wells criticizes More's *Utopia* for suppressing individualities by imposing a common pattern on them. Unlike More, Wells does not believe that men have a common nature that can be satisfied by one activity. The uniformity that, for More or for Plato, results from men's acting upon that which is best in their nature, appears merely oppressive to Wells.

Wells is aware that the values by which he organizes utopia are private ones and that he cannot assume that other and different human natures will find them compelling:

There are works, and this is one of them, that are best begun with a portrait of the author.[39]

Thank Heaven this is my book, and that the ultimate decision rests with me. It is open to him [the botanist] to write his own Utopia. . . .[40]

Wells complains that the botanist, his unimaginative companion in utopia, cannot begin to appreciate that society as long as he is a prisoner of the

---

[37]H. G. Wells, *The New Machiavelli* (London: Lane, 1911), quoted in Brooks, *The World of H. G. Wells*, p. 146.

[38]Wells, *A Modern Utopia*, p. 20.

[39]Ibid., p. 13. Henry James is critical of Wells's literary work for the same reason: it is too closely tied to its author's personality. He claims that "the ground of the drama is somehow most of all the adventure for *you*—not to say *of* you—the moral, temperamental, personal, expressional, of your setting it forth. . . .'' Henry James, *The Letters of Henry James*, ed. Percy Lubbock (2 vols.; London: Macmillan and Co., Ltd., 1920), II, 272.

[40]Wells, *A Modern Utopia*, p. 71. In *First and Last Things*, Wells is even more explicit:

Now I make my beliefs as I want them. I do not attempt to distil them out of fact as physicists distil their laws. I make them thus and not thus exactly as an artist makes a picture so and not so. I believe that is how we all make our beliefs. . . .

Wells, *First and Last Things*, pp. 38–39. This passage also appears in the 1908 edition of *First and Last Things*.

accidental events and unreasoned affections that have shaped him in the past. The complaint pinpoints Wells's difficulty: if men have no common nature and therefore do not recognize any common values, there is no reason for them to find his picture of a perfect society an attractive one.

The same sense of dissatisfaction that resulted from Wells's inability to explain why innovations continued to be valuable in utopia occurs when one contemplates the finished utopian picture. Surveyed in retrospect, utopia looks like the arbitrary effort of one man to legislate for the future. There is a great deal of poignancy in Wells's admission: "It will not be like *my* dream, the world that is coming. My dream is just my own poor dream, the thing sufficient for me."[41] Wells does not, however, let himself be limited by the implications of such a statement. He proceeds, a few lines later, to place the utopias that will be written after his in a time sequence, suggesting that each one will be more complete and real than its predecessor and "closer to the problems of the Thing in Being." What the "Thing in Being" is meant to designate is not clear inasmuch as God is said to differ in the measure of every man's individuality.[42] It is probably intended to stand for Wells's belief in some form of progress, for though he does not think history inevitably results in utopia, he does believe that his utopia is in line with the direction the future will take.

Wells's utopians have rejected the doctrine of original sin for the belief that, on the whole, man is good. A sense of sin, Wells remarked elsewhere, is "neither more nor less than the natural discomfort of an imperfectly adapted animal to its environment."[43] Wells also seems to hold

[41]Wells, *A Modern Utopia*, p. 353 (Wells's italics).

[42]Ibid., p. 354. By examining a number of parallel texts from 1891 to 1917, Connes shows that by 1917, when Wells published a revised edition of *First and Last Things,* he had modified his earlier nominalism enough to allow that general concepts, such as "man," have a meaning. However, Wells included in the concept "man" only what he considered were positive qualities. Smith, to use Wells's own example, represents man in his generality when he philosophizes; when he boasts, he represents only Smith. The same sort of procedure may explain Wells's ordering of future utopias, unsuccessful ones representing their authors' weaknesses rather than limitations in the utopian genre of writing. Wells, *First and Last Things*, pp. 49–50. Cf. Connes, *Étude sur La Pensée*, pp. 36–38.

The description of the future race of utopians as the receptacle of successful past experiments in individuality may be roughly analogous to what Wells means by the "Thing in Being." If so, it is subject to the same criticism as his qualified realism in language. There is no reason to assume that either Smith or the future race of men is more representative of man in general or more efficacious in determining the future when exhibiting those traits which Wells considers desirable.

[43]H. G. Wells, *You Can't Be Too Careful* (London: Secker and Warburg, 1941), quoted in Norman Nicholson, *H. G. Wells* (London: Arthur Barker Ltd., 1950), p. 96.

this belief, in a qualified way, with respect to preutopian society. Man is good to the extent he can dream of a better future; the potential *samurai* of utopia exist, although they do not know it, in twentieth-century London. Wells finds it hard, however, to discover any good in people who can remain indifferent to his utopia:

People of this sort do not even feel the need of alternatives. Beyond the scope of a few personal projects . . . they do not feel that there is a future. They are unencumbered by any baggage of convictions whatever, in relation to that.[44]

What is there to prevent a . . . movement of all the civilized Powers in the world toward a common ideal and assimilation?

Stupidity—nothing but stupidity, a stupid brute jealousy, aimless and unjustifiable.[45]

Wells has a very human tendency to gather all good and justice on his side. The reader is not left free to accept or reject Wells's utopia on its own merits; he risks being accused of willful stupidity if he demurs. The freedom that Plato and More offered their audiences to use utopia as a form of thought experiment depended on utopia's not being taken primarily as a blueprint for future change. Wells's hopes for the future are too intense for him to allow the reader any such latitude.

The reader's suspicion that, if he does not accept Wells's utopia, Wells's utopia will not accept him shifts the level of discourse back to a direct confrontation of different value judgments. (The author indicates that he is aware that his logic has shifted by remarking that the argument's form has changed to a direct address to the reader.) The strength of the utopian picture lies in its attempt to communicate at a level that avoids such direct confrontations. But if the men in the present, to whom utopia is addressed, are assumed to have fundamentally different natures and values, such confrontations seem unavoidable. Nor are they to be taken lightly, for if utopia does come into being, the reader who has rejected it will be proved not only stupid but immoral. Wells's warning to those who remain indifferent to his utopia is less strident than Bellamy's, but it is felt just as strongly.

For the modern utopian author, to investigate an ideal in thought is a way of coming to know the implications of a value by imagining a reality that accommodates and reflects it. The ideal is known more adequately when a set of implications has been drawn from it and examined in detail. The

[44]Wells, *A Modern Utopia,* p. 330.
[45]Ibid., p. 336.

knowledge that results from holding an ideal apart from an overcomplicated reality has a special—and limited—coherence of its own. It is thought at the opposite end of the spectrum from Wells's unfortunate botanist friend who "thinks in little pieces that lie about loose, and nothing has any necessary link with anything else in his mind."[46]

Wells has tested his value by seeing whether an adequate social organization could be built upon it. When he finishes, he describes himself as experiencing "something of the satisfaction of a man who has finished building a bridge; I feel that I have joined together things that I had never joined before."[47]

The exercise of investigating an ideal in thought gives it a new force and cogency for the author. "You cannot," Wells remarks to the disaffected botanist with some exasperation, "focus all good things together."[48] The botanist is, of course, free to attempt to do so; his refusal risks leaving the author in possession of the field of combat.

[46]Ibid., p. 329.
[47]Ibid., p. 338.
[48]Ibid., p. 228.

William Dean
Howells's
*A Traveller
from Altruria*
and
*Through the Eye
of the Needle*

Howells's *A Traveller from*
Altruria and *Through the Eye*
of the Needle

170

William Dean Howells's utopian novels first appeared as a series of twenty-three essays, "Letters of an Altrurian Traveller," written for *The Cosmopolitan* and published between 1892 and 1894.[1] In 1894 Howells republished the first twelve of these essays in book form: *A Traveller from Altruria*. Six of the remaining letters were used to make Part One of *Through the Eye of the Needle*, which Howells completed in 1907.

Howells's utopia differs from Bellamy's and Wells's by being situated in space rather than time. It is on a large, inaccessible, and economically self-sufficient island located somewhere in the South Seas.[2] Although Altruria's origins are Hellenic, Howells disassociates it from utopias based on the legend of the lost island of Atlantis (Altruria has no tradition of submergence). In addition, the civilization has been Christian for a long time, for soon after the death of Christ the gospels were made known by a Christian communist who was shipwrecked on the coast. Howells does acknowledge that in simplicity of dress and dwelling there is some resemblance between his utopia and those of both More and Bacon, the crucial difference being that Altruria has undergone the discipline of competitive capitalism.

The matter-of-fact, pragmatic spirit that Howells associates with competitive capitalism is one explanation of his decision to locate Altruria in the present. The best of the business and professional types that the Altrurian traveler meets during his visit to the United States are hardheaded, down-to-earth men with a great respect for achievement. A banker, whom Howells portrays as both shrewd and reflective, speaks for this group when he remarks that if Altruria were not an accomplished fact, he would think it impossible, but that he always feels bound to recognize the thing done.[3]

[1] William Dean Howells, *Letters of an Altrurian Traveller*, ed. Clara M. Kirk and Rudolf Kirk (Gainesville, Fla.: Scholars' Facsimiles & Reprints, 1961).

[2] William Dean Howells, *A Traveller from Altruria* (New York: Sagamore Press, Inc., 1957); William Dean Howells, *Through the Eye of the Needle: A Romance* (New York: Harper & Brothers Publications, 1907).

[3] Among other modern utopias, the most notable one to be located in the present (and in America) is B. F. Skinner's experimental community, *Walden Two*. Skinner defends this choice on grounds that are similar to those of Howells: the strength of *Walden Two* consists in showing that the good life exists as a fact, not a theory, and that it has experimental, and not merely rational, justification. B. F. Skinner, *Walden Two* (New York: The Macmillan Company, 1948), p. 133. Despite the shift to a spatial location, the reader of Skinner and Howells is just as dependent on an inquisitive outsider for information about these down-to-earth utopias as they were for their knowledge of future-oriented utopias. (Skinner adds, as a further justification for locating his utopia in the present, that progress and expansion, through direct

Another advantage of making utopia contemporary with America is that it permits Howells to bring his Altrurian to the United States. The naïveté of the visitor allows him to discover, inadvertently, the contradictions in American civilization. By a rather Socratic combination of simplicity and astute questioning, the Altrurian transforms the familiar conventions and practices of American life into rituals as elaborate and exotic as anyone might expect to encounter in the South Seas. Using utopia as a distancing device, Howells is able to criticize contemporary civilization on the spot, so to speak, and not just through the remembered experience of the visitor to utopia. Altruria itself, by contrast, is much less substantial and detailed; it is described in a series of rather disjointed letters from an American who has married the Altrurian visitor and goes with him to his country.

Howells was chosen to complete the study of modern utopias because he is more aware than either Bellamy or Wells of the difficulties of describing a utopia that is convincing and attractive enough so that people want to live in it. If it is possible to answer the objection that Bellamy's and Wells's utopias are unconvincing because they are not painted with a fine enough brush, Howells should be able to do so. Bellamy is a novelist of only secondary importance, and Wells is very uneven in his work, with a tendency to lapse into didacticism. But Howells's talents as a novelist need no defense; if his utopia is unconvincing, the explanation cannot be a lack of literary skill.

Howells is perhaps the least "modern" of the modern utopian authors included in this study. He most certainly hoped that America would come to resemble Altruria. But, like his classical predecessors, he was more interested in understanding utopian values and applying them to the present than in proselytizing for the coming of utopia in the future.

The Ideal of A Traveller from Altruria and Through the Eye of the Needle
Howells's utopia is most directly described in the second part of *Through the Eye of the Needle*, when Eveleth Strange marries the Altrurian visitor and returns to his home with him. Eveleth is typical of a certain class of Americans in having more money than she can use intelligently. She is "strange"

competition with other types of society, are necessary if Walden Two is to avoid the weakness of preceding utopias, which were satisfied to achieve and maintain a stable state of happiness. Ibid., pp. 173–174. Skinner neglects, however, to explore the interesting consequences of this claim for *Walden Two* when it has made enough converts to become universal.)

because she realizes that giving part of her money away is no solution to problems of unemployment and poverty and because she is willing to give up her money and all her other possessions in order to live in Altruria.

Before the scene shifts to Altruria, the reader already has gained some knowledge of that country from a public lecture given by the Altrurian visitor, Aristides Homos, and, by implication, from his criticisms of American society. The audience for the lecture is composed of wealthy summer residents of a New Hampshire resort hotel and the underemployed or out-of-work natives from the surrounding area. Both the idle rich and the work-hungry poor are expected to find the description of Altruria relevant, for the Altrurian ideal is physical labor in congenial surroundings.

The foundation of the Altrurian economy is biblical: "For even when we were with you this we commanded you, that if any would not work, neither should he eat."[4] The Altrurians work in semipastoral surroundings; their once-crowded cities have been progressively depopulated in favor of decentralized towns and villages serviced by regional capitals. All buildings, including homes, are owned by the state; the inhabitants are more concerned that their buildings appear beautiful (they favor the Greek style of architecture) than with the mere fact of possession.

Laborsaving devices have fallen into disuse, except for electric trains which are used in the capitals when speed is necessary:

. . . everything has tended to simplification here. They [*the Altrurians*] have disused the complicated facilities and conveniences of the capitalistic epoch, which we are so proud of, and have got back as close as possible to nature.[5]

In *A Traveller from Altruria*, Howells says that the Altrurians have retained machines, even though their needs are simple and can be met by handwork, because machine work is more thorough and more beautiful. The discrepancy can be explained by the length of time that elapsed between the writing of *A Traveller from Altruria* and the second part of *Through the Eye of the Needle*, combined with Howells's ambivalence toward monopoly capitalism. While he was writing *A Traveller from Altruria*, Howells thought that business would develop into a monopoly that, when taken over by government, would result in economic equality. This explanation of Altruria's economic evolution reflects the influence of *Looking Backward*; Howells had initially been a member of the group interested in

[4]Howells, *Through the Eye*, p. 205.
[5]Ibid., p. 157.

The Ideal of *A Traveller from*   173
Altruria and *Through the Eye*
of the Needle

preparing for the speedy implementation of Bellamy's utopia. The second part of *Through the Eye of the Needle*, written in 1907, omits any mention of such a takeover; machinery and the superfluous goods it produces are seen as maintaining the artificial class distinctions of capitalist society.[6]

Clothing style has also been simplified and made beautiful; individual taste is exercised in the choice of color, but if the result is too atrocious, the local art commission may issue a gentle admonition to the offender. As manual labor has caused a great improvement in physical fitness, garments need very little alteration to accommodate advanced age or ungainly shapes.

Work in Altruria is divided into "obligatories" and "voluntaries," each of three hours' duration. The work credits earned in the obligatories are sufficient to supply all the Altrurians' material needs; goods are bought at government-owned army and navy stores located in the regional capitals. Housework, which is a cooperative enterprise, counts as obligatory work. Also in this category are the public missions that Aristides Homos undertakes upon his return: lecturing to the Altrurians on what he has learned from his travels.

The work that the Altrurians value most is manual rather than mental labor. Farm work, stone quarrying, road and building construction, all cooperative enterprises, are highly esteemed. Working on public buildings and monuments arouses such enthusiasm that the Altrurians use the voluntaries for it as well as the obligatories. When Eveleth Strange sees a series of road arches being built in commemoration of Altrurians who had served their country exceptionally well, she relates that the work

. . . was all joy and all glory. They say there never was such happiness in any country since the world began. While the work went on it was like a perpetual Fourth of July or an everlasting picnic.[7]

At the end of the three-hour morning obligatories, the Altrurians hold religious services in the temples and consecrate the day's work with hymns and offerings from the field.

In *A Traveller from Altruria* Howells acknowledges the influence of William Morris, and indeed the similarities between their utopias are strik-

[6]See Robert L. Hough, *The Quiet Rebel: William Dean Howells as Social Commentator* (Lincoln: University of Nebraska Press, 1959), pp. 57–62. For the influence of Bellamy, see Howells's essay on Bellamy: William Dean Howells, "The Romantic Imagination," *European and American Masters*, ed. Clara M. Kirk and Rudolf Kirk (New York: New York University Press, Collier paperback, 1963), pp. 184–189; also pp. 94, 180 ff. (editors' commentary).
[7]Howells, *Through the Eye*, p. 187.

Howells's *A Traveller from*
Altruria and *Through the Eye*
of the Needle

174

ing. The authors are one in their dislike of a competitive society that creates class antagonisms, shoddy production, and conspicuous consumption by the wealthy. Morris's *News from Nowhere* is located in the future, but by equating Altrurian simplicity with that still enjoyed by rural Americans, Howells is also able to link his ideal to America's past. Even more important, for both authors the artist who finds satisfaction in his work and gives pleasure by it is the ideal of human development.[8] Consequently in both utopias industrial development is deliberately curtailed to conform to the artistic temperament, which is thought to develop better in a rural environment. Nor is this temperament the preserve of a fortunate few; any form of useful and wholesome labor is beautiful, in contrast to the shoddy work and meretricious goods produced by the capitalist system. Although less concerned than Morris with handicrafts, Howells follows him in emphasizing the aesthetic character of the utopian work product:

. . . when the labor of the community was emancipated from the bondage of the false to the free service of the true, it was also, by an inevitable implication, dedicated to beauty and rescued from the old slavery to the ugly, the stupid and the trivial. The thing that was honest and useful became, by the operation of a natural law, a beautiful thing.[9]

From his description of the utopian work process it becomes clear that Howells intends to do more than equate beauty with utility. Because the Altrurians have been relieved of the pressures of deadlines and quotas and the need to think of monetary returns, they are able to rediscover the satisfaction of making a product beautiful. Every man, to the extent of his talents, is described as working in the spirit of the artist, performing work for its own sake and for the satisfaction of accomplishment. For Howells the artist is the human type most like the divine, and he makes his creative

[8]See Clara M. Kirk, *W. D. Howells and Art in His Time* (New Brunswick, N. J.: Rutgers University Press, 1965), for a detailed discussion of Howells's attitude toward art. Kirk also identifies aesthetic work as the ideal of Altruria. Ibid., pp. 194–195.

[9]Howells, *A Traveller*, p. 185. It is noteworthy that the emphasis on beauty within utopia and on the beauty of utopia appears in modern utopias, which are blueprints for change, and not in classical utopias, which are unattainable ideals. A partial explanation may be the nineteenth century's preoccupation with art as an "imaginative truth" and the artist as a specially gifted human being. See Raymond Williams, *Culture and Society: 1780–1950* (Middlesex: Penguin Books Ltd., 1963), pp. 15–16. For a similar emphasis on the aesthetic, see Wells, *First and Last Things*, p. 39, and *A Modern Utopia* (for Wells's ideal of creative innovation); Aldous Huxley, *Island* (New York: Bantam Books, Inc., 1963); W. H. Hudson, *A Crystal Age* (London: T. Fisher Unwin, 1906); and Herbert Read, *The Green Child* (New York: New Directions Publishing Corporation, n. d.).

The Ideal of *A Traveller from*   175
Altruria and *Through the Eye*
of the Needle

activity the norm for industrial and shop work, as well as for work in the fields.

In Altruria only manual labor counts as work. Composing music, writing plays, and painting pictures are considered pleasures, and as these activities do not equalize the work load, they are relegated to the voluntaries.[10] In a passage reminiscent of Marx, Howells notes that the poet may well be a shoemaker in the obligatories and the shoemaker a poet in the voluntaries. In utopia no one occupation is honored over others except cultivation of the soil, in which all Altrurians engage. Because agriculture is not performed with a view to profit, Howells expects such work to strengthen men's love of country and arouse their natural piety by making them grateful to God for his bounty.

Howells's criticism of capitalism is a moral and humanistic one whose inspiration is from Tolstoy rather than Marx. Although Howells believed socialism would be more efficient than capitalism, his major interest was in a social system that permitted fuller human development. The mainspring of Howells's socialism has been well described by Hough as "a barn-raising, housewarming kind of cooperation between rural neighbors."[11]

Howells's ideal of dignified and wholesome labor is appealing in terms of what it replaces. The criterion of beauty is not indigenous to utopia but rather implicit in the contrast with the shoddy workmanship of the past. When Aristides Homos visits the Columbian exposition of 1893 in Chicago, he comments that had such a city been constructed in Altruria, "every man who drove a nail, or stretched a line, or laid a trowel upon such a work, would have his name somehow inscribed upon it. . . ."[12] Presumably Howells did not wish to imply such discrepancies in individual development in Altruria that some would find hammering a nail a sufficient form of self-expression while others would need to design entire buildings or plan whole cities. It is more likely that he wished to point out that all work is satisfying when it is willingly done for a common and worthwhile purpose without the need for monetary return, for he calls the highest quality of

---

[10]Howells, *Through the Eye,* p. 177. Howells is not altogether consistent, for he includes studies and intellectual pursuits in the obligatories, probably because he thought these occupations were more directly useful to the community. Ibid., pp. 183–184. And in *A Traveller from Altruria* artists are also able to be released from obligatories. Howells, *A Traveller,* p. 189.

[11]Hough, *The Quiet Rebel,* p. 63; cf. pp. 51–56. See also Howells, "Leo Tolstoy," *European and American Masters,* pp. 96–108.

[12]Howells, *Letters,* p. 27.

beauty a spiritual one, the result of giving one's talent without expecting material rewards.

The same difficulty that arose in understanding Bellamy's ideal of emulation or Wells's ideal of innovation also exists with Howells's ideal of beautiful and useful labor. The reader is not shown any motive for such activity (other than supplying material needs) or given any explanation of its significance. The motive of competition has, of course, been eliminated from utopia; men have been found to work willingly on their own initiative when their purpose is to provide common necessities. No Altrurian has or wishes to have private interests distinguishable from the common good, which might tempt him to take advantage of another Altrurian.

It may be that Howells eliminated laborsaving devices from *Through the Eye of the Needle* so that work would retain some relation to biological necessity and not appear entirely gratuitous:

Art, indeed, is beginning to find out that if it does not make friends with Need it must perish. It perceives that to take itself from the many . . . and to give itself to the few whom it can bring no joy in their idleness [*sic*], is an error that kills.[13]

But as Orwell has commented, to walk forty miles to London with buses speeding by is not the same as to walk to London for want of any other means of conveyance. The first case leads to an overly self-conscious back-to-nature mentality.[14]

To the extent that work goes beyond supplying the simple Altrurian necessities, it appears to have no rationale. Aristides Homos describes Altruria as a society "where the sciences and arts and letters are cultivated for

[13]William Dean Howells, *Criticism and Fiction and Other Essays,* ed. Clara M. Kirk and Rudolf Kirk (New York: New York University Press, 1959), p. 85.

[14]George Orwell, *The Road to Wigan Pier* (New York: The Berkley Publishing Corporation, paperback, 1961), pp. 164–167. Orwell's comment centers on the major problem of Morris's *News from Nowhere.* In Howells the problem is less in evidence either because his description is vaguer and more impressionistic than Morris's or because he is more aware of the difficulty. Howells's own criticism of Morris's poetry comes very close to Orwell's more general comments. In 1875 he described Morris's poetry (he later revised his opinion) as rather

like looking through a modern house . . . adorned with tiles, and painted in the Pompeiian style, or hung with Mr. Morris' own admirable wall-papers; it is all very pretty indeed; charming; but it is consciously medieval, consciously Greek, and it is so well aware of its quaintness, that, on the whole, one would rather not live in it.

Howells, *Atlantic Monthly* (August 1875), p. 243, quoted in Kirk, *W. D. Howells and Art in His Time,* p. 187.

The Ideal of *A Traveller from*   177
Altruria and *Through the Eye*
of the Needle

their own sake. . . ."[15] Howells blurs the question of whether work in utopia could be significant by contrasting it, for the most part, to the American inability to conceive of work that is not motivated by economic rewards. There is no problem in understanding that the Altrurians work only to satisfy consciously limited needs. The difficulty is to understand what significance, beyond supplying their needs, their work can possibly have for them. Science and the arts, for instance, pursued for their own sake, appear at best to be irrelevant to a society in which man's wants are fulfilled and his purposes established independently of these activities.

Howells describes the Altrurians as entirely content and at ease with the arrangements of their society. There is no indication that the Altrurians have any motives or purposes not adequately accommodated by existing social arrangements which would account for either their work activity or their common aesthetic inclination. Their activity seems capable of explanation only in terms of a society designed and organized to encourage it. It may be Howells's own aesthetic preferences that are expressed in utopia (he favored Greek architecture). But if so, he does not discuss the reasons for his preference or why it is adopted as the criterion of what is beautiful in utopia.

Howells's utopian ideal is work that produces both beautiful and useful results. His emphasis on the aesthetic, while no doubt congenial to his own temperament, is also very well suited to the static character of utopian society, for some forms of artistic activity are very plausibly seen as the result of pleasure and delight in the present. Altrurian recreation provides a good example. Homos calls premeditated pleasures stupid and mistaken and says the Altrurian ideal is spontaneous recreation.[16] By emphasizing spontaneity, Howells can avoid describing the forms in which pleasure occurs in utopia. Were he to describe them, Howells might risk having to admit that different tastes can at times become conflicting tastes.

What is missing in Altruria is the awareness that one form of expressing harmony or completeness, taken seriously, might exclude others. In Wells's utopia creative innovation was, by definition, always incomplete. In Howells's utopia, spontaneous pleasure is complete and sufficient in itself. In both utopias, the lack of any criterion for innovation or for pleasure

[15]Howells, *A Traveller*, p. 54.
[16]Morris also emphasizes spontaneity and links it to creativity by comparing art to the imaginative play of children. "It is the child-like part of us that produces works of imagination. When we are children time passes so slow with us that we seem to have time for everything." William Morris, *News from Nowhere* (New York: Longmans, Green, and Co., 1905), p. 113.

appears as an unwillingness to discriminate at all or as the type of indifference that occurs when choices have no consequences. By not having such criteria utopias avoid controversy, perhaps at the expense of significance.

The Altrurian ideal is social because both the motive and the purpose of making beautiful products can be adequately accounted for only as a response to the norms of already established utopian arrangements. The ideal is also pervasive; it determines all other activity in Altruria. The exclusive dominance of the ideal of aesthetic work occurs almost by default in Howells's description of utopia. Short of the organization of work into the obligatories, and its frequent extension into the voluntaries, the author tells us remarkably little about Altruria. The reader learns that children are raised in the family only from Howells's remark that couples who quarrel continually and show themselves unfit to be parents will have their children taken away from them.

Despite some sketchiness, Howells's handling of such topics as the afterlife, the arts, and criminality offers evidence of the pervasiveness of his social ideal. Although there are no religious denominations, and religious ceremonies are limited to hymns and work offerings, the Altrurians believe in the immortality of the soul. They consider death natural and just, rather than something to be feared. Having had no experience of cruelty, the Altrurians cannot conceive of death as unkind and accept its arrival with equanimity. Their equanimity points to the limitations of Altrurian experience. Homos tells his American audience:

"We do not say that the dead have gone to a better place, and then selfishly bewail them, for we have the kingdom of heaven upon earth, already, and we know that wherever they go they will be homesick for Altruria. . . ."[17]

If death is not cruel, it appears at least to be a rather inexplicable and arbitrary removal from one state of bliss to another. Such problems, however, would not trouble the Altrurians, for whom, Homos says, religious differences are temperamental and aesthetic rather than theological and essential. Like William Morris's utopians, the Altrurians are too happy, individually and collectively, to trouble themselves about the next life.

The Altrurians spend their leisure time reading for entertainment and attending social meetings characterized, Howells says, by their wit and playfulness. The great national amusement is dancing, which retains a religious

---

[17]Howells, *A Traveller*, p. 200.

The Ideal of *A Traveller from*
Altruria and *Through the Eye*
of the Needle

179

significance. Although plays are performed, Howells wisely limits them to comedy, for life in Altruria is so happy that tragedy would not be true to it. The possible fate of tragedy in utopia is suggestively sketched by Huxley in *Island*. He reinterprets *Oedipus Rex* as a marionette show called *Oedipus in Pala* which is presented with a new ending: a boy and girl from Pala talk Jocasta out of suicide.[18]

But if comedy involves some form of inappropriate activity (the result, for instance, of an inadvertent disparity between a situation and the actor's conception of it), Altruria does not offer much material for comedy either. Howells describes only one play, and its subject matter is not Altrurian but American: a millionaire's daughter escapes with her impoverished suitor to Altruria. The humor derives from the caricature of the millionaire (he is covered with dollar signs) and from his inability to visualize Altruria and thereby to understand his daughter's motives. The visitor to Morris's utopia suggests why the literature of the past is more alive than any the utopians can produce. The latter, like Gulliver's Houyhnhnms, have become too rational, and in the process, have lost the ability—or adaptability—to extract good from evil.

There are criminals in Altruria, but their crimes do not result from desires that Altruria cannot fulfill or from dissatisfaction with its social arrangements. The only murders that take place are the result of jealous rage, and the murderer, "consumed with an undying pity for the man he slew," provides his own punishment through remorse.[19] Again Morris supplies the explanation, observing that society punishes the criminal only when it fears for its own safety; it has nothing to fear from "inadvertent" criminals who fully accept society's values.[20]

Howells's position is logical; if there is no incentive or provocation to act antisocially, crimes should be considered accidents. When the cause of crime is a momentary aberration, and the criminal can be counted upon to fully recognize the wrong, punishment is superfluous. One might wonder whether the murderer's remorse for an act he did not intend makes much sense. But it is not at all surprising that the remorse is endless, since the criminal cannot show contrition by reforming himself for an act that was an accident.

In sum, neither criminalty nor the arts appear to offer the possibility

[18]Huxley, *Island,* p. 251.
[19]Howells, *Through the Eye,* p. 167.
[20]Morris, *News from Nowhere,* pp. 89–93.

Howells's *A Traveller from*
Altruria and *Through the Eye*
of the Needle

180

of behavior or thought whose motive or purpose is at variance with Howells's social ideal. Aesthetic work seems to be the only principle that determines activity in Altruria. Howells's ideal, like Bellamy's and Wells's, seems to be a completely social ideal because there is no adequate explanation for utopian activity beyond the fact that it maintains a society that in turn has been organized to permit such activity. When man is not considered in relation to a reality transcending his own nature and his society, utopia appears either as a ceaseless quest for arbitrary individual self-expression or as an uncritical contentment with the present state of affairs. Wells's quest for self-expression is unsuccessful because the mechanism designed to produce difference appears futile in the absence of any judgment about the significance or value of different human development. Thus Howells, like Bellamy, is not successful in making a variety of motives appear plausible in utopia. What is not included in utopia appears to be deliberately excluded in such a way that the results do not fulfill the modern utopias' promise to describe both an adequate and an attractive human reality.

The Static Character of A Traveller and Through the Eye of the Needle
In 1907 Howells was working on the second part of *Through the Eye of the Needle*, in which most of the description of Altruria occurs. During this period he wrote a letter to Charles Eliot Norton, which included the following comment:

. . . I have given my own dream of Utopia, which I fancy your not liking, unless for all its confessions of imperfections even in Utopia. All other dreamers of such dreams have had nothing but pleasure in them; I have had touches of nightmare.[21]

Unfortunately, the author does not explain what about his utopia was causing him nightmares. Perhaps it can be inferred from an earlier remark Howells made about the characters in Bellamy's *Looking Backward:* "His people are less objectively than subjectively present; their import is greater in what happens to them than in what they are."[22]

Howells makes two closely related points in his comment on *Looking Backward*. The first, to paraphrase an observation that Henry James made in an essay on Howells, is that when imagination leaves its anchorage in the im-

[21]Letter to C. E. Norton written April 1907 in *Life in Letters of William Dean Howells*, ed. Mildred Howells (2 vols.; Garden City, N.Y.: Doubleday Doran & Company, Inc., 1928), II, 242.
[22]William Dean Howells, "The Romantic Imagination" (essay from the *Atlantic Monthly*, August 1898) in *Criticism and Fiction and Other Essays*, pp. 251–252.

The Static Character of *A*
Traveller and *Through the Eye*
of the Needle

181

mediate, familiar commonplace and attempts to deal with the rare and
strange bordering on fantasy, it tends to become vague and arbitrary.[23] Or, in
Wells's words, the present, no matter how illogical it appears, seems substantial and real in comparison to the untried future.[24] Second, the inhabitants of
utopia do not seem either anchored or involved in their environment. They
tend to represent humanity instead of being human. They have become typical, generalized people rather than particular individualized agents.

Howells is very much aware of the difficulty of making utopia appear
real and viable. At the end of an emotion-charged description of Altruria in *A
Traveller from Altruria*, Homos himself wonders whether his country is more
than a dream, for he finds it increasingly difficult to recapture the Altrurian
reality, the longer he lives in radically different surroundings. The element of
nightmare that Howells acknowledges feeling toward his utopia may well derive from a novelist's frustration at the insubstantiality of his creation. Eveleth
Strange conveys a like frustration when she writes from Altruria:

Life here is so subjective . . . that there is usually nothing like news in it. . . . But
now we have had some occurrences recently, quite in the American sense,
and these have furnished me with an incentive . . . to send you a letter.[25]

And at the end of her series of letters describing Altrurian life, Eveleth Strange
again voices her uneasy feeling that Altruria is a dream, constantly requiring
for its reality the fresh confirmation of more visitors.

The two occurrences that stimulate Eveleth Strange to continue her
chronicle are both events originating "outside" utopia. A millionaire's pleasure yacht is shipwrecked on the Altrurian coast, and its recalcitrant passen-
gers are made to conform to the Altrurian mode of life. One of the few dis-
plays of ill temper to be found in modern utopias occurs when Eveleth
Strange is confronted with the obtuse and disagreeable millionaire's wife. Af-
terward she is duly contrite.

The other incident is the mutiny of the crew of the *Little Sally*, a trading ship that has docked in Altruria. The mutiny becomes the occasion for a
public meeting in which captain and crew both present their cases, agree that
life outside Altruria is miserable, and arrange one final voyage to retrieve the
captain's family and bring them to live permanently in Altruria.

[23]Henry James, "William Dean Howells," *The American Essays*, ed. Leon Edel (New York:
Vintage Books, Inc., 1956), p. 152.
[24]Wells, *A Modern Utopia*, p. 20.
[25]Howells, *Through the Eye*, p. 128.

Howells is unusual both because he is aware that the placid tenor of utopian life is inescapable and because he is uneasy about it. Eveleth Strange writes:

It is no use to pretend that in little over a year I have become accustomed to the eventlessness of life in Altruria. I go on for a good many days together and do not miss the exciting incidents you have in America, and then suddenly I am wolfishly hungry for the old sensations. . . .[26]

Altrurian newspapers offer little relief for Eveleth Strange's tedium. They report on plays, public works in progress, and the results of any scientific inquiry. But for news they rely primarily on capitalist history and current developments, such as war, pestilence, and white slavery. Any amelioration is cited as progress toward the Altrurian ideal.

The eventlessness of utopia presents Howells with a dilemma. The author's own logic forces him to disapprove of the events he introduces to disturb the utopian calm. But the shipwrecked millionaires are really interesting only before they are assimilated into Altruria. Because the example of idleness that they offer is intolerable to the utopians, the millionaires are obliged to work for their living; later, when they have learned to enjoy their work, they become indistinguishable from the Altrurians.

A similar lack of comprehension characterizes the Altrurian reaction to the sufferings of the mutinous sailors. They feel horror and pity, the emotions of the uncomprehending spectator, when they hear of the squalid conditions in which the sailors have lived. Howells comments that even their pity is a luxury, as Altruria offers so little occasion for wrongdoing.[27] But like the remorse of the criminal, the pity and the horror the Altrurians experience are based on incomprehension and do not work in the direction of a greater understanding or an enlarged sympathy.

Altrurians do not find the evidence from their own past any more meaningful than the events that are described to them from the American present. Homos, noting this indifference toward the past, suggests very sensibly that the capitalist cities that have been left as a cautionary example of former conditions in Altruria be razed. (Altruria's development paralleled America's until the Altrurians decided on reform.) And in *News from No-*

---

[26]Ibid., p. 218.
[27]Howells, *Through the Eye,* p. 143. In one of Wells's utopias a woman is described as a throwback for having discovered in herself the emotion of pity without finding any person on whom to exercise it. Wells, *Men Like Gods,* p. 157.

where a reflective utopian points to the thin line that separates total stability from total change when the former state is based on ignorance:

... people are too careless of the history of the past ... happy as we are, times may alter; we may be bitten with some impulse towards change, and many things may seem too wonderful for us to resist, too exciting not to catch at, if we do not know that they are but phases of what has been before; and withal ruinous, deceitful and sordid.[28]

Not only are the Altrurians *not* bitten with an impulse to change, but they are unable to understand such change when it intrudes upon them in the form of an unwelcome shipwreck. Obliged to use force in the form of mild electric shocks to persuade the least work-prone of their visitors, the Altrurians rightly fear its adverse effect on themselves. Without the ability to understand what they are attempting to change, the "humaneness" of the Altrurians' method of persuasion is poorly grounded; it appears to be a most fragile barrier against the use of more drastic forms of persuasion. The two conditions that Howells terms "illogical" in Altrurian existence are their use of force and their discouragement of immigration.[29] (The latter is defended as in the interests of capitalist countries whose citizens, once having visited Altruria, would refuse to leave.) In both cases what is at issue is the adequacy of a civilization incapable of understanding what it is obliged to pass judgment upon.

Under such conditions, it is difficult to conceive of politics in utopia, and Howells does not attempt it. He mentions administrative officials, alternated every year, who live in the regional capitals, but tells us nothing of how they are chosen or what they do. Warfare no longer exists, as the neighboring capitalist countries submitted to the Altrurian example soon after the country was established. Disease and vice have vanished with the capitalist conditions that caused them; and chance, having been eliminated from economic life, manifests itself only in accidents of physique and disposition.

But although government is no longer needed, even to maintain a stable utopian environment, Howells does not attribute this stability to a greater spiritual or mental development on the part of the Altrurians. The Altrurians, he says, are certain that their civic ideals are perfect, but they are

[28]Morris, *News from Nowhere*, p. 218.
[29]Howells, *Through the Eye*, p. xii. Cf. *A Traveller*, p. 191.

Howells's *A Traveller from*
Altruria and *Through the Eye*
of the Needle

184

not certain that their civilization is. Boston was probably the prototype for Altruria, and the comments of a Bostonian banker throw light on Howells's rather enigmatic distinction between civic ideals and civilization:

Boston has the public spirit and Boston has the money, but perhaps Boston has not the ambition. Perhaps we give ourselves in Boston too much to a sense of the accomplished fact. If that is a fault, it is the only fault conceivable of us. Here in Chicago they have the public spirit, and they have the money, and they are still anxious to do; they are not content as we are, simply to be. Of course, they have not so much reason![30]

It has been observed that when enjoyment is separated from labor, the means from the end, man's experience is fragmented, and he himself becomes only a fragment.[31] But the converse may also be true. When enjoyment and labor are indistinguishable, when means and ends coincide entirely, man is equally limited to a fragment of what is humanly possible for him. Altruria is, as Howells comments, no more civilized than heaven.[32]

A Traveller and Through the Eye of the Needle as a Critique of the Present

The pragmatic Americans who meet Aristides Homos during his travels call him subjective and no more tangible than a bad conscience:

Was he really a man, a human entity, a personality like ourselves, or was he merely a sort of spiritual solvent, sent . . . to precipitate whatever sincerity there was in us, and show us what the truth was concerning our relations to each other?[33]

As Altruria is not described until the end of each novel, the contrast between America and utopia is, for the most part, implicit. Before Altruria is presented in detail, utopia is used mainly to make credible the innocent astonishment of Homos at the discrepancy between what America is and what it purports to be.

Howells's method is different from Bellamy's or Wells's. He first

[30]Howells, *Letters*, p. 28.
[31]Friedrich Schiller, *The Aesthetic Letters, Essays, and the Philosophical Letters,* trans. J. Weiss (Boston: Charles Little and James Brown, 1845), p. 46.
[32]Howells, *Through the Eye*, p. 231. *Walden Two* illustrates another facet of the means-end dilemma. Skinner claims his utopia is not static but motivated by "a fervent urge to push forward. . . ." Skinner, *Walden Two*, pp. 241–242. The urge is caused by the desire to create a perfect science of behavior, which science has been presented as the means to achieving utopia. As the means become the end, *Walden Two* doubles back on itself and becomes self-contained. Unlike Howells, Skinner appears to be blissfully unaware of what has occurred.
[33]Howells, *A Traveller*, p. 113.

A Traveller and *Through the*   185
Eye of the Needle as a
Critique of the Present

contrasts American practice with American ideals; only after the discrepancy between the two has been made clear is utopia offered as a blueprint for social change. This method enables Howells to make his criticism of existing society much more independent of the proposed utopian solution than is the case with Bellamy and Wells, whose criticisms rely directly on the contrast between utopia and the present. Homos' initial anonymity is reminiscent of the classical utopian narrator. He is unwilling to make direct comparisons between utopia and the present and is content to imply that he knows, from Altrurian experience, that American ideals can be put into practice. To the extent that utopia is not an attractive blueprint for future change, Howells's criticisms of America are all the more forceful for being relatively independent of utopia.

Homos discovers, during his visit, that the major contradiction in American society is the juxtaposition of a democratic political tradition and an aristocratic social tradition. He finds it difficult to understand how his well-to-do hosts reconcile social stratification, unequal opportunity, and the business ethic of each man for himself with the ideals to which Americans pay lip service: Christian doctrine and the Declaration of Independence. Homos' questions about the quality of American family life, social ambition, and religious belief derive from his taking his sophisticated hosts' ideals more seriously than they do. He observes, for instance, that rural and urban poverty exist in the midst of plenty, and he wonders how both organized business and labor can accept such conditions and still assume that people enjoy any real equality.

The brunt of Homos' criticism is directed against the well-to-do urban middle class who perpetuate an economy based on self-interest and egoism. The pragmatic American answer is that some inequality is inevitable, that a system without incentives based on material rewards and deprivations is against human nature. When pressed, Americans point for proof to the existing social structure of which they are the beneficiaries.

Homos' final answer to American skepticism about the possibility of change is to describe Altruria, how it came into being, and what it is. Altruria's history is a thinly disguised sketch of Western development. It began with a temporary conversion to Christian brotherhood and developed through political tyranny to a democracy, first based on competitive and later on monopoly capitalism. Contemporary America is compared to the stage in Altrurian history when monopoly capitalism had gained control of the courts and legislature and used them to further its own interests.

Howells's A Traveller from
Altruria and Through the Eye
of the Needle

186

But Altruria did not remain at this stage of development. Once the deprived became aware that their suffering was unnecessary, they used the one weapon monopoly capitalism had forgotten about, "the despised and neglected suffrage."[34] Monopoly capitalism was voted out of existence, and its power was transferred to a government that, guided by the new civic consciousness, proceeded to establish Altruria in its present form.

When Howells describes Altruria's history, his approach becomes that of the modern utopian, concerned with development in time. Homos accordingly warns his audience that to understand Altruria they must understand the conditions from which it has evolved. And in effect, Altruria makes best sense when contrasted to its own past or to the American present, for Altruria is really America without the latter's arbitrary and inequitable economic arrangements. The differences between the two countries, Homos declares, are differences of degree, not of kind:

Logically, the Americans should be what the Altrurians are, since their polity embodies our belief that all men are born equal, with the right to life, liberty, and the pursuit of happiness; but that illogically . . . they still cling to the economical ideals of Europe, and hold that men are born socially unequal. . . . It is in their public life and civic life that Altruria prevails; it is in their social and domestic life that Europe prevails. . . .[35]

As the description of Altruria is developed, it becomes a symbol of what is still possible for America, or for those of her inhabitants who desire a more humane social order in which poverty has been eliminated and men enjoy their work, assured of a sufficient livelihood. And the resemblance is perhaps even closer than Howells realized, for despite its name altruism has not replaced egoism in his utopia. Altruria is far too prosperous and content with itself to afford very frequent occasions for the exercise of altruism:

Illogical and insensate as their [the shipwrecked sailors'] system was, their character sometimes had a beauty, a sublimity which was not possible to Altrurians even, for it was performed in the face of risks and chances which their happy conditions relieved them from.[36]

That aesthetic and satisfying work, rather than altruism, is Howells's social ideal is evident when the author actually describes life in utopia and

[34]Ibid, p. 180.
[35]Howells, Through the Eye, p. 25.
[36]Ibid., p. 149.

A Traveller and Through the
Eye of the Needle as a
Critique of the Present

187

seemingly becomes aware that it offers even less scope for altruism than does America. At times Howells suggests that Altruria's superiority consists in a broader exercise of sympathies than is possible in America, where sympathy is limited to the immediate family. But the indiscriminate emotionalism with which the Altrurians react to the tale of the shipwrecked soldiers is not very edifying, and Howells rightly does not insist on this point.

Howells is equally aware of another facet of the problem. Those who condone poverty because it offers an opportunity for charity display an egoism that more than vitiates the moral value of charity:

"Do you really think Christ meant that you *ought* always to have the poor with you?" [Homos] asked.
"Why, of course!" she answered triumphantly. "How else are the sympathies of the rich to be cultivated?"[37]

But Howells finds it difficult to admit the consequences of this logic for Altruria, and shifts to the different question of whether compassion has greater moral value when it is difficult to exercise than when it is easy. He concludes that moral actions have greater value when they are easy and therefore more prevalent. The conclusion is reached by an analogy: Homos compares infrequent moral acts to rare and beautiful buildings that become lost in their ugly and squalid environment.

The consequence of Howells's architectural analogy is to make the ethical quality of an act depend on the pleasure it affords the observer. Howells's dilemma is awkward. He is not at ease with the implications of his analogy, which substitutes aesthetic for moral criteria or makes the two identical. But if the value of moral activity is made to depend on its efficacy, on its ability to change things for the better, America has the advantage over Altruria. For moral activity to have value apart from its results, Howells needs an objective criterion of value independent of utopia and serving to measure activity within it. Without such a criterion, whether Howells's ideal is aesthetic objects produced by the work process or aesthetic moral acts, the measure easily becomes the subjective pleasure of the observer.

Like Wells, Howells finds the utopian ideal already prefigured in American life, in spite of prevailing conditions and not because of them. Howells is not, however, as explicit as Wells in identifying the sources of possible change. He suggests that those members of the middle class who feel

[37]Howells, *A Traveller*, p. 100 (Howells's italics).

themselves threatened by the trusts and syndicates might be willing to "Altrurianize" America. But Homos stumbles when he tries to explain how middle-class egoism will produce Altruria:

> . . . it will not be wonderful that this Altrurian miracle should have been wrought here in the very heart, and from the very heart of egoism. . . . We know that like produces like only up to a certain point, and that then unlike comes of like since all things are of one essence. . . .[38]

Eveleth Strange is representative of the type of social consciousness Howells hopes will become more widespread in America. But in marrying Homos, she in effect abandons America to its own fate. Howells makes a tale of romantic indecisiveness from the millionairess's inability to decide between her wealth and her Altrurian. The story glosses over the social implications of her decision, which Homos seconds by insisting that he could live happily only in Altruria. The attitudes of both appear to be one of *sauve qui peut*. To the extent that Homos is more than a disembodied conscience, the edge of his criticism is badly blunted by his indifference to helping change the conditions he has found so unsatisfactory.

Unlike Bellamy, who describes history as moving inexorably in the direction of utopia, Howells considers it quite possible that America will either continue to muddle along in its present fashion or develop a new form of slavery in which the proletariat is legally owned by the state. What he hopes is that Altruria will make men increasingly aware of the defects and anomalies in their social organization. Howells's answer to the question of how such social awareness can be developed is that conditions in America are "unconsciously provisional."[39] Man has always been better than his environment, for if such were not the case he would still be a savage.

Altruria is a "testimony of a potential civility in all states,"[40] says Homos. This civility is still present in rural Americans who make their living from the soil and have not had their consciences blunted by an economic system that rewards the few at the expense of the many. Howells has been criticized for his overromantic description of rural America.[41] But if this is the group Howells finally selects to achieve utopia, the romantic description may not have been a mistake.

---

[38]Howells, *Letters*, pp. 20–21. Cf. *A Traveller*, p. 197.
[39]Howells, *Through the Eye*, p. 160.
[40]Ibid., p. 3.
[41]George N. Bennett, *William Dean Howells: The Development of a Novelist* (Norman: University of Oklahoma Press, 1959), p. 204.

A *Traveller* and *Through the*
Eye of The Needle as a
Thought Experiment

189

A Traveller and Through the Eye of the Needle as a Thought Experiment

Howells is more aware than either Bellamy or Wells of the difficulties of conceiving of utopia as a viable, actually existing society. In the introduction to *Through the Eye of the Needle,* he contrasts the sociological value of the first part of the book, in which Homos exposes the contradictions implicit in American life, with the insufficient sense of reality conveyed by Eveleth Strange's description of Altruria in the second part:

Either we have no terms for conditions so unlike our own that they cannot be reported to us with absolute intelligence, or else there is in every experience of them an essential vagueness and uncertainty.[42]

Somewhat defensively, therefore, Howells suggests that Eveleth Strange's letters from Altruria will be of interest to the reader primarily because they complete the story of her love affair with the enigmatic Mr. Homos.

The sociological value of *Through the Eye of the Needle,* its critique of the present, troubles Howells because it is so unrelated to the description of utopia proper. The ideal is so different from the actual that he calls Altruria a civilization fundamentally alien to the American one, leaving "a sort of misgiving as to the reality of the things seen and heard."[43]

The author never indicates that he thought of Altruria as a way of exploring the implications of his ideals in thought, an experiment requiring distance from the constraints and anomalies of the present. As a novelist, Howells was more concerned with his inability to make the two parts of *Through the Eye of the Needle* into a coherent story. However, if utopia is considered, not as a romance, but as a thought experiment, the value of constructing it is in its very difference and distance from the present, its ability to offer both the author and his reader a standpoint outside of their own society from which they can question and criticize it. Aristides Homos has already taken this critical position when, as a spiritual solvent, he shows Americans what is wrong with their plutocratic country. But, as Homos notes, he has few imitators:

Only once have I happened to find anyone who questioned the situation from a standpoint outside of it, and that was a shabbily dressed man whom I overheard talking to a poor woman . . . she listened without rancor to the man as he unfolded the truth to her concerning the conditions in which they lived, if it may be called living.[44]

---

[42]Howells, *Through the Eye,* pp. xii–xiii.
[43]Ibid., pp. xii–xiii.
[44]Howells, *Letters,* p. 45.

Howells's *A Traveller from*
Altruria and *Through the Eye*
of the Needle

190

Howells has the banker remark irritably that whenever Homos is asked how Altruria has solved the problems that beset America, the latter replies that the problems do not exist in Altruria. While the coherence of utopia, its lack of problems, is a defect for those interested in immediate change, it becomes an asset if utopia is used to visualize a society in which values are realized fully and without contradictions. Homos is describing just such an absence of limitation in utopia when he compares the new civic consciousness that accompanied the birth of Altruria to a "disembodied spirit released to the life beyond this and freed from all the selfish cares and greeds of the flesh."[45] In *A Hazard of New Fortunes,* Howells's spokesman, Basil March, objecting to "this economic chance world in which we live," expresses a similar desire to simplify:

It ought to be law as inflexible in human affairs as the order of day and night in the physical world, that if a man will work he shall both rest and eat. . . . Nothing less ideal than this satisfies the reason.[46]

In his perception of the fragility of Altruria, Howells is closer to the classical tradition, which views utopia as a device for gaining perspective on the present, than to the modern tradition, which regards utopia as a means of transforming it. He is also closer to the classical utopians in the manner in which he held Christianity to be valuable: "We shall not have fraternity, human brotherhood without trying for it. From nature it did not come; it came from the heart of man, who in the midst of nature is above it."[47] If Howells believes that human nature has values available to it independently of its environment, the Americans whom Homos describes most certainly do not. They share a common environment but no agreement about what human nature should be, which may explain why they cling so tenaciously to their common environment.

A likely explanation for Howells's reticence about whatever religious beliefs he held and for his restraint in picturing them in Altruria is his desire, despite the lack of any agreed upon view of human nature, to influence "the popular fancy of our enormous commonplace average."[48] He attributed the

[45]Howells, *A Traveller,* p. 181.
[46]William Dean Howells, *A Hazard of New Fortunes* (New York: The New American Library, Signet paperback, 1965), p. 380.
[47]William Dean Howells, *Century,* LI, 935, cited in Hough, *The Quiet Rebel,* p. 63.
[48]Howells, essay from the *North American Review,* December 1900, in *Criticism and Fiction,* p. 246.

A Traveller and Through the
Eye of The Needle as a
Thought Experiment

191

uccess of *Looking Backward* to Bellamy's unerring grasp of how the average man thought and felt.[49] And Basil March, wondering whether man changes at all and if so by what agency, says:

Well, it won't do to say, the Holy Spirit indwelling. That would sound like cant at this day. But the old fellows that used to say that had some glimpses of the truth. They knew that it is the still, small voice that the soul heeds, not the deafening blasts of doom.[50]

As Howells can no longer appeal to a public, commonly held notion of what is good, the joint exploration of ideals in thought by both writer and reader, one of the strengths of the classical utopias, is not available to him. The alternative—a private investigation of ideals that clarify or reinforce the author's personal beliefs—Howells may have found unnecessary. Or he may have tried such an exercise and thought it futile if posterity has replaced God as judge and justifier of men. Howells's values are Christian ones and consequently meant to be public and shared by all men. But the reference must be seen as private, rather as if Howells admits to missing the mark, when he says somewhat noncommittally of his utopia: "It is, however, an interesting psychological result, and it continues the tradition of all the observers of ideal conditions from Sir Thomas More down to William Morris." When Christian values evoke no public response, they do, of necessity, become private. Howells perhaps is indicating as much when he warns "the thoughtful reader" to expect "imperfect glimpses of a civilization fundamentally alien to her [sic] own. . . ."[51]

The lesson that modern utopian authors can learn from experimenting with values in thought is rather ambiguous. The ideals that utopias embody without contradiction or ambiguity lose their meaning if they are not eventually brought to bear upon the present. Values require the resistant factuality of the here and now in order to remain useful. When they are either completely divorced from the present or entirely identified with it, they appear futile and unnecessary. Perhaps what is best learned about values from investigating them in thought is their limitations. Thought experiments and the values that both form and inform them need to be held in tension with the world of particulars that they try to remake in their image.

[49]Howells, "The Romantic Imagination," *European and American Masters*, pp. 186 ff.
[50]Howells, *A Hazard of New Fortunes*, p. 422.
[51]Howells, *Through the Eye*, p. xiii.

An exchange between Homos and his banker friend indicates that Howells might have sensed the ambiguity of his thought experiment, without being too dismayed by it:

"You can't have unselfishness till you have Altrurianism," I returned. "You can't put the cart before the horse."

"Oh, yes we can," he returned in his tone of banter. "We always put the cart before the horse in America, so that the horse can see where the cart is going."[52]

[52]Howells, *Letters*, p. 31.

Conclusion

10

Twentieth-Century Utopias

The paradox of progress, Northrop Frye has suggested, is that its only conceivable goal is greater stability, an order more secure and predictable than the present one.[1] In a similar fashion, one's vision of a better world (and here perhaps may be a dividing line between utopias and science fiction) is predicated upon a constant and ample supply of what is already known and valued: peace, plenty, intellectual and emotional development. Thus Bellamy attempted to provide a secure environment for equality and Wells for innovation by eliminating the oppressive aspects of social life that distorted these values or impeded their realization.

As beneficiaries of the battle of the ancients and the moderns, those who lived in the nineteenth century knew that their era was qualitatively different from preceding times, and that the future was capable of bringing even greater qualitative change. Moreover, the span of future time available to man appeared to be vastly increased, the result of new geological theories that extended the period of man's presence on earth from a few thousand years of biblical history to the hundreds of millions of years of geological time.[2] Theories of biological evolution gave structure and significance to the vast stretches of time through which men were now understood to have lived and developed, and became part of the climate of opinion that influenced Bellamy, Wells, and Howells alike.

One of the best examples of the sense of multiple possibilities that accompanied the new awareness of time is Olaf Stapledon's Last and First Men (1930).[3] Man's future development is traced through eighteen different transformations over a period of two billion years, during which heights of technological and intellectual brilliance are attained and then supplanted by other cultures, more primitive, or empathic, or sensual. Among the species that evolve (including the last, caught in the waning solar energy of the sun's decay) are some with such different mental and spiritual equipment as to seem barely human; they appear to be not so much either good or evil as simply strange and even alien.

Stapledon's vision of mankind's spacious futures, on earth or among the stars, still reflects the late nineteenth-century climate of progressivism, with its confidence in man's ability to handle change and shape it to ends of his own devising. In more recent utopias a note of urgency, of time running

[1]Northrop Frye, The Modern Century (Toronto: Oxford University Press, 1967), p. 33.
[2]H. Bruce Franklin, "Fictions of the Future," Stamford Today, Series 1, No. 17 (Summer 1966), 8.
[3]Olaf Stapledon, Last and First Men and Star Maker (New York: Dover Publications, reprint, 1968).

out, begins to be clearly heard. T. H. Huxley had already sounded the warning by 1880: cosmic evolution does not of itself issue in social and moral improvement; the latter depends not on imitating but on combating and checking the cosmic process.

Wells's *samurai* are one answer to Huxley's challenge. Another response, in utopias such as *Islandia* (1942) and *Sedge* (1963), is the simpler society that reasserts human proportions and purposes in a world increasingly recalcitrant to men's designs.[4] These utopias, frequently spatially rather than temporally located, present themselves as oases of sanity and calm in an age when such qualities are given short shrift. Their criticism of contemporary society is really from the perspective of a simpler and more humane past, even when it is recognized that the population is already too great, the technology already too developed, to permit such alternatives as an agrarian economy to be more than a nostalgic dream of what might have been. While individuals may always choose to leave their uncongenial surroundings to live permanently in such utopias, there is a greater recognition than, for instance, in Howells's utopia that it is not so easy for society to dismantle or abandon its inherited social apparatus.

Utopias such as *Islandia* and *Sedge* rely on civilized surroundings to produce civil human beings, and in their emphasis on a decent environment as a prerequisite for decent behavior they are quite within the modern utopian spirit. When these utopias are not in jeopardy from the economic or territorial imperialism of outside powers, they are pleasant, humane societies in which the essential drama is that of the human life cycle: birth, love, and death. Like Howells's utopia, they appear to be private societies without public purposes or collective goals, unless called upon to defend their existence against outside threats.

Mention should be made of two other types of twentieth-century utopian writing. W. H. Hudson's *A Crystal Age* (1906) and Herbert Read's *The Green Child* (1935) both portray utopias dedicated to the aesthetic life.[5] In these societies men are primarily artists, absorbed in creating timelessly beautiful objects and in contemplating the endless variations and nuances of beauty to be found in them. The contemplation of beauty is, of course, an

[4]Austin Tappan Wright, *Islandia* (New York: Holt, Rinehart and Winston, Inc., 1942); Louis J. Halle, *Sedge: The Anthropologo-Psychologico-Socio-Politico-Cultural Complex of This Remote and Little-Known Country* (New York: Frederick A. Praeger, 1963).
[5]W. H. Hudson, *A Crystal Age* (London: T. Fisher Unwin, 1906); Herbert Read, *The Green Child* (New York: New Directions Publishing Corporation, n.d.).

activity that is well suited to a changeless society. Unlike their classical counterparts, Hudson and Read do not claim that their ideal satisfies the true requirements of all men's natures or that it transcends the society that sustains it. They do imply that a perfection of sorts is entirely present within their ideal societies. It is as if men had become gods, free to create in their own or any other image and, like gods, were held to no standards or limits except of their own making. In such visions, the line between utopia and fantasy is stretched very thin, for in their perfect self-sufficiency, their ability to incorporate an entire universe of significance in a single artifact, these future utopians seem no longer recognizably human.

Another type of utopia, exemplified by Huxley's *Island* (1962) and Marcuse's *Eros and Civilization* (1955) can be labeled experiential utopias.[6] Whether through Huxley's *moksha* medicine (a mind-expanding drug) or through Marcuse's increased libidinal freedom, the ideal of this type of utopia is to augment man's self-awareness, his capacity to feel and to enjoy his feelings. Both Marcuse's utopia, which presupposes an increasingly self-sufficient technological capacity, and Huxley's, based on a deliberately simplified standard of living, are protests against a technology that absorbs man's energies, dulls his perceptions, and assimilates his creative capacities to its own mechanical and repetitive processes.

Skinner's *Walden Two,* despite its behavorial emphasis on reinforcing "desirable" activity and its reticence about the significance or even the existence of psychic states, should also be included among the experiential utopias:

In Walden Two no one worries about the government except the few to whom that worry has been assigned. . . . The only thing that matters is one's day-to-day happiness and a secure future. Any infringement there would undoubtedly "arouse the electorate."[7]

Although he claims that men with goals and projects, the problem solver and the men with grand designs, will not be neglected in his utopia, Skinner's society is most plausible when it claims to satisfy the majority of people who "if they have any long-time plan it's little more than the anticipation

---

[6]Aldous Huxley, *Island* (New York: Bantam Books, Inc., 1963); Herbert Marcuse, *Eros and Civilization: A Philosophical Inquiry into Freud* (New York: Alfred A. Knopf, Inc., and Random House, 1962).
[7]B. F. Skinner, *Walden Two* (New York: The Macmillan Company, 1948), p. 225.

of some natural course—they look forward to having children, to seeing the children grow up, and so on."[8]

Like the antiutopias of Zamiatin, Huxley, and Orwell, twentieth-century utopias are criticisms of a civilization in which human purposes are blunted or thwarted by the social arrangements that should serve them. These utopias remain part of the modern utopian tradition, not so much because they share the conviction of their nineteenth-century predecessors that society will change in the direction of utopia, but because of their belief that what is valuable for man is distorted by the present environment but could be more fully expressed or more adequately enjoyed in a society with different social arrangements.

While there is less emphasis than in the nineteenth-century utopia on continued innovative activity once utopia is achieved, twentieth-century utopias still require some form of development to circumvent the inhuman perfection of the fully achieved utopia. With the partial exception of the aesthetic type of utopia, twentieth-century utopias continue to believe in the desirability of change, but its locus is shifted from the public act to the private psychic state. There is no doubt that this shift constitutes a considerable advantage in portraying utopia, for the psychic state is interior and private, not susceptible to the same type of portrayal or the same sort of judgment as the public act. But the difficulty confronting Wells in his desire to construct a dynamic utopia remains unresolved. By what standard is psychic development or psychic satisfaction to be measured? Is a common standard possible for men of diverse capacities and a variety of endowments? If so, how could such a standard be justified as more than the private preference of the author? And if there is no common standard, what does it signify to talk of development when it would be impossible to establish regression?

Twentieth-century utopias are more cautious than their nineteenth-century predecessors in voicing any claim to universality in the future. Nor can they command men's attention on the grounds that the values they exhibit fulfill universal requirements of men's nature. Twentieth-century utopias are private both in their emphasis on inner human development and satisfaction and in their awareness that the ideals they recommend are culturally and historically determined—and to that extent transitory. The societies they build are civil and humane societies, emphasizing fairness,

[8]Ibid., p. 138.

cooperation, and tolerance. But as Alasdair MacIntyre has observed, tolerance and fairness are secondary virtues: their existence in a moral universe
is secondary to or dependent upon a primary set of virtues relating to the
goals men pursue.[9] The secondary virtues permit us to go about our
projects, but their cultivation does not help us to discover in what activities
we ought to be engaged. And in the absence of such activities within the
twentieth-century utopia, in the portrayal of societies in which being is
emphasized over doing and no one exists at the expense of another, upon
what is tolerance to be exercised or fairness employed?

The Two Utopian Traditions
The concern of this study has been to suggest some salient differences
between classical and modern utopian thought. The most important difference is between the classical utopian author, who views his utopia as a
permanent state of being that answers the requirements of man's nature,
and the modern utopian author, who considers his utopia to be a stage in
man's continued development. Despite the important differences that derive from their assumptions about human nature, classical and modern
utopias have common uses. Both are instruments with which the authors
can investigate the implications of particular ideals, and both are persuasive
devices that attempt to show that a value is desirable by picturing a society
in which it is fully realized.

The developmental view of man's nature presumes that new problems and new challenges will continue to present themselves in upopia and
that men will continue to develop in response to those challenges. The
difficulty is that the character of utopian reality, in which the author has
included all the values he believes are important for men, does not readily
allow either novelty or serious change to be convincingly portrayed. In his
desire to see utopia achieve realilty, the modern author concentrates his
attention on those motives or aspirations of men which are thwarted by
present social arrangements and which are to be allowed adequate expression when utopia arrives. But in his eagerness to show that utopia can be
attained, the author neglects to describe how those characteristics of man's
nature will provide the needed impetus for continued development once
utopia is achieved.

H. G. Wells exemplifies the problems that the utopian structure

[9]Alasdair MacIntyre, *Secularization and Moral Change* (London: Oxford University Press, 1967),
pp. 24 ff.

makes for a modern author. He tries to provide the impetus for develop-ment by calling innovation a permanent characteristic of man's nature; he is not convincing because he fails to show the reader that this innovative potentiality is capable of bearing results in any cause other than the estab-lishment of utopia. When describing the nonutopian present, Wells views man as a historical animal without fixed traits or constant characteristics—a man as flexible as the environment that he molds to meet his changing needs and demands. Yet in utopia Wells postulates that creativity will be-come the dominant trait in man's nature, even though, once preutopian problems have been solved, creativity is without substance upon which to work. Despite Wells's claims, creativity appears to be either a case of special pleading, an unsuccessful attempt to circumvent the static utopian format, or simply an indication of the author's faith that the future will not let men down.

The unchanging character of utopian reality is better adapted to classical utopian assumptions about human nature. When human nature is thought to have permanent requirements that all men share in common, the static character of utopian reality is an asset in portraying a society designed to satisfy these permanent requirements. While the values through which men find self-completion in the classical utopia are expressed in utopian social arrangements, their existence is not dependent upon those social arrangements. Utopian social arrangements are congruent with and serve as a support for the good that transcends utopian reality, and it is the nature of the good which gives primary meaning and value to the activity that takes place within utopia.

The classical utopian author believes that there is a good that will prove permanently satisfying to men if they can be made to see or if they are able to understand its real nature. Classical utopian authors remain aware, moreover, of men's limitations. They do not expect that utopia's realization is imminent, and the utopian enterprise remains valuable for them even if utopian social arrangements never come into existence. Socrates is able to show Glaucon and Adeimantus something about the nature of justice and about the Good from which justice derives its meaning; the greater under-standing they obtain from Socrates' picture is valuable in itself, even if the society in which they live remains indifferent or even antagonistic to such knowledge.

The modern utopian author, in his eagerness to see the ideal state become reality, portrays the utopian ideal through utopian institutions. By equating the good with particular social arrangements, he implicitly identifies what is valuable in existing society with the ability to move in the direction of utopia. Once utopia is achieved, the problem of how man is to find new enterprises and purposes is left unresolved. The problem is all the more unsettling for the modern author for whom the utopian status quo offers no permanent value; the value of utopian arrangements is, rather, that they continue to offer malleable material through which the innovative traits of man's nature express themselves. Almost against his will, the modern utopian author gives the stamp of finality to what he intends as provisional, thus freezing future utopians into a permanent and arbitrary mold, which he is unable to justify.

This study makes no claim that either classical or modern utopias exhaust the ways of critically examining whether a value is worth holding. Utopias are one way of trying to understand a particular value by holding it apart and developing its implications in isolation from competing values. The permanent importance of classical utopias lies in their attempt to convince someone else of the desirability of an ideal by drawing a picture of what a society would be like were it molded entirely to the specifications of that ideal. The classical utopian author justified his enterprise by the belief that his picture of the utopian ideal would evoke recognition in his reader, whose nature required such a good for its permanent satisfaction.

The modern utopian author who uses utopia as a persuasive device encounters a different problem. To the extent that he believes that man's nature is characterized by the *diversity* of legitimate ends it seeks, and by the *variety* of different values by which it can be guided, he cannot expect that the values he portrays in utopia will necessarily evoke recognition from his interlocutor. The modern utopian picture can reinforce the belief of someone who already holds the values it portrays, or it can persuade someone who comes to it without any particular convictions about what is desirable for men in the future. But when two men hold divergent and conflicting values, or when they hold different priorities within the same set of values (all of which cannot be realized at once), the modern utopia cannot persuade them to change either their values or their priorities.

Modern utopian authors believe that the common environment men share directly influences the nature of the values they hold and the ends they desire. Because man's future environment will continue to influence his values, it is important that its creation be a joint endeavor, and it is this cooperative aspect of the modern utopian enterprise that causes difficulty.

The lack of prior agreement about which values the future society will accommodate can prevent change in the direction of utopia from occurring, and because such change is the strong suit of modern utopias, the enterprise accordingly flounders.

While modern utopias may not be able to resolve disagreements about value preferences, they can function as thought experiments in which the implications of any one value is explored. To the degree that the utopian picture continues to make men more conscious of the implications of their values and more aware of what those values exclude as well as what they permit, the modern utopian enterprise is valuable. If human nature is indeed of the provisional, continually changing character that modern utopian authors describe, a cautious and tentative adherence to any one set of values is a sensible, indeed a desirable, course.

Utopias as Play

The entire utopian enterprise may also be thought of as a form of serious play. Like children with building blocks, utopia builders reconstruct existing social arrangements as if they were transparent to the will. Utopian play is a serious game, however, with rules and an objective: to find those social arrangements in which human nature will be most free to carry on the activities that endow it with value and significance.

Like any form of play, utopia building is as important for what it excludes as for what it includes. This particular type of play includes a willingness to suspend disbelief about human nature, to relinquish old assumptions, and to explore new ones. Play is a disinterested form of activity with no concern for everyday needs and desires. In Johan Huizinga's description, play is a temporary world within the ordinary world dedicated to the performance of an act apart. The act of play "creates order, *is* order. Into an imperfect world and into the confusion of life it brings a temporary, a limited perfection."[10]

It might be added that not to build utopias is to risk acquiescence in another type of game. Politics has sometimes been described as an activity in which the players become so absorbed in scoring points that they forget that the survival of their side is not the only result for which they may be held responsible. The risk may be all the more present in politics because, unlike the more self-conscious utopian form of play, it has no natural termi-

[10]Johan Huizinga, *Homo Ludens: A Study of the Play Element in Culture* (Boston: Beacon Press, Beacon paperback, 1955), p. 10 (Huizinga's italics).

nal point. When the gaming aspect of politics becomes prevalent, the skill and foresight required are capable of absorbing the energies of the players and satisfying one part of man's intelligence.

There is another part of man's intelligence which the exercise of skill and foresight does not saitsfy. Whether thought mirrors an intelligible order that exists independently of it or attempts itself to impose meaning on the world, in both cases the mind obeys its own directives of coherence, harmony, or stability. If these requirements of thought were merely idiosyncrasies of the mind, one would question the mind's attempt to confer meaning on a reality whose nature may be of an entirely different sort. There seems to be, however, a part of man's intelligence which is not satisfied unless it can postulate the existence of values that accord with the requirements of mind but do not exist merely to satisfy those requirements.

Classical utopian thought, as this study has interpreted it, assumed the existence of an intelligible, stable, and harmonious order that mind could attempt, always inadequately, to interpret. For utopian thinkers after Kant, unable to *confirm* their belief in an order that is intelligible, much less stable and harmonious, such beliefs took the form of postulates. In both cases, of course, the conviction or the hypothesis that there is a stable and coherent order independent of the knowing mind in no way explains *why* stability or coherence is valuable.

If utopia building is conceived as a form of play, it would be well to insist on the seriousness of play, which the participants can choose to extend into real life. As either a standard of judgment or a critique, utopias invite their readers to a fresh appraisal of the present. Indeed, were they to shunt aside this task of reappraisal, utopias would be indistinguishable from fantasy. To lose the tension between utopia and the real world is to risk making the content of utopia

. . . merely typical, formal, and *representative,* and thus losing one term of the dialectic that goes on between spirit and the conditioned. . . . [To lose] the actuality of the conditioned, the literality of matter, the peculiar authenticity and authority of the merely denotative . . . is to lose not a material fact but a spiritual one, for it is a fact of spirit that it must exist in a world which requires it to engage in so dispiriting an occupation as hunting for a house.[11]

[11]Lionel Trilling, *The Opposing Self: Nine Essays in Criticism* (New York: The Viking Press, Compass paperback, 1959), p. 93 (Trilling's italics). Trilling's comment occurs in a discussion of *A Hazard of New Fortunes,* in which the house hunting mentioned is an episode.

Classical and modern utopias represent the two terms of this dialectic. Classical utopias make free with the literality of matter. They are based, not on desire, but on a disdain of desire. They belong to a time when men thought they knew what human nature was. The form of change in which they were interested was change from potentiality into actuality, the two terms marking the limits within which men could move. If the classical utopia maintained a deliberate distance from its own society, it was no less aware of the distance that separated all man-made objects, including utopia, from the fully actual or the ideal.

Modern utopias are based on desire—the desire to change an unpalatable present that fetters men's spirit, while reserving a place in the future for further desire. If their future contains no limits, not even the limits imposed by the past, in a modern utopia like Howells's there is a rueful recognition that such a future may exceed man's ability either to make or to imagine.

If is surely no accident that when men became interested in social change, their sense of the source of complexity shifted from the ideal to the actual. Classical and modern utopias may be compared to two persons on a seesaw. The classical utopian is at ease in the air; he uses the complexity of utopia's ideals to maintain a tension and distance from the inadequate present. The modern utopian feels the weight of the present and uses it to anchor his feet on the ground, to give weight and direction to his ideal. In their distinctive ways, both traditions acknowledge the weight of the present even while building utopias on ideals that testify to its inadequacy.

Today it may be that the modern utopian has blocked the view of his more distant predecessor. It is with the hope of shedding some light on what is distinctive in both traditions that this study has been written.

Bibliography

The bibliography includes only the utopias and the commentaries on utopia cited in footnotes to this study.

Adkins, Arthur W. H. *Merit and Responsibility: A Study in Greek Values.* Oxford: At the Clarendon Press, 1960.

Andreae, Johann Valentin. *Reipublicae Christianopolitanae descriptio.* Argentorati: Sumptibus Laeredum Lazari Zetneri, 1619.

――――. *Christianopolis: An Ideal State of the Seventeenth Century.* Translated by Felix Emil Held. New York: Oxford University Press, 1916.

Arendt, Hannah. *The Human Condition.* New York: Doubleday & Company, Anchor paperback, 1959.

Aristotle. *The Basic Works of Aristotle.* Edited and with an introduction by Richard McKeon. New York: Random House, 1941.

Bacon, Francis. *The New Atlantis* in *Ideal Commonwealths.* Edited by Henry Morley. New York: The Colonial Press, 1901.

Barker, Ernest. *From Alexander to Constantine: Passages and Documents Illustrating the History of Social and Political Ideas: 336 B.C.–A.D. 337.* Oxford: At the Clarendon Press, 1956.

Becker, Carl L. *The Heavenly City of the Eighteenth-Century Philosophers.* New Haven: Yale University Press, 1932.

Bellamy, Edward. *Doctor Heidenhoff's Process.* London: William Reeves. 183 Fleet Street, E. C., n.d. [not before 1880].

――――. *Equality.* New York: D. Appleton and Company, 1897.

――――. *Looking Backward: 2000–1887.* New York: Grosset & Dunlap, n.d. [ca. 1909].

――――. *Looking Backward: 2000–1887.* Edited with an introduction by John L. Thomas. Cambridge, Mass.: The Belknap Press of Harvard University, 1967.

――――. *The Religion of Solidarity.* Edited by Arthur E. Morgan. Yellow Springs, Ohio: Antioch Bookplate Company, 1940.

――――. *Selected Writings on Religion and Society.* Edited by Joseph Schiffman. New York: The Liberal Arts Press, 1955.

Bennett, George N. *William Dean Howells: The Development of a Novelist.* Norman: University of Oklahoma Press, 1959.

Bergonzi, Bernard. *The Early H. G. Wells: A Study of the Scientific Romances.* Manchester: Manchester University Press, 1961.

Bierman, Judah. "Science and Society in the *New Atlantis* and Other Renaissance Utopias," *Publications of the Modern Language Association of America,* LXXVIII (December 1963), 492–500.

Blitzer, Charles. *An Immortal Commonwealth: The Political Thought of James Harrington.* New Haven: Yale University Press, 1960.

Boas, George. *Essays on Primitivism and Related Ideas in the Middle Ages.* Baltimore: The Johns Hopkins Press, 1948.

Bodin, Jean. *The Six Books of the Commonwealth.* Abridged and translated by M. J. Tooley. Oxford: Basil Blackwell, n.d.

Bredvold, Louis I. *The Natural History of Sensibility.* Detroit: Wayne State University Press, paperback, 1962.

Brooks, Van Wyck. *Howells: His Life and World.* New York: E. P. Dutton & Co., Inc., 1959.

———. *The World of H. G. Wells.* New York: Mitchell Kennerley, 1915.

Brüggemann, Fritz. *Utopie und Robinsonade.* Weimar: A. Đuncker, 1914.

Burnet, John. *Greek Philosophy: Plato to Thales.* London: Macmillan & Co., Ltd., 1961.

Burtt, Edwin Arthur. *The Metaphysical Foundations of Modern Physical Science.* Garden City, N.Y.: Doubleday & Company, Inc., Anchor paperback, 1932.

———. *Types of Religious Philosophy.* Revised edition. New York: Harper and Brothers, 1951.

Butler, Samuel. *Erewhon and Erewhon Revisited.* New York: Random House, 1927.

Cabet, Étienne. *Voyage en Icarie.* Paris: Au Bureau du Populaire, Rue Jean-Jacques-Rousseau, 14, 1848.

Campanella, Thomas. *City of the Sun* in *Ideal Commonwealths.* Edited by Henry Morley. New York: The Colonial Press, 1901.

Cassirer, Ernst. *The Philosophy of the Enlightenment.* Translated by Fritz C. A. Koelln and James P. Pettegrove. Boston: Beacon Press, Beacon paperback, 1955.

Chambers, R. W. *Thomas More.* New York: Harcourt, Brace and Co., 1935.

Chappuis, Jean-Claude. *Le Plan Social de Jean-Claude Chappuis: Une Utopie Socialiste au XVIIIe Siècle.* Edited by Jacques Tout. Paris: Librairie du Recueil Sirey, 1942.

Close, A. J. "Commonplace Theories of Art and Nature in Classical Antiquity and in the Renaissance," *Journal of the History of Ideas,* XXX (October–December 1969), 467–486.

Cochrane, Charles Norris. *Christianity and Classical Culture: A Study of Thought and Action from Augustus to Augustine.* New York: Oxford University Press, 1957.

Condorcet, Marquis de. *Esquisse d'un tableau historique des progrès de l'esprit humain.* Posthumous work. Paris: Chez Agasse, L'An III de la République.

Connes, Georges, *Étude sur La Pensée de Wells.* N.p.: Librairie Hachette, 1926.

Cornford, Francis M., trans. *The Republic of Plato.* New York: Oxford University Press, 1945.

Cushman, Robert E. *Therapeia: Plato's Conception of Philosophy.* Chapel Hill: University of North Carolina Press, 1958.

Den Boer, W. "Graeco-Roman Historiography in Its Relation to Biblical and Modern Thinking," *History and Theory: Studies in the Philosophy of History,* VII (1968), 60–75.

Donner, H. W. *Introduction to Utopia.* Upsala, Sweden: Sidgwick & Jackson, Ltd., 1945.

Doughty, F. H. *H. G. Wells Educationist.* London: Jonathan Cape Ltd., 1926.

Duhamel, Albert P. "Medievalism of More's *Utopia*," *Studies in Philology,* LII (April 1955), 99–126.

Elliott, Robert C. "Saturnalia, Satire, and Utopia," *The Yale Review,* LV (Summer 1966), 521–536.

Engels, Friedrich. *Socialism: Utopian and Scientific,* in Karl Marx and Friedrich Engels, *Selected Works.* 2 vols. Moscow: Foreign Language Publishing House, 1962.

Erasmus, Desiderius. *The Praise of Folly.* Translated with essay and commentary by Hoyt Hopewell Hudson. Princeton: Princeton University Press, 1941.

Ferguson, Arthur B. Review of *The Complete Works of St. Thomas More,* Vol. IV: *Utopia,* in *Journal of the History of Ideas,* XXIX (April–June 1968), 303–310.

Forster, E. M. *The Eternal Moment and Other Stories.* New York: Grosset & Dunlap, Universal Library paperback, 1964.

Foster, M. B. *The Political Philosophies of Plato and Hegel.* Oxford: At the Clarendon Press, 1935.

Frank, Erich. *Philosophical Understanding and Religious Truth.* New York: Oxford University Press, 1945.

Franklin, H. Bruce. "Fictions of the Future," *Stamford Today,* Series 1, No. 17 (Summer 1966), 6–11.

Friedländer, Paul. *Plato: An Introduction.* Translated by Hans Meyerhoff. Bollingen Series, Vol. LIX. New York: Bollingen Foundation, 1958.

Frye, Northrop. *The Modern Century.* Toronto: Oxford University Press, 1967.

Gould, John. *The Development of Plato's Ethics.* Cambridge: At the University Press, 1955.

Grene, David. *Greek Political Theory: The Image of Man in Thucydides and Plato.* Chicago: The University of Chicago Press, 1965.

Gunnell, John G. *Political Philosophy and Time.* Middletown, Conn.: Wesleyan University Press, 1968.

Hale, J. R., ed. *The Evolution of British Historiography from Bacon to Namier.* Cleveland: The World Publishing Company, Meridian paperback, 1964.

Halle, Louis J. *Sedge: The Anthropologo-Psychologico-Socio-Politico-Cultural Complex of This Remote and Little-Known Country.* New York: Frederick A. Praeger, 1963.

Harrington, James. *The Commonwealth of Oceana* (reprint of the 1771 London edition) in *Works: The Oceana and Other Works.* Darmstadt: Scientia Verlag Aalen, 1963.

———. *The Political Writings of James Harrington: Representative Selections.* Edited with an introduction by Charles Blitzer. New York: The Liberal Arts Press, 1955.

Heiserman, A. R. "Satire in the *Utopia,*" *Publications of the Modern Language Association of America,* LXXVIII (December 1963), 163–174.

Held, Felix E., trans. *Christianopolis: An Ideal State of the Seventeenth Century,* by J. V. Andreae. New York: Oxford University Press, 1916.

Hertzka, Theodor. *Freeland, A Social Anticipation.* Translated by Arthur Ransom. London: Chatto & Windus, 1891.

Hexter, J. H. *More's Utopia: The Biography of an Idea.* New York: Harper & Row, Publishers, Torchbook edition, 1965.

Hough, Robert L. *The Quiet Rebel: William Dean Howells as Social Commentator.* Lincoln: University of Nebraska Press, 1959.

Howells, William Dean. *Criticism and Fiction and Other Essays.* Edited by Clara M. Kirk and Rudolf Kirk. New York: New York University Press, 1959.

———. *European and American Masters.* Edited by Clara Marburg Kirk and Rudolf Kirk. New York: New York University Press, 1963.

———. *A Hazard of New Fortunes.* New York: The New American Library, 1965.

———. *Letters of an Altrurian Traveller.* Introduction by Clara M. Kirk and Rudolf Kirk. Gainesville, Fla.: Scholars' Facsimiles and Reprints, 1961.

———. *Life in Letters of William Dean Howells.* Edited by Mildred Howells. 2 vols. Garden City, N.Y.: Doubleday Doran & Company, Inc., 1928.

———. *Through the Eye of the Needle: A Romance.* New York: Harper & Brothers Publishers, 1907.

———. *A Traveller from Altruria.* New York: Sagamore Press Inc., 1957.

Hudson, W. H. *A Crystal Age.* London: T. Fisher Unwin, 1906.

Huizinga, Johan. *Homo Ludens: A Study of the Play Element in Culture.* Boston: Beacon Press, 1955.

Huxley, Aldous. *Island.* New York: Bantam Books, Inc., 1963.

Jaeger, Werner. *Paideia: The Ideals of Greek Culture.* Translated by Gilbert Highet. 3 vols. New York: Oxford University Press, 1943–1945.

Jagu, A. "La conception platonicienne de la liberté," *Mélanges de Philosophie Grecque offerts à Mgr Diès,* pp. 129–140. Paris: Librairie Philosophique J. Vrin, 1956.

James, Henry. *The American Essays.* Edited with an introduction by Leon Edel. New York: Vintage Books, Inc., 1956.

———. *The Letters of Henry James.* Edited by Percy Lubbock. 2 vols. London: Macmillan and Co., Ltd., 1920.

Joachim, Harold H. "Truth as Coherence," *Contemporary Philosophic Problems: Selected Readings,* pp. 213–222. Edited by Abraham Edel and Yervant H. Krikorian. New York: The Macmillan Company, 1959.

Jones, Richard Foster. *Ancients and Moderns: A Study of the Background of the Battle of the Books.* St. Louis: Washington University Studies, 1936.

———. *Ancients and Moderns: A Study of the Rise of the Scientific Movement in Seventeenth-Century England.* 2d edition. Berkeley: University of California Press, 1965.

Jouvenel, Bertrand de. "Utopia for Practical Purposes," *Utopias and Utopian Thought,* pp. 219–238. Edited by Frank E. Manuel. Boston: Houghton Mifflin Co., 1966.

Kateb, George. *Utopia and Its Enemies.* New York: The Free Press of Glencoe, 1963.

———. "Utopia and the Good Life," *Utopias and Utopian Thought,* pp. 239–259. Edited by Frank E. Manuel. Boston: Houghton Mifflin Company, 1966.

Kirk, Clara Marburg. *W. D. Howells and Art in His Time*. New Brunswick, N. J.: Rutgers University Press, 1965.

Lachèvre, Frédéric. *Les Successeurs de Cyrano de Bergerac*. Paris: Librairie Ancienne Honoré Champion, 1922.

Langer, Susanne K. *Philosophical Sketches*. New York: The New American Library, 1964.

Laslett, Peter. *The World We Have Lost*. London: Methuen & Co., Ltd., University paperback, 1965.

Lovejoy, Arthur O. *Reflections on Human Nature*. Baltimore: The Johns Hopkins Press, 1961.

Löwith, Karl. "The Philosophical Concepts of Good and Evil," *Evil*. Edited by The Curatorium of the C. G. Jung Institute. Evanston, Ill.: Northwestern University Press, 1967.

MacIntyre, Alasdair. *Secularization and Moral Change*. London: Oxford University Press, 1967.

Mannheim, Karl. *Ideology and Utopia: An Introduction to the Sociology of Knowledge*. New York: Harcourt, Brace and Company, 1957.

Manuel, Frank E., ed. "Toward a Psychological History of Utopias," *Utopias and Utopian Thought*, pp. 69–98. Boston: Houghton Mifflin Company, 1966.

Manuel, Frank E., and Fritzie P. Manuel, eds. and trans. *French Utopias: An Anthology of Ideal Societies*. New York: The Free Press, 1966.

Marcuse, Herbert. *Eros and Civilization: A Philosophical Inquiry into Freud*. New York: Alfred A. Knopf, Inc., and Random House, Vintage paperback, 1962.

Marx, Karl. *Theses on Feuerbach*. Moscow: Progress Publishers, 1972.

Mercier, Louis Sébastien. *L'An Deux Mille Quatre Cent Quarante. Rêve s'il en fût jamais: suivi de L'Homme de Fer, Songe*. 3 vols. N.p., n.n. 1791.

Momigliano, Arnaldo. "Time in Ancient Historiography," *History and Theory: Studies in the Philosophy of History*, Beiheft 6, Vol. 5 (1966), 1–23.

More, Thomas. *The Complete Works of St. Thomas More*. Vol. IV: *Utopia*. Edited by Edward Surtz, S. J., and J. H. Hexter. New Haven: Yale University Press, 1965.

————. *St Thomas More: Selected Letters*. Edited by Elizabeth Frances Rogers. New Haven: Yale University Press, 1961.

————. *Utopia*. Edited with introduction and notes by Edward Surtz. New Haven: Yale University Press, Yale paperback, 1964.

Morgan, Arthur E. *The Philosophy of Edward Bellamy*. New York: King's Crown Press, 1945.

Morris, William. *News from Nowhere*. New York: Longmans, Green, and Co., 1905.

Morrow, Glenn R. *The Ethical and Economic Theories of Adam Smith: A Study in the Social Philosophy of the Eighteenth Century*. Cornell Studies in Philosophy, No. 13. New York: Longmans, Green, and Co., 1923.

————. "Plato and the Law of Nature," *Essays in Political Theory*, pp. 17–44. Edited by Milton R. Konvitz and Arthur E. Murphy. Ithaca, N.Y.: Cornell University Press, 1948.

————. *Plato's Cretan City: A Historical Interpretation of the Laws*. Princeton: Princeton University Press, 1960.

Morton, A. L. *The English Utopia*. London: Lawrence and Wishart Ltd., 1952.

Murdoch, Iris. "The Idea of Perfection," *The Yale Review*, Vol. 53 (Spring 1964), 342–380.

Murphy, N. R. *The Interpretation of Plato's Republic*. Oxford: At the Clarendon Press, 1960.

Negley, Glenn, and J. Max Patrick. *The Quest for Utopia: An Anthology of Imaginary Societies*. New York: Doubleday & Company, Inc., 1962.

Nettleship, Richard Lewis. *Lectures on the Republic of Plato*. London: Macmillan & Co., Ltd., 1963.

Nicholson, Norman. *H. G. Wells*. London: Arthur Barker Ltd., 1950.

Orwell, George. *The Road to Wigan Pier*. New York: The Berkley Publishing Corporation, 1961.

Parrington, Vernon Louis, Jr. *American Dreams: A Study of American Utopias*. New York: Russell & Russell, Inc., 1964.

Plato. *The Collected Dialogues of Plato*. Edited by Edith Hamilton and Huntington Cairns. Bollingen Series, Vol. LXXI. New York: Bollingen Foundation, 1963.

————. *The Republic of Plato*. Translated with introduction and notes by Francis MacDonald Cornford. New York: Oxford University Press, 1945.

Pocock, J. G. A. *The Ancient Constitution and the Feudal Law: A Study of English Historical Thought in the Seventeenth Century*. Cambridge: At the University Press, 1957.

Polanyi, Michael. "A Postscript," *History and Hope: Progress in Freedom*, pp. 185–196. Edited by K. A. Jelenski. London: Routledge and Kegan Paul, 1962.

Poulet, Georges. *Études sur le temps humain*. Paris: Librairie Plon, 1949.

Raknem Ingvald. *H. G. Wells and His Critics*. Oslo: Universitetsforlaget, 1962.

Randall, John Herman, Jr. *The Career of Philosophy*. Vol. I: *From the Middle Ages to the Enlightenment*. New York: Columbia University Press, 1962.

Read, Herbert. *The Green Child*. With an introduction by Kenneth Rexroth. New York: A New Directions Book, n.d.

Rowley, H. H. *The Relevance of Apocalyptic: A Study of Jewish and Christian Apocalypses from Daniel to the Revelation*. Second edition, revised. New York: Association Press, 1963.

Ruyer, Raymond, *L'Utopie et les utopies*. Paris: Presses universitaires de France, 1950.

Schiffman, Joseph. "Edward Bellamy's Altruistic Man," *American Quarterly*, VI (Fall 1954), 195–209.

Schiller, Friedrich. *The Aesthetic Letters, Essays, and the Philosophical Letters*. Translated by J. Weiss. Boston: Charles C. Little and James Brown, 1845.

Shklar, Judith N. *After Utopia: The Decline of Political Faith*. Princeton: Princeton University Press, 1957.

————. "The Political Theory of Utopia: From Melancholy to Nostalgia," *Utopias and Utopian Thought*, pp. 101–115. Edited by Frank E. Manuel. Boston: Houghton Mifflin Company, 1966.

————. "Rousseau's Two Models: Sparta and the Age of Gold," *Political Science Quarterly*, LXXXI (March 1966), 25–52.

Shorey, Paul. *The Unity of Plato's Thought.* Chicago: University of Chicago Press, 1903.

Skinner, B. F. *Walden Two.* New York: The Macmillan Company, 1948.

Stapledon, Olaf. *Last and First Men and Star Maker.* New York: Dover Publications Inc., 1968.

Thompson, C. R. *The Translations of Lucian by Erasmus and St. Thomas More.* Ithaca, N.Y.: Vail-Ballou Press Inc., 1940.

Toulmin, Stephen, and June Goodfield. *The Discovery of Time.* New York: Harper & Row, Publishers, Torchbook paperback, 1965.

Trevor-Roper, H. R. *The Crisis of the Seventeenth Century: Religion, the Reformation and Social Change.* New York: Harper & Row, Publishers, 1968.

Trilling, Lionel. *The Opposing Self: Nine Essays in Criticism.* New York: The Viking Press, Compass paperback, 1959.

Tuveson, Ernest Lee. *Millennium and Utopia: A Study in the Background of the Idea of Progress.* New York: Harper & Row, Publishers, paperback, 1964.

Vallentin, Antonina. *H. G. Wells: Prophet of Our Day.* New York: The John Day Company, 1950.

Vyverberg, Henry. *Historical Pessimism in the French Enlightenment.* Cambridge, Mass.: Harvard University Press, 1958.

Walsh, W. H. "Plato and the Philosophy of History: History and Theory in the Republic," *History and Theory: Studies in the Philosophy of History,* II (1962), 3–16.

Wells, H. G. *Anticipations.* London: Chapman and Hall, 1901.

———. *First and Last Things.* Revised and enlarged edition. London: Cassell and Company, Ltd., 1917.

———. *The Future in America.* London: Chapman and Hall, 1906.

———. *Men Like Gods.* New York: The Macmillan Company, 1923.

———. *A Modern Utopia.* London: Thomas Nelson and Sons, Ltd., 1905.

———. *The Time Machine: An Invention.* New York: Random House, 1931.

———. *When the Sleeper Wakes.* London: Harper & Brothers, 1899.

West, Anthony. "H. G. Wells," *Encounter,* VIII (February 1957), 52–57.

Williams, Raymond. *Culture and Society: 1780–1950.* Middlesex: Penguin Books Ltd., 1963.

Wolin, Sheldon S. *Politics and Vision.* Boston: Little, Brown and Company, 1960.

Wright, Austin Tappan. *Islandia.* New York: Holt, Rinehart and Winston, Inc., 1942.

Index